GAME IN THE DESERT

Nine hundred and fifty copies of

GAME IN THE DESERT REVISITED

have been published

by the Amwell Press for

THE NATIONAL SPORTING FRATERNITY LIMITED

This copy is number *353*

Jack O'Connor
Jack O'Connor

President, N.S.F.L.

GAME
IN THE DESERT
REVISITED

BY JACK O'CONNOR

ILLUSTRATED BY

RICH HAUSER

FOREWORD BY

JIM RIKHOFF

THE AMWELL PRESS • CLINTON, N.J.

DEDICATION

ONE September night a little over fifty years ago I dressed to look my most dashing and went to what was known as a "Get Together Dance," an institution through which the University of Missouri encouraged students to embrace and rub together in the dance and to give each other garbled and insincere accounts of their past lives.

I was then twenty-four and I was planning to get a Master's degree. With the cynical eye of a middle-aged *roue* I looked the girls over. Two caught my fancy. One was a skinny but beautiful blonde. The other was a little chick with short-bobbed reddish light brown hair of a shade which I believe is called "light chestnut." She had large gray-green eyes, full lips, a cute nose, and high cheek bones. She also had beautiful legs and everything else was properly proportioned and in exactly the right place. I cut in on the blonde first. She let me know that her father owned about half the oil wells in Oklahoma but although she talked a lot she didn't say much.

Actually I didn't pay a great deal of attention to her. I was watching the little gal with the light brown hair. I gave her a couple of romantic smiles as we passed but she ignored my leers and grimaces.

When someone relieved me of the skinny blonde, I cut in on the little girl. I learned her name was Eleanor Barry, that she was from St. Louis, and that she was a pledge to the Chi Omega sorority. I also found out she was in a very sour mood. Her sorority had got her a blind date. She said the guy was a real oaf and was drunk. I cut in on her several times. When an intermission came I walked her around outside. I thought of trying to kiss her but in the mood she was in I thought she might break my neck. I offered to take her home, but she said the older girls would probably be sore if she ditched that clown they had got her a date with. I told her I'd like to come by and see her soon. She did not swoon for joy. Instead she said, "Give me a ring." I got the impresson that she was not going to sit up waiting for the call. Apparently she could take dates with elderly graduate students or leave them alone.

The next day was Sunday. I went to the usual chicken dinner at the Sigma Chi house. Throughout the meal one of the brothers, a medical student, raved about a beautiful little doll he had met a couple of days before, a St. Louis girl named Eleanor Barry. He was thinking of going over to the Chi Omega house to lay his heart at her feet.

I beat him to the draw. As soon as I had finished my canned-peach-in-Jello dessert I shot into the telephone booth, called Miss Barry, and made a date for that afternoon.

Exactly one week later I told her I thought I was in love with her. A week after that I told her that she ought to give some consideration to marrying me. She told me to act my age. We still weren't exactly "going steady."

About a month after that I gave her my Sigma Chi pin and we were "engaged." Her parents did not relish their daughter's choosing her life mate at the age of eighteen. But we both persisted. Our marriage in September 1927 was an elopement. She had no trousseau and we got no wedding presents. I had borrowed $300 to get married on. We shared a upper berth (it was cheaper) from Kansas City to Alpine, Texas, where I had a job. My wife had never met my family and from all she knew I might have been descended from a line of bankrupt cretins. She had never been in the Southwest where I was taking her, and she wasn't even sure I could support her. She packed her trunk with her few clothes, some sheets, and a couple of blankets, put her little hand in mine and headed west with me. The nest-building instinct among young women had always amazed me. Beset by the mating urge they will follow men who are almost strangers, men who will probably neglect them and beat them, to the ends of the earth.

But in our case it has worked out pretty well. We have pulled each other's hair on occasion but we've always kissed and made up. Small events decide our destinies. If I had not gone to that get-together dance (and I almost stayed away) my wife's life would have been very different. We moved in different circles and might never have met.

Another thing that has amazed me about young women is the length they will go to share their husband's lives. To be good companions they will embrace the most grotesque hobbies. I have seen tender and beautiful girls take up frog spearing, skin diving, quarter horse breeding, trap shooting, collecting Eighteenth Century Irish silver, mountain climbing, and what not.

Since I was a hunter I encouraged my wife to join me in my hobby. She wept the first time she killed a cottontail rabbit. She was nauseated the first time she saw me butcher a deer but she became interested when she saw the chops laid out on wax paper ready to broil. She killed with one shot the first deer she ever shot at—an enormous buck mule deer. She has hunted from Yucatan Peninsula to Alaska and the Yukon, from Washington to India, in Spain, Scotland, and Iran. She has slept in leaky huts in Mexico, on a wheezy fishing boat in Alaska, and has traveled hundreds of miles by packtrain. She is one of the few women in the world that has shot tigers and the only one I know who has taken a 44-inch North American ram. She has been on eight safaris. On three of them our son Bradford was along. She is a crack shot and a good sport and my favorite hunting companion.

Since I dedicated the first edition of *Game in the Desert* to her I might as well do the same with this book!

JACK O'CONNOR

FOREWORD

THERE are very few living legends around, which is probably a pretty good thing then one considers the possible consequences of too many egos abroad at one time. A lot of people think they are legends, but very few are genuine bonafide "living legends" and even fewer are nice about it. Jack O'Connor is one of those rare last ones.

I have known Jack O'Connor for twenty years. As the foreword to *The Rifle Omnibus* pointed out last year:

"Jack O'Connor and I have hunted a number of States and a couple of Canadian Provinces—in fact, I have accompanied him on two of his celebrated 'farewell' sheep hunts. (He gives up sheep hunting almost as frequently as Sarah Bernhardt used to give up the stage.) We have also hunted Mexico, Scotland, Spain and Italy ... sometimes even with a bit of success."

Jack is seventy-five years old now. We were hunting sheep together in the Yukon and the Cassiar range of British Columbia when he was in his early seventies. It is the measure of the man that he collected another (I won't say his last) Stone sheep after our last hunt a couple of years ago. Unlike some others in the outdoor writing trade, he is reluctant to admit a tally on the number of sheep he has taken over some fifty-odd years of hunting, but when he is called the "Dean of American Sheephunters", the accolade rests with some security.

While Jack has hunted the world over—from Alaska to Zambia—his primary identification has always been with his native Arizona and Southwest, including Northern Mexico. He is an expert on African safaris and Indian shikars, but old-timers and young whippersnappers alike still picture Jack's familiar Hibernian mug peering through wire-rimmed glasses out from under an old beat-up cowboy hat. And well it should be for, regardless of all of his world travel and sophisticated cultural and educational achievements, he remains the quintessential Southwestern hunter.

As it happens, I used to live in Arizona so my words are not simply the inane ramblings of an Eastern book reviewer. I know a little of the country in which Jack was born and matured, finally seasoning into the most experienced writer-hunter the Southwest has ever seen. The times are gone when one could savor the hunting Jack has known and his like will not be witnessed again.

Jack, both born and bred in the Arizona Territory, was educated at the University of Arizona and the University of Arkansas, graduating from the latter in 1925. He received his Master of Arts from the University of Missouri in 1927. Since then he has been a newspaperman, a director of public relations, a novelist, and a professor of journalism.

Few of his fans know that he also served in both the United States Army and Navy for some years at the tail-end of World War I, including a memorable stint as a 15-year-old, obviously under-age, private in the Arizona National Guard, activated as the 158th Infantry. He was known as "Cactus Jack, the ass-less wonder"—a description, I might add, still incredibly apt.(One recalls an historic occasion a few years back when Winchester took the gun writers to Italy to view their new ammunition plant; on the way over we were standing in the plane's aisle discussing ballistics when a stewardess had to go by Jack, who promptly pulled in his stomach to allow this pleasant passage and found to his dismay that his pants fell down.)

Perhaps Jack is most closely identified with his many years (starting in 1937) with *Outdoor Life*, primarily as Arms and Ammunition Editor from 1941 until his retirement from that position in 1972. He stayed on as Hunting Editor after his retirement until 1973 when he grew weary of changing editorial policy and took his talent and prestige to *Petersen's Hunting Magazine*, where he still resides as Executive Editor. He contributes a full feature article every month and I am told his name on the cover insures considerable additional newsstand sales, which is hardly surprising when one reflects on the almost unique respect Jack O'Connor's name commands in the shooting sports. (I remember both older men and youngsters hanging around the lobby of the plush Mountain Shadows resort in Scottsdale, Arizona, waiting for Jack to pass by so they could have their books autographed.)

Jack's first books were novels—*Conquest*, published in 1930, and *Boomtown*, published in 1938. He is also the author of many standards in the hunting and shooting field—including *The Art of Hunting Big Game in North America*, *The Big Game Rifle*, *The Rifle Book* and *The Shotgun Book*, *The Hunting Rifle*, *Sheep and Sheep Hunting* and his unforgettable autobiography of his early days in Arizona, *Horse and Buggy West*.

His first hunting book was the classic *Game in the Desert*, published in 1939 by the renowned, though now sadly defunct, Derrydale Press in a beautiful edition limited to 950 copies, numbered but strangely left unsigned. That first edition is now a collector's prize, bringing some $75 to $100 on the rare book market and much more if one can be found signed by the author.

Alfred Knopf, the publisher of one of Jack's novels and many of his hunting books, brought out a trade edition of *Game in the Desert* in 1946 under the title *Hunting in the Southwest*. Outside of a new preface, the content of the book is the same but the manufacture, though excellent by trade standards of the time, no way approaches the quality of the Derrydale original. Even *Hunting in the Southwest,* long out-of-print, commands a premium over its original retail price and can be found for about $10-20, depending on condition.

It brings particular personal pleasure to me to bring out a new limited edition of Jack O'Connor's first hunting book—fittingly entitled *Game in the Desert Revisited.* This new version has all of Jack's original text plus two important new sections and superb new illustrations by the noted wildlife artist, Richard Hauser. (O'Connor admits The original drawings in the first edition leave a little to be desired; the late artist was Jack's brother-in-law.) This new custom, slipcased edition will also be limited to 950 copies, but this time the books will be signed by the author as well as numbered.

There will be many more hunting books, both lavish and less so, in the years to come. Some will be classics in their own right; others will become standards in their field. There will be only one *Game in the Desert Revisited* because, quite simply, there is only one Jack O'Connor.

JIM RIKHOFF, *President*
National Sporting Fraternity Limited

February 19, 1977
Speakeasy Hill
High Bridge, New Jersey

INTRODUCTION

I put *Game in the Desert* together in the winter of 1937-38. I was then living with my wife Eleanor in a house owned by my mother in my old home town of Tempe, Arizona. I had taken a year off from my job as the one and only professor of journalism at the University of Arizona. I might add that during my year off I got no pay from the university and indeed during my eleven years on the faculty there was no such thing as a sabbatical leave with pay. That was one of the economies brought about by the depression. If a professor wanted some time off to write a book, to do some research, or simply to cultivate his soul, he had to finance it himself. This, I might add, took some doing. When I left The university in 1945, I still was making less than $3,000 a year. My own leave was financed by a sneaky little deal I made with Ray Brown, the editor of *Outdoor Life*.

I look back on that year's leave of absence with considerable nostalgia. In those days Phoenix was still a small city; Tempe, a small town. The summer climate of the Salt River Valley would fry a salamander, but the winters are among the world's best. Days are warm and sunny, nights often nippy, sometimes frosty. During most of the long quail season, I used to get up early and write for about three hours. Then my wife and I would take some bread, butter, lard, flour, a frying pan, generally some beer, and our shotguns and head for a favorite quail area about thirty-five miles away on the lower Verde River upstream from Granite Reef Dam. That the the greatest quail year I have ever seen.

We would start seeing conveys of quail in the Fort McDowell Indian reservation and we would start hunting as soon as we hit the national forest beyond. That year there were quail everywhere. It used to take us all of fiteen or twenty minutes to get a couple of these lovely Gambel's quail each. Then we would skin them, flour them, fry them, and eat them with bread and butter, washed down with beer. Then we would go ahead and complete our limits of fifteen birds each. We must have hunted quail three or four times a week. There were literally thousands of quail—but all the time we hunted there on the lower Verde we saw only one (1) lonely hunter. We had no dog. Neither did the lonely hunter. In those innocent days it was firmly believed that the hard-running little Gambel's quail of the desert could not be hunted with dogs. Today, Arizona hunters have found that Brittany spaniels work very well on them.

My wife and I each got a fine buck mule deer in northern Arizona that Fall. I went into Sonora for a hunt in January, I believe, got a couple of Mexican desert mule deer and a very fine Coues whitetail. In the Spring I collected an excellent desert ram in the San Francisco mountains with my old friend Charlie Ren. If I ever get around to writing autobiographical material about those days, old Charlie will have a prominent place. That was our last trip together. He died later that year.

As anyone who reads the chapter on the desert bighorn will no doubt notice, I am pretty general in writing about the hunting of the bighorn. The season was then officially closed but the sheep were shot by everyone who was in possession of a rifle when he encountered sheep. Cowboys shot them for meat with .22s, fishermen shot them off the mountainsides overlooking the Gulf of California, prospectors and miners lived on them. For a time I used a somewhat irregular but effective "permit" for everything including sheep. It was a letter addressed to all concerned Mexican officials in northwestern Sonora saying that I was to be aided and abetted in anything I undertook. It was signed by the general in charge of the military district and it was as good as gold.

I have not hunted in Sonora since 1947 and only a few times for birds in Arizona since I moved away in 1948. In the 1930's and early 1940's it was possible to find fairly fresh sheep sign on almost any rough hill in northwestern Sonora or southwestern Arizona. Charlie Ren, who at that time knew more about the sheep of Sonora than any other man, estimated that in 1937 there were about 5,000 desert bighorn in Sonora. Today a very intelligent sheep hunting Mexican friend of mine estimates that there are about 500 in the state. I understand that the sheep are better protected now than they were forty or fifty years ago, but I would still hate to be a bighorn within range of a hungry Mexican with a .30/30.

After doing absolutely nothing to preserve the bighorn in Arizona for a couple of generations, the state began to make some motions along in the late 1930's. Now Arizona has had a limited season on desert bighorn for around twenty years. Water in sheep ranges has been developed. Herds have been reestablished. Nevertheless, the preservation of the desert bighorn seems to be a losing fight. Total numbers continue to decrease. There is more and more interference with sheep habitat. Power lines are driven through the mountains. Roads, irrigation canals, mines, and resort development block migration routes and access to feed and water. Cattle continue to overgraze fertile valleys where the desert bighorns like to browse when they come down off the heights. For a long time the wild and semi-wild burro (donkey) has been a serious competitor of the sheep. Now, since the Bleeding Hearts are championing the burro and the wild horse, they have in effect entered the lists against the bighorn.

Sheep hunting has since the war become a big ego trip and of the four varieties of North American sheep, the desert bighorn has the most prestige. He is the rarest. Getting a legal permit to take one is the most difficult, and hunting him is the toughest. The late Grancel Fitz, New York commercial photographer, head-hunter, and writer, made sheep hunting a prestigious caper and getting a "Grand Slam" (trophies of the four varieties of North American sheep) the most prestigious caper of all. Many hunters who have shot no more than one whitetail deer want to start their sheep hunting with a desert ram! Many are finding that the securing of a permit does not necessarily mean that the permittee will get a ram. Many a legal sheep hunter has sweated and stumbled over some of the roughest, toughest mountains in the world, has filled his knees, his hands, and his fanny full of thorns and has never seen a ram. I started hunting desert sheep over forty years ago and I never saw Sonora sheep hunting when it was not tough.

A legal sheep license in the United States is very chancey. I understand that in Arizona and Nevada there are several hundred applicants for every nonresident permit granted. In Mexico a permit costs one thousand dollars or more and if the ram taken is not of the highest record class the head is confiscated by Mexican officials and the hunter heavily fined. I shot my last desert ram in Sonora in 1946. The stalk was an interesting one. I was careful enough to sneak right into a bunch of sheep at the head of a boulder strewn canyon. I am now content to live with my memories—and besides at my age a full day in a desert bighorn range would probably kill me.

At the time I was gathering material for the articles which became the chapters in *Game in the Desert* the Southwest was blessed with many deer. The great herd of Rocky Mountain mule deer in the Kaibab

Forest north of the Grand Canyon had its die-offs, its problems with over-browsing and under-harvesting, but in the middle 1930's the forest contained many deer and fine trophies. There were many areas of fine and well-populated deer range in the state that were lightly hunted. In the early 1930's, I was on the staff of what is now Northern Arizona University at Flagstaff. I used to hunt excellent mule deer country north and west of the San Francisco Peaks and I shot some fine bucks there in three seasons. I saw only one other hunter!

The interesting desert mule deer were plentiful in Arizona south of the Mogollon rim and down into the Sonora desert. These are fine big deer somewhat lighter in color than the Rocky Mountain mule deer of northern Arizona but almost as large. It is my understanding that these "burro" deer are maintaining their numbers in Arizona reasonably well. How they are doing in Sonora I cannot say. Sonora is an altogether different place from the Sonora I knew and loved. The public domain has been grabbed by smart Mexican operators and fenced off. Water holes and wells have been pushed clear out to the once completely uninhabited coast of the Gulf of California. There are paved roads now where there were cow trails in my day. Like the members of any other race they are a mixed lot. Some are fine hunters and fine sportsmen. Some are game hogs. One very rich Mexican told me how he had machine-gunned from an airplane antelope in the plains and sheep off of ridges.

The Arizona whitetail (*Odocoileus cousesi*), one of my favorite big game animals, has, according to my Arizona friends, decreased in the oak-clad hills of southern Arizona. During most of the 1930's these handsome little deer were very plentiful in suitable range in Arizona. They were mostly found in hills carpeted with grama grass and spotted with live oaks. Manzanita, cliff rose, and coffee berry grew in the draws. On many occasions I have seen from thirty to fifty of these lovely deer a day in Arizona and more than that in some areas in Sonora. For years my wife and I hunted deer in Sonora an average of twice each year and we always hunted during the season in Arizona. The Arizona whitetail is a foxy little creature, the smartest deer I have ever encountered. When he decides to move, he blasts off like a rocket. Once I almost stepped on a buck that had taken refuge in a dead oak that had fallen down. He took off a few feet away and showered me with dead leaves. He also just about scared the wits out of me.

My friends in Arizona, mostly old timers who remember the good old days I wrote about in *Game in the Desert*, tell me the Arizona whitetail is not doing well. His numbers, they say, have greatly decreased. The trouble lies, they tell me, in "any deer" seasons that were held some years ago. Killing off the does gave the whitetails a permanent setback, they think. On the other hand, the biologists in the Arizona Game Department blame the reduced numbers on overbrowsing in years past by deer and cattle. Biologists in other states link the general decline of deer throughout the West to the gradual exhaustion of the nutrients in the soil brought about by long continued overgrazing by cattle and consequent erosion.

At any rate, Arizona's deer have decreased since the time of *Game in the Desert*. Arizona and Sonora are arid and semi-arid states. Long periods of drought are followed by torrential rains. Plants grow slowly. The fragile soil is easily washed away. Too many demands are being put on this parched land, where in some areas there is less than two inches of rainfall a year. When I was growing up in Tempe, the Salt River a mile or so from my home ran the year around, a clear, pleasant, willow-shaded stream. Now it is a dusty waste of dirt and sand strewn with tin cans, old automobile casings, and garbage. In areas where it was possible to strike water at forty and fifty feet fifty years ago, wells several hundred feet deep are now dry. Much of the underground water in the Southwest was "fossil" water put down during the Pleistocene era when the Southwest was much better watered than it has been in historic times. When this water is pumped out for irrigation, that's all there is—there isn't any more. A project is under way to bring water from the poor, robbed, exploited Colorado River into centra Arizona by an enormously expensive series of canals and tunnels. There is even talk of diverting water from the Snake and the Columbia Rivers to make up the water deficit in the Southwest.

Game in the Desert was first published by Derrydale Press in 1939. Derrydale specialized in deluxe editions, but I doubt if Derrydale was ever a very profitable venture, as back in the 1930's not many people had enough walking-around money to buy deluxe editions. As a matter of fact, not many had enough money to buy shotgun shells. That is the reason my wife Eleanor and I saw only one other quail hunter that wonderful fall of 1937. *Game in the Desert* was bound in imitation lizard skin, had a frontispiece in color, and was printed on hand-laid rag paper. The edition was limited to 950 copies and sold for $15. Some years later, after Derrydale went out of business Alfred A. Knopf, Inc., brought the book out under the title *Hunting in the Southwest*. It has been out of print for many years. The original Derrydale edition has long been a collector's item. I have heard of copies selling for well over one hundred dollars.

When Jim Rikhoff and I first started talking about a new edition of *Game in the Desert* we thought about "bringing it up to date". I decided against it. If I did so it would be an entirely new book. As a consequence, I am letting the text stand. What bringing up to date there is resides in the "Introduction" and in the chapter called "Retrospect and Survey".

I still have a sister in Arizona. I likewise have a couple of cousins and many friends. I have gone back to hunt morning and whitewing doves several times and once I went back to hunt Mearns quail near Patagonia. There are a few bright spots. The state still produces some fine mule deer, desert bighorn, and antelope trophies. There is still pretty good quail shooting. But on the whole a visit to Arizona leaves me depressed and unhappy. Seeing Arizona as it is today is a bit like encountering an old sweetheart in a bordello.

JACK O'CONNOR

Lewiston, Idaho
January 1, 1977

CONTENTS

CONTENTS

ACKNOWLEDGMENTS

MANY people have been very helpful to me in the preparation of this book, and I wish here to thank them. Some must necessarily go unnamed—cowboys, trappers, Mexican *vaqueros*, and Hopi, Navajo, Pima, Papago, Yaqui and Apache Indians. But there are a number of my friends to whom I am genuinely and deeply indebted, and to whom I can give specific thanks:

A. A. Nichol, formerly of the University of Arizona faculty and now of the National Park Service, is a man with an enormous amount of information on the range conditions and the wildlife of the Southwest. He has given me much new information and he has verified many of my own observations. I am deeply grateful to him.

To John C. McGregor, of the staff of the Museum of Northern Arizona, I must also give my thanks. A gifted observer and an old hunting *compadre* of mine, McGregor is a man of good suggestions and fertile ideas, an excellent observer and a genuine scientist.

I am indebted to C. C. Ren, Mexican outfitter of Ajo, Arizona, and Sonoyta, Sonora, for much of my information on the Mexican bighorn. An old sheep-hunting companion of mine, Charlie is a keen observer and a man with a genuine romantic understanding of the out-of-doors. He has hunted and guided in Sonora for a score of years and he probably knows more about the game of the Sonora coast than any living man.

To Dr. W. S. Lackner of Tucson I am indebted for a great deal of my information on the habits and the hunting of the mountain lion, for the Doctor is a lion-hunting enthusiast of the first water and an authority on lions. Most of my knowledge of the Mexican jaguar or *tigre* comes from the incomparable Lee brothers. Ernest is my principal informant.

Nor can I well forget my friend Fern Chaipetti, the turkey hunter, or Epifanio and Alfonso Aguierre of El Datil, Sonora, with whom I have discussed the habits of the lordly desert mule deer.

I wish I could thank all those from whom I have learned—Jose Juan, the best sheep hunter I know of, for instance, and Polacio Gomez, the *hombre* who can find more whitetail deer than any guide I have ever seen, and the blond Mayo Indian boy who took me on my first Mexican hunt twenty years ago.

To Ray Holland, editor of *Field & Stream*, I am grateful for permission to reprint several of these chapters.

But most of all I want to thank Eleanor, my wife, the coolest big-game shot I have ever hunted with, who has frozen with me on elk hunts, who has roasted when hunting desert *javelinas*, who has camped with me from 9,000 feet to sea level, and who has listened to me while I have articulated my notions on everything from shooting antelope to writing novels.

JACK O'CONNOR

PREFACE

IT was my maternal grandfather, I am convinced, who made a hunter out of me. He was a close-knit, gray-bearded man with glittering steel-blue eyes. He looked a little like General U. S. Grant; and, like the typical *paterfamilias* of the 'eighties and 'nineties, he was silent, uncommunicative. He was also the deadliest hand with a shotgun I have ever seen. His pose was that of the calm, completely masculine and unsentimental man of the great open spaces, and I was always greatly in awe of him. But I am convinced now that he was a sentimental romantic playing a part.

As a very young man, he sold his fertile Kentucky farm, and took his frail wife and two young children into the Rocky Mountains of Colorado. Ostensibly he made the move because he wanted to become a cattleman instead of a farmer, because he wanted to grow up in a country richer with financial opportunities. That is what he told other people. Possibly he believed it himself; but if he did believe it, he was doing what modern psychologists call rationalizing. He really uprooted his family, I know now, because he loved to hunt and his native Kentucky was shot out. After a few years, he moved from Colorado to northern New Mexico—because the hunting was better there. Then in the late 'eighties, he sold his cattle and came to Arizona's Salt River Valley.

Again he seemed to have a perfectly logical reason. Inadvertently he had settled on the famous Maxwell grant, and hired gunmen were shooting the nesters. But Grandfather was a courageous man. He didn't mind shooting at people or getting shot at. Besides,

he had been thinking about the move before the trouble broke out—
ever since a traveler had told him about the myriad quail, the whitewings, the doves in the valley and about the bighorn sheep on the
surrounding desert mountains. It was the bighorns that decided him.

I don't know how old I was when I first started going out with
him. Probably I was barely six. I was not a hunter those first few
years; instead I was my grandfather's bird-dog. I wasn't much of a
pointer, I'll admit, but I was an excellent retriever. He broke me in
on whitewings first. All afternoon long we'd sit under cottonwoods
while the birds streamed swiftly over. Grandfather would shoot and
I'd shag. Sometimes he'd have four or five birds down at once. Sometimes other men would hunt with him, and I always took pride in
the fact that the old man could shoot circles around them.

"You sure can shoot, Granddad," I used to tell him when he had
killed fifteen or twenty birds straight, taking everything up to fifty
yards.

"Humph!" he would answer. But I knew I had pleased him.

In turn he used to say to his friends: "This little kid is the best
dad-blamed retriever I've ever seen. He's worth two dogs!" How I
did swell with pride at those words of praise!

I must have been about seven when he handed me his double
twelve one day and suggested that I assassinate a whitewing on a
fencepost. The gun practically kicked me out of a year's growth, but
I hit the bird; and from then on I lusted to become a full-fledged
hunter instead of a mere bird-dog. Not long after that he bought me
a 20-gauge shotgun, then a .22 Marlin pump. I was still a bird-dog,
but I was an armed one; and gradually I learned to shoot.

But I learned more than hunting and shooting from my grandfather. I also learned to love game and to love the country. I remember one afternoon when a quail fluttered out of our path as if it had a broken wing, and I tried to run it down.

"Stop, son," he told me. "Let's look about."

A moment later he was pointing out the tiny striped newly hatched quail immobile on the ground. He picked one up very tenderly and showed it to me. "Cute little trick!" he commented. He put it down then and we backed off, taking great care not to step on the little creatures, and a moment later we saw the mother returning. He showed me nests of quail and doves and whitewings, taught me what a deer-track looked like, filled me full of the lore of wild lands and wild things.

Grandfather died while I was in my early teens, but his influence has surely shaped my life. I have been a hunter since the first day I saw a whitewing crumple before the blast of that old Lefever twelve, an amateur naturalist from the time I saw that fluffy little quail in my grandfather's gentle old hand.

I have hunted all my life. I have read everything I could find about the birds and animals I have hunted, and I have spent more time in the field simply observing than I have with a gun and deadly intent.

In this book, *Game in the Desert*, I have tried to communicate some of the feeling I have about the creatures of the Southwest, as well as some of the information I have gathered. It is frankly a book for the sportsman, for the man who likes to go afield in the fall to harvest with gun and rifle his little share of the annual crop of game, but whose interests are not confined wholly to the hunting season. It is a book by a hunter for the man who likes to know more about the game he hunts, or would like to hunt—what it looks like, what it eats, what sort of country it lives in, what its habits are, how it is standing the impact of civilization, and how it may best be hunted.

Such men are not the enemies of the game. They take some, surely, but they save more than they take, and almost all of the legislation designed to perpetuate game has come at their instigation.

"There are two classes of persons who are interested in wild life," Ernest Thompson Seton has written in *Lives of Game Animals*, "—the sportsmen and the sentimentalists. Of course, the creed of the former is, on the face of it, 'to kill,' and of the latter, at any price, anywhere, all the time, 'to save.' And yet it is a curious fact that it has been the sportsmen who have originated and made effective nearly every movement and law that has operated to save our big game from extinction, and greatly to increase their numbers, even near settlements."

So I feel that I need not apologize that I am a hunter writing for other hunters. My grandfather, who used to kill deer by the wagonload, did his part to help deplete our game resources. We of the second and third generation of Southwestern hunters are doing all in our power to help the game reëstablish itself in its former numbers.

Some of the information in this book has come from reading, and where it has been possible I have checked my observations with those of others. But the great part of it has come straight from what I have seen in the field and what I have learned from talking to guides, trappers, cowboys, Mexican peons. Some of the things may not agree with what certain scientists have had to say; but, while I have been all over the Southwest, many of the scientists who have written about it have not. When I have observed something in the field which disagrees with the books, I have preferred to believe my own eyes instead of the printed word. Game animals and birds do not read the books about themselves, and hence do not always conform.

But, as a matter of record, very little is known about many of the large desert mammals, and even less has been written. Almost nothing worth reading is in print about desert sheep or antelope, for example; little is known about the Arizona whitetail as it exists in Mexico; and almost everything I have had to say about these three species comes straight from the deserts themselves.

I am perfectly aware that there are serious holes in this book. I do not devote much space to bears, for example, because I don't know too much about them. I've only hunted elk a couple of times, so I pull in my sails in that chapter. I skip lobo wolves because they are practically extinct, and dusky grouse for the same reason. In a book of this sort, nothing which did not come largely from observation would be of much value. Too many books are simply a rehash of other books that are a rehash of still other books.

So *Game in the Desert* is offered without apology by a man who has hunted and observed all over the Southwest and northern Mexico; who has killed much game, but who could have killed far more had he been a truly bloodthirsty fellow; and who loves those creatures whose lives he takes.

GAME IN THE DESERT

CHAPTER I

THE SOUTHWEST AS A GAME COUNTRY

I AM writing this book about the game birds and animals of the Southwest, a section whose boundaries are exceedingly elastic. So before I go further, I had better stop and define my term. To some the Southwest begins in Arkansas and extends clear to Southern California. But to me the Southwest begins in western Texas and ends with the Coast range of Southern California. On the north, it stops at the Utah and Colorado borders and on the south at the Sierra Azul de los Indios opposite Tiburon Island on the Sonora coast.

I have chosen these boundaries for biological rather than geographical and cultural reasons. My section contains several species found nowhere else in the United States and unique adaptations of more widely distributed species. The Mearn's and Gambel's quail and the javelina are examples of the former, the desert mule deer and the Sonora antelope of the latter.

East of the Pecos River in Texas, most of the quail are Eastern bob whites, the deer are the Texas variety of Virginia whitetail. West of the Pecos, these typically Eastern forms are replaced by the mule deer, the Arizona whitetail, and by the Western quails. The same thing holds true of my western boundary. On the Pacific side of the Coast range, the desert Gambel's quail is replaced by the California valley quail and the big plumed mountain partridge, the big desert mule deer by the smaller California mule deer and, a little farther north, by the Columbian blacktail.

[1]

The Southwest about which I am writing, then, is all of Arizona and New Mexico, part of western Texas, the northern half of Sonora and Chihuahua, and parts of Nevada and Southern California. In reality this is a desert country. To be more exact, it is a desert country spotted with mountains and plateaus. The lowlands are without exception very dry and warm, but altitude takes the place of latitude in forming the climate and the high-flung ranges catch the moisture from lofty clouds. This great variation results in rainfall that ranges from extremely light to fairly heavy, in temperatures that range from hot to cool. In Arizona, for example, Yuma, near sea level on the Colorado River, often reports the highest temperatures in the United States at the same time that Flagstaff, at nearly 7,000 feet, reports the lowest. The Southwest is a land of variety in climate, in vegetation, in bird and animal life.

The Southwest has every type of climate and almost every type of vegetation found within the continental United States, and a Southwesterner with the leisure can, if he wishes, live the year round in an ideal climate. Furthermore, he can do it by traveling from fifty to seventy-five miles from almost any place in which he happens to find himself. In many instances he will not have to go that far. Stand on the brink of the Grand Canyon of Arizona. You are at 7,000 feet, and even in midsummer the nights are so cold as to require two or three blankets. Look down. Far below you is a hot desert. On the rim the temperature may be a bit over 70°, but down there it is well over 100°, perhaps as much as 114°.

The Grand Canyon is far from being the only place where you can change your climate with a trip of a few miles. In Tucson, famed winter resort, a tourist can bathe in an unheated swimming pool and bask in the warm January sun in the morning and go skiing on top of the nearby Catalina Mountains that same afternoon. So it goes.

One summer day a few years ago, I drove in a little over forty miles through every type of climate found within the United States. When I left the Verde Valley the thermometer was at 108°. I was in desert country, the lower Sonoran zone of the scientist—a land of no snow and little rain, a land of catclaw, mesquite and cactus. In a few miles it was distinctly cooler. I had risen a thousand feet into the upper Sonoran zone and had shed several degrees of temperature. I encountered piñon, juniper and red cedar, and I still saw a few of the Gambel's quail which were thick in the valley itself. In a few more miles I was in the transition zone and still higher. Great yellow pines more than a hundred feet tall rose on every side. Gambel oaks and hoary alligator-bark junipers spotted rolling hills and aspens were light green in old burns.

For twenty miles I drove through a great pine forest across the rolling plateau before I started up the road which leads to the top of the San Francisco peaks. Soon the pines began to give way to the Douglas fir of the Canadian zone. Now it was definitely chilly even if it was midday in August. As the narrow road climbed higher and higher, the thermometer continued to drop, and I entered a dense dark forest of Englemann spruce and cork-bark fir, the same sort of forest found near the Hudson Bay. Finally I reached timberline, where a few stunted ground pine lay tortured along the ground, barely able to maintain their existence against the deep snows, the high winds, and the terrible cold of winters at more than 11,000 feet. The road ended then and I left the car and walked over gray shale and slide rock to the very top of the peak, 12,610 feet above sea level, and the highest point in Arizona. Only mosses, lichens and arctic willows grew there, and from all appearances I was within the arctic circle. Below me was a great basin spotted with old snow and filled with the rotting corpses of trees which had tried to grow there but had lost the struggle. A sharp wind made my nose tingle and my eyes water, and below me I saw the shoulders of the great mountain stretching massively out, merging into the enormous pine forest that covers the Coconino plateau. The dark green of the forest became blue with distance, smoky, vague. To the south it merged with the series of mighty mountain ranges that runs clear to the Mexican boundary. To the north the pines became thin, scattered, lost themselves in the blue, yellow, red and ochre sands of the Painted Desert. And I could see a red crevice that was the Grand Canyon, lined with the distant blue that was the north rim and the Kaibab.

A good portion of the Southwest lay spread beneath my feet, canyon and mountain, desert and forest, mesa and plateau. Clouds patterned it with shifting purple shadows. Below me and far in the distance lightning stabbed bright from thunderheads that trailed blue-gray curtains of rain. I was on top of the world, as far-seeing and as aloof as a god.

And in all this wide lovely country, in all these diverse climates, birds and animals live and move, find their own food, escape their enemies, love briefly and violently like the deer or long and tenderly like the quail, guard and cherish their young, and finally die, usually horribly, for Nature, lovely though she is, has no love for the awkward, the slow, the old and the weak.

And these birds and animals are to me as much a part of the

country as the very trees themselves. The spruce forests are to me more interesting because they contain the dusky grouse, the bandtail pigeon and the great Rocky Mountain mule deer. The pine forests and the open grassy parks of the transition zone are twice as romantic because they contain the swift, boldly colored antelope, wild turkeys, massive elk, gray deer fleeing through the timber. The upper Sonoran zone of the southern Arizona mountains is an interesting country—yellow gramma grass spotted with the dusty green of live oaks, with twisted junipers, flowering yucca. But it is the elfin whitetail which makes it live—the whitetail and that curious, trusting, stupid fellow, the Mearn's quail.

And the deserts—the tangle of cholla, ironwood, mesquite, long arroyos where the water flows beneath the surface to escape the sun, the tall terrible mountains rising sheer from the valley floor, the yellow sandy playas. . . . The massive bighorn, the great light-gray desert mule deer, the wheeling antelope, the pugnacious little javelina, the quail, the doves, the whitewings—all these animate the deserts for me, lend them interest and mystery.

With the exception of the moose, the white goat and the Columbian blacktail deer, the Southwest contains examples of all the large game animals commonly found in the United States.

There are bighorn sheep there, and at one time they ranged clear from West Texas to Southern California. The regular Virginia whitetail invades eastern New Mexico and his little Mexican cousin comes across the Mexican border. The native elk were shot out in the 'nineties, but imports from the Northwest have brought those grand animals back. Antelope range over most of the whole great area, and the mule deer of some subspecies or other is found wherever he can obtain food, moisture and cover. Lions live wherever deer are found, and even the great Mexican *tigre*, the largest of New World cats, occasionally crosses the border.

Lobo wolves once ran elk and deer and later the cattle of the pioneer ranchers. Most of them are gone now, along with the surly grizzly. But the shy clownish black bear is coming back over most of its range, wherever it can find oak and piñon mast.

But even more than a big-game country, perhaps, the Southwest with its multiple climates is a land of game birds. The great wild turkey, largest of the world's pheasants, summers in the yellow pines and winters in the juniper and piñon of lower elevations. Mourning doves and bandtail pigeons migrate from elevation to elevation with the seasons. The dusky grouse lives in thick spruce and the white-wing dove comes annually up from Mexico to feed in southern Arizona's wheatfields. Three kinds of quail are found in Arizona and New Mexico. The most plentiful, the Gambel's, is a bird of the thorny desert lowlands, where cacti, mesquite and *palo verde* furnish him protection from hawks and the smaller predatory animals. The scaled quail loves the more open grassy plains and rolling foothills, and depends more on his protective coloring than does the Gambel's quail. On the tops of hills and mountains, in the land of oak and juniper, piñons and gramma grass, lives the round buttery Mearn's or fool quail, so tame he can often be killed with sticks. At one time, in the valley of the Santa Cruz River in southern Arizona, the masked bob white, only far Western cousin of the merry bob white of the East, piped his cheery call. Though he still exists in Sonora, he is no longer found in Arizona. The cattle that ate off his grassy cover spelled his doom.

Every type of country has its birds and animals, then, and all wildlife its favorite country. But gradually the various species have changed their habits in order to exist. If open water is handy, quail, for example, will drink daily. If it is not, they don't seem to mind greatly so long as they can get moisture from insects and green vegetation. In the chapter on the pronghorn antelope I have told the story of the southern Arizona herd which moved into Sonora and learned to do entirely without open water in order to escape the persecution of men with rifles. Evolution brought about by the battle for existence is in progress even today. Mountain sheep, I suppose, were originally animals of high cold country in their ancestral home in Asia. Yet in Arizona they were once found throughout the entire range of climatic zones, wherever the country was rough and relatively free from timber. They used to run on the San Francisco peaks above timberline, but their cousins get along equally well 13,000 feet lower on the deserts of southwestern Arizona and Sonora. It would take an expert to tell the difference in appearance between a Kaibab and a Yuma County mule deer, but it would be hard to imagine creatures of more different habits.

Watching these birds and animals, noting their efforts to adapt themselves to a country of little rain and many enemies, seeing them for the most part slowly triumph over a hostile environment, over predatory animals and man, has long been my favorite pastime. In the succeeding chapters I'll tell you about them.

CHAPTER II

GRAY GHOSTS OF THE MOUNTAINS

ALMOST thirty years ago, when I was a child of six or seven, I saw my first mule deer. The sight affected me profoundly and I have no doubt that it was a turning point in my life. As luck would have it, the animal was a magnificent buck. His summer coat was just beginning to turn to the gray of the fall mating season and his great antlers were still heavy with velvet. I shall never forget him. I had been toiling painfully up a talus slope toward a rimrock not more than a half-mile from our summer cabin when the buck came out. He had been bedded down there and he crashed from the scattered oaks that shielded him. For a moment he stood there looking at me, brave, defiant, magnificent. But I was a man, though a small one, so the old buck threw back his heavy antlers and ran.

I stood there watching as he disappeared and then came out on another ridge far above, trotting freely and easily. Suddenly he faded into a patch of scrubby timber, and I never saw him again. He had appeared like a ghost and he vanished like one. He left me breathless, strangely frightened, curiously moved. I returned to our cabin as pop-eyed as if I had seen a miracle and told my family I had jumped a deer. Deer? How nice. Sure, there were deer in the mountains. They had seen tracks and droppings about.

From that day on I have been a lover of mule deer. Later I began to hunt them, and for years I have studied them, in season and out, in high cold forests of spruce and fir and in the hot waterless

[9]

deserts of Mexico. Never have they ceased to interest me. They were my first love and still remain my strongest. As the years have passed I have learned to love the swift antelope that wheel and maneuver like so many wind-borne things across the juniper-studded plains of Arizona and New Mexico and the sandy playas of Sonora. I regard the great brown sheep of the desert ranges and the elfin Arizona whitetails with the deepest affection. But somehow the sight of an old mule deer buck, head high, antlers lying along his broad back, returns me definitely to my childhood and the day I first felt the mystery of wild game and wild country.

I first knew mule deer as blacktails, and blacktails they are still called in the southern part of their American range, in Arizona, New Mexico and West Texas. In California, where the true black-tail is found, they go by their correct name and they are also known as "mule-tailed" deer. In parts of Arizona and New Mexico where most of the land is in national forest, natives have been trained by scientific-minded rangers to call them mule deer, but to the old-timer along the Mexican border they are still blacktails.

In Arizona there are three subspecies of mule deer—Rocky Mountain mule deer, Mexican mule deer and the burro deer, known to scientists respectively as *Odocoileus hemionus marcotis*, *Odocoileus hemionus canus* and *Odocoileus hemionus eremicus*. New Mexico has no examples of *eremicus*, which is distinctly a low desert species, and Texas has only *canus*. Besides these subspecies there are very definite families with very definite family characteristics. The bucks of the Kaibab on the north rim of the Grand Canyon are very different from those of the south rim, and time and time again I have proved that I can pick out the Kaibab heads in collections. Scientists have not recognized any Kaibab subspecies, but almost all observant hunters are aware of this difference which I have noted, and some of them insist that the Kaibab bucks are "mule deer" and their Mogollon Plateau cousins are "blacktails." I can spot heads from the Big Bend of Texas, too. The deer there are classified as *canus* but they are as different from the examples of *canus* found around Tucson, Arizona, as the north-rim bucks are from the big fellows on the Sonoran desert. But that is a problem for the scientific classifiers to work out and not something to worry a romantic sportsman.

But wherever they are found, mule deer of whatever subspecies have definite characteristics in common—light gray muzzle, dark brisket, large ears, dichotomous, or evenly branched antlers, and the funny little white tail, almost hairless, and tipped with black on the end. The tail is nearly all white, except for that little black tip, yet the curious misnomer "blacktail" has persisted since Lewis and Clark first saw the species and fastened the name upon them in 1804. I once went into Coahuila with an old whitetail hunter from Texas who had never seen a mule deer, but who had always heard them referred to as blacktails. On the first day of our hunt he came into camp at noon completely goggle-eyed and said he had shot a new species of deer.

"You must have got a blacktail," another member of the party suggested. "Blacktails and whitetails both range in these hills."

"No, it ain't a blacktail," he said emphatically. "It's some kind of a whitetail. It's got a dinky little white tail with a black tip on it."

It has been estimated that there were at one time 10,000,000 mule deer within the boundaries of the United States. The estimate

may be correct, or nearly so. Oldtimers speak of them in almost incredible numbers, yet it has been my experience that oldtimers are
romantics to whom the old days are always best. I know that I have
hunted in a good many absolutely primitive areas and I have never
found game nearly so plentiful as I had expected it to be. In a true
wilderness there are always too many predatory animals.

Be that as it may, mule deer were common and sometimes extremely plentiful over a vast area of country—from West Texas and
the badlands of the Dakotas to California, and from the Mexican
border to the Canadian line. A majority of the great herd, perhaps,
belonged to the division of Rocky Mountain mule deer. They were
there by the million, at any rate.

The impact of civilization dealt the race a tremendous blow.
Settlers lived off them, cattle overran their range and brought in
diseases, market hunters killed them by the hundreds, hide hunters
shot them by the thousands for a paltry two bits and fo' bits a hide.
On Arizona's Mogollon Rim as late as 1906 two market hunters
took 600 hides—of bucks, does and fawns—in one winter. Other
more businesslike market hunters killed them by the hundreds, jerking the meat as well as saving the hides. For any armed native to
see a deer at any time of the year was to kill it.

At the turn of the century and for many years thereafter almost
everyone was willing to admit that the mule deer was doomed. Any
man who had been much in the hills had seen the herds decrease
year by year until they were but a small remnant of their former
numbers. The oldtimers had seen the buffalo go. They saw that the
antelope were going, and they could see no reason why the mule
deer should not follow suit.

[12]

My own grandfather, who came West in the 'seventies and who killed mule deer for the market by the wagonload, was as sure of it as anyone else. He regretted it, but he felt that it was an inevitable part of the conquest of the West. So firmly was he convinced that in 1911 when he showed me a herd of young bucks in the mountains, he said, "Look carefully, son, because you may never see a sight like this again, and by the time you are as old as I am you can tell your own grandchildren that you once saw a herd of wild blacktails." I looked again, as thrilled and excited as I had been the day I saw my first buck.

Grandfather died, I suppose, still convinced, if he ever thought about it, that game would continue to decrease. Like all the members of his generation, he was a great bewailer who never felt like doing anything about it. He would have snorted in disbelief if anyone had told him that even then the deer were staging a comeback and that within a few years they would in many sections be even more plentiful than they were under wilderness conditions.

By the early years of this century the mule deer had about finished playing their part as a purely economic resource. They had been the meat supply of all Westerners from the mountain men of the eighteen-thirties to the nesters of the 'eighties and 'nineties. And earlier than that they occupied the same position in the economy of the mountain Indians as the buffalo did in that of the plains Indians.

Early settlers in the mountain states used to kill a dozen deer in November when they were fat and hang their carcasses on the north side of their houses where they would freeze and remain fresh through the winter. Much frontier clothing was made of buckskin, and selling deer meat and hides in town was one of a pioneer's surest sources of cash income. Many a wagonload of venison went to pay for cartridges and clothes and medicine used by my own pioneering ancestors.

Under this constant pressure it is no wonder that the deer grew so scarce that their extinction was but a matter of time. The efficiency of the repeating rifle, the over-grazing of their summer and winter range by hordes of cattle and sheep, the forest fires that swept the mountain areas in the 'eighties and 'nineties, all formed a combination the big gray deer could not cope with.

But by 1915 the deer themselves were showing that those who foresaw their doom were poor prophets indeed. Now they are on the increase in almost every section with which I am familiar. The establishment of regular seasons has meant a great deal. So has the buck law. Oldtimers out here in Arizona are now agreed that mule deer are more plentiful than they were in 1900, and many are so bold as to declare that they are more plentiful than they ever were. In certain parts of their range, such as the Kaibab Plateau in northern Arizona and the Black range of New Mexico, they have become so plentiful as to menace their own food supply—something which never happens under true wilderness conditions.

Several factors besides the regulation of hunting have contributed to the increase of the herds. In the first place, the deer themselves are far wiser than their ancestors whose numbers were thinned by the pioneers and market hunters. They have changed their habits to conform to civilization, and gradually they are acquiring the sophistication that has enabled their Eastern cousins, the Virginia whitetails, to survive in close contact with civilized man, the most relentless and dangerous of predatory animals, for three hundred years. If anyone still believes the present-day mule deer to be a dullard and a fool, I invite him to take a fall hunt with me out here in Arizona and learn the true state of affairs.

Then again, the coming of man has enabled the deer, in many places at least, to extend their range. Until the American settlers on Arizona's great Mogollon Plateau began to build "tanks" for the impounding of water, places where the water-drinking Rocky Mountain mule deer could drink were few and far between. Large areas of country well adapted to deer had no deer population at all because there was no available water. On the other hand, what deer there were clustered thickly around the few streams and springs and were consequently easily hunted. Now tanks have been built all over the plateau and the herd is so scattered that the animals range over the entire wooded section. Here their food supply, for fall and summer at least, is assured, as the United States Forest Service no longer allows the over-grazing characteristic of Western sheep and cattle business in the old days of unregulated and rugged individualism.

The last factor in the increase of the animals is that man has hunted the mountain lion—the deer's worst and almost only natural enemy—even more relentlessly than he has the deer. Since each adult mountain lion kills about fifty deer a year, it is easily seen that the thinning out of the predators has been important.

At Flagstaff, Arizona, where I used to live, bucks are regularly shot almost within the city limits—and Flagstaff is a city of five thousand inhabitants where almost every male citizen owns a rifle. Dozens of places within ten miles of the town are good for at least one shot during an afternoon of hunting, and many a buck has been jumped by surprised golfers on the country club course.

I have seen as many as thirty or forty deer in one day's ride through the pine forests of northern Arizona, and on an elk hunt on the Mogollon Rim in 1935 I saw at least two hundred deer every day I was out. I may possibly have seen some of the same deer twice, but any way you take it that's a lot of deer. I have yet to see that many deer even in the famed Kaibab. Another time I saw thirty-seven deer, mostly bucks, on one day's hunt near Flagstaff. I could repeat such tales endlessly.

So the mule deer is back, and back to stay—and never again will he arrive at the point where he is in danger of following the footsteps of the passenger pigeon and the great auk.

How does the Rocky Mountain mule deer differ from the other subspecies of his race? For one thing, he is larger than most of them. For another, he is darker. The summer coat of the mountain deer is almost as red as that of a bay horse, whereas bucks found on the desert vary from an orange tan to a pale yellow during the hot months. In the winter all species are gray, but again the mountain deer are darker. The shape and weight of antlers differ widely, even with bucks taken in the same immediate locality, but as a rule the Rocky Mountain mule deer grows the best ones, and the Mexican mule deer the poorest. Yet even an expert might find it hard to distinguish individual members of the various subspecies, particularly in the winter.

And what sort of country do Rocky Mountain mule deer like? That's far from a simple question. As a rule they like rough, broken, partially timbered country, and they are not nearly the thick-country animal that the Eastern whitetail is. If you asked me to choose typical country I would take rolling hills cut with canyons, dotted with piñons and junipers, and supporting scattered patches of cliff rose, or buck brush as the natives of the Arizona mountains know it. Springs and pot-holes would enhance the picture somewhat, as the deer of the mountains go to water two or three times a week, particularly in the warmer months. You'll find deer in such country the year round, and you'll find them particularly plentiful there in the winter.

Yet in the summer and early fall the deer are found in great numbers in the cold dark forests of spruce and fir at altitudes from 8,000 to 9,000 feet. I have even seen them on the shale and slide rock above timberline. In the summer a great portion of the deer herds near a high mountain range starts following the melting snow to the top of the peaks. They feast on tender aspen leaves, on mushrooms, and on dozens of annual plants that spring up during the brief hectic summer of the high elevations. Often they remain at high elevations clear into the middle of November, but the first good snow sends them flocking into the low country, through the yellow-pine forests of the transition zone and down into the piñon and juniper of the upper Sonoran to join the stay-at-homes who have never left their friendly canyons.

Where they are not hunted too hard, they can get along with very little cover, and I have found them plentiful in deep, almost barren canyons which to an Eastern whitetail hunter would seem the most unlikely deer country possible. If the country is rough and rocky enough, they need but little brush and timber for protection, and I have seen wise old bucks that looked as big as small horses fade from sight in a patch of chaparral which I'd swear wouldn't harbor a jackrabbit.

[17]

Of all American deer, the mule deer is to me the most impressively beautiful. His antlers are the largest and most symmetrical, and his coloration the best designed. The big bucks have a massive dignity even in death, and to see one bounding off across a deep Arizona canyon is one of the most thrilling of all sights. Beside the lithe grace of one of these big bucks, the elk is ungainly and the moose grotesque. Perhaps members of the family *cervidae* cannot grow larger than mule deer and still retain their grace. In any event, I have never seen a graceful elk or moose. A big bull elk is beautiful in repose, yes. But let one start to run. . . .

The mule deer are the largest of the American *cervidae* bearing the name deer, but they are not so large as some observers, many of them well qualified, would have us believe. Although Vernon Bailey, author of *Mammals of New Mexico*, writes that he has heard of a large desert buck which weighed 425 pounds dressed, I am inclined to doubt his informant. I have seen hundreds of bucks, and I have killed my share; but I have no actual record of one that weighed more than 260 dressed when it was actually put on the scales.* Perhaps giants of the species would weigh as much as 300 if extremely fat, though I have never seen one. I do know that I have a photo of a desert buck which was killed by my father in the early nineteen-hundreds and is the largest I have ever seen. It was not actually weighed, but its *estimated* dressed weight was 300 pounds. Estimates, though, have a habit of going wrong—and usually in the direction of too much weight. An average full-grown,

---

* I am speaking of the Rocky Mountain mule deer as found here in Arizona. In the Northwestern states the animals grow much larger, and bucks weighing 300 pounds dressed are relatively common.

four-point buck (ten points to Easterners) will weigh about 165 pounds dressed, and any deer going above that is exceptionally large. A 200-pounder is a prize indeed. At Flagstaff, Arizona, a local hardware store has sponsored a big-buck contest for a dozen years or so. Each year the prize winner is around 200 pounds and the heaviest one ever brought in weighed 215 pounds.

Curiously enough, the heaviest bucks seldom have the largest antlers. Usually the big heads come from old decadent bucks which are thin and run down, and whose energy has all gone into the production of those magnificent antlers. A typical head from a fine, fat mature buck is what Westerners call a four-pointer. That is, it has four points to a side and two equally branching beams. In the East he would be called a ten-pointer, as Easterners count the brow-tines or "guards" as points and count every point on each antler. However, on mule deer the guards are much smaller than on whitetails and sometimes they are absent altogether. One of the biggest heads I ever took had five points on one side, four on the other, but no guards at all. In late maturity, when the buck is from seven to nine years old, his horns begin to freak. They flatten or palmate, and they grow more points. I have seen absolutely symmetrical heads with nine points, counting the guard, to a side. After that, if the buck can get through the winter and dodge lions with his stiffening muscles, his head begins definitely to freak. It loses its symmetry, grows an enormous number of points, turns this way and that. In a country where predatory animals are not plentiful and where there is little snow, hunters find great numbers of freak heads, weird and fantastic, and some collectors prize them.

I think it has been established beyond reasonable doubt that the best heads come from a limestone country. I am certain that the best sets of antlers I have ever seen come from the Kaibab, which is practically all limestone, and from the Sonoran deserts below Altar, Mexico, where limestone is common. Experiments conducted at Tucson, Arizona, show that even a young buck will grow a magnificent head if he is stuffed with lime and protein at the time he is growing his new set of antlers.

From my own experience, I am convinced that really big mule-deer heads are far commoner than the record books would seem to indicate. Only a small proportion of deer hunters are out after big heads. Many of them think so little of their trophies that they throw them away, and only a few know a record head when they see it. The natives who live illegally off the game both in Arizona and in Mexico are after meat rather than trophies, and seldom bother to save the heads. I have shot two big bucks with heads that rank high in the records, but I have seen literally dozens of unrecorded heads that were better than either of them. One of them I killed in the Kaibab. He was a fine buck, with a 36-inch spread, a 26-inch main beam, and thirteen points; but on that same day in the same area two bucks with heads slightly better than mine were taken. Neither, so far as I know, was recorded. Mine was, and as a consequence, he ranks better than he deserves.

What then is a good head?

One with a 25-inch spread and a 25-inch main beam will win plenty of prize competitions; but it is my opinion that such a head, though it is a fine trophy, is not exceptional. Bucks with heads exceeding those measurements are fairly rare, and one with a 30-inch main beam is something to guard and cherish. I have seen dozens of heads with spreads of more than 35 inches, and I have seen a very few which exceeded 40 inches. The record, I believe, is around 45 inches in spread; and that, ladies and gentlemen, is *some* head. Counting points is a poor way to determine the value of a head, for I have seen some sets of antlers with thirty or more points that I wouldn't bother to carry home except as a curiosity.

Some heads are close-pinched with long beams and small spreads. Others are almost all spread. The shape of the antlers seems to be an individual family characteristic rather than a subspecific difference; and I have shot bucks running together with the two varieties of heads. For my part, I am partial to wide spreads. They are, to say the least, more spectacular.

The common notion that a buck mule deer adds a point to each side with every year of his age must be taken with considerable salt. Roughly, perhaps, it is true—but only roughly. A yearling may be a spike, a two-pointer, or even a three-pointer. Two-year-olds sometimes have four points. The size, the heaviness, the "wartiness" of the antlers is a far better indication of age than points.

It is commonly believed, especially by those who have never hunted them, that the mule deer are the fool hens of the family *cervidae*. They may have been unsuspicious in the early days when they were unused to the ways of white men, but now they are as keen and crafty as could be desired. T. S. Van Dyke, who hunted them and studied their habits for years, never underestimated their intelligence, and it does not pay one to do so now. They gamble with their lives every day during the hunting season and they do so shrewdly and coolly, all too often outwitting the hunter, as the fact that they are increasing everywhere proves.

Let me tell a story to illustrate my point. Several years ago I was hunting with a friend of mine in Arizona's White Mountains when, late in the afternoon, I got on the track of a big fat buck as full of guile as a fake oil-stock promoter. Several times during the afternoon I saw him, but always too far away for a shot. Finally toward dusk, absolutely dead beat, I topped a ridge overlooking a little valley thinly timbered with yellow pine, and with a few thick patches of scrubby oaks along the bottom. My buck had headed straight for the bottom of the valley and I knew that he was there somewhere, so I sat down and began to use my binoculars.

The first moving object I saw was not the buck but my friend swinging along at the head of the valley. Presently when my friend was fifty yards or so from one of the clumps of oaks, the buck emerged as quietly as a ghost from the other side. At the same time, through the glasses, I saw my friend peer interestedly into the oaks. The buck did not move. Then buck and man began a slow march around the oaks, the buck keeping exactly on the opposite side from my friend. Finally the man stopped, put the butt of his rifle on the ground, and lit a cigarette. Sizing up the situation, the buck sneaked quietly up the opposite hill, waiting till he was two hundred yards away before he broke into the easy floating bounds that carry a mule deer up and down hill as if by magic. Just before the buck went out of sight my friend saw him and went into action. But the buck was lucky and the light was poor, so my friend only wasted his shots.

Now that is the case of a buck who used his head. He risked his life and won. I could relate a hundred others.

When an Eastern hunter whose sole acquaintance with mule deer comes from the sporting magazines tells me that mule deer will not skulk, I have to laugh. When he tells me that they always stop for one last look, I give vent to another chortle. An old buck can out-plan, outthink and outgeneral the average hunter. Another hunting story will illustrate my point.

One fall my wife and I jumped a bunch of large bucks, which we were fortunate enough to outmaneuver. I shot one as the herd dashed through a small open flat between two hills. While my wife skirted the hill on which the herd had disappeared, I dressed my buck and hung him up in a piñon to cool and drain. With the job finished I decided to go along the foot of the hill hoping to run a buck over the top to my wife. Now I had been noisy at my job of dressing my deer. I had grunted and had probably sworn, as the buck was heavy, and I had made no small amount of noise breaking off ends of cedar branches to fill the belly cavity and keep out flies. But within fifty yards of where I had worked something not quite natural in a bunch of cedars attracted my attention. When I examined it I discovered it to be another buck, hugging the ground, frozen for all the world like a sly cottontail. I had seen him only by the most remote chance. Nine times out of ten I would have walked past him, never suspecting there was a buck within a quarter of a mile. My wife had shot at him and he had decided to hide to escape the bombardment. His tactics had enabled him to elude her and he had almost eluded me. When he realized by my attitude that I had seen him, he made off with a great crashing of brush and all the speed he could muster, skillfully keeping timber between him and me. No one can tell me that he didn't know all about rifles and bullets. He had seen one buck out of his bunch go down, and he had no desire to share his fate.

[23]

It is my firm conviction that the mule deer is as difficult to hunt as the Virginia whitetail when they are hunted in similar country. As a matter of fact, the mules are more often found in semi-open country and are consequently more easily seen and shot; but when they are in thick spruce and aspen, as they often are at the beginning of the season, they are as tough a proposition as anyone could ask for. The early writers on the species made much of the mule deer's habit of standing and gaping at hunters, giving perfect shots. They have also made the statement that mule deer will run off for a little way, then stop for a last look. I have seen them behave this way; but in almost every instance they were back-country animals which had never been hunted hard. I have also seen whitetails act the same way in the Sierra Madres of Mexico where hunters molest them only occasionally.

Sometimes a whistle will stop a running mule deer, but it will stop a whitetail about as often. Entirely too much has been made of the curiosity of the big Western deer. All too often—for the good of the hunters—they display little or none at all.

I have encountered many old bucks that were almost incredibly smart, bucks that seemed to show a high order of genuine intelligence and a firm grasp of the problem they were facing in their battle of survival against men with guns.

A few years ago I was hunting on horseback with a party in northern Arizona when we approached the thickly timbered head of a canyon. It looked "deery," so we stopped. Presently a little two-pointer came dashing out. One of the members of the party dropped him. Then his companion, a three-pointer of about the same age, came out on a dead run and went down across the canyon.

We dressed out the first buck, hung him in a piñon, and went over to the second, leaving our horses and rifles across the canyon. A foolish thing to do, perhaps, but we did it. Presently I happened to glance down the canyon and saw two enormous bucks sneaking along through the cedars. In a fraction of a second they were out of sight, but their tracks in the bottom of the canyon told the story. All the time we had been bombarding the two jittery little fellows, the old ones had gambled quietly with their lives by sitting tight. Then, when we turned our attention to dressing their late companions, they took advantage of the diversion and left for a safer locality. Smart? You're telling me!

Old bucks that have been shot at and missed several times soon begin to learn what rifle bullets are, how they work, and all about them. They learn so much, in fact, that reason seems to get the better of instinct.

A habit of wise old bucks, noticed by most Southwestern hunters, illustrates this. A brushy point is a favorite bedding ground for smart bucks. Strategically such a place is almost perfect. As the buck drowses through the warm hours of the day, he can see below him and he can catch the rising scent of an enemy. If the hunter tries to approach from below, he can sneak back along the timbered arm of the point and leave only his tracks and his warm bed to betray his presence. The only way to get at such a buck is to come down the arm toward the point and hope to get a shot as he runs off.

A young buck so bedded will nearly always run directly off and tear out across the flat to the timber. That to me would seem the natural and instinctive thing to do. But the old ones do not. Often they will go down off a point, affording the hunter a brief glimpse or the sound of cracking brush, but instead of crossing the open ground below they turn, stick to the timber, and run past and behind the hunter.

I remember one smart old buck on whom I turned the tables. I had seen him twice in three days and his big tracks were all over a rough section of canyon country. Both times he had got away by running around the point and getting behind me. The third day I decided to get him or break a leg in the attempt. I was certain he had not left the section, as I had not shot at him and he had never seemed particularly frightened. Late that afternoon, just as I worked along a ridge ending in a point about three hundred feet above the surrounding country, I heard the scrape of dry brush and saw magnificent antlers going down to the left. Instead of trying to follow, I ran swiftly to the right, went down the ridge and waited. Presently I heard the *thump, thump, thump* of his trotting feet, and he came in sight fifty yards away. His great antlered head was thrown back and his powerful muscles rippled under sleek hide. At twenty yards I raised my rifle and he saw me for the first time.

He was a fine buck—old, wise and very fat. The lower part of his massive irregular antlers were heavily warted and his teeth were going bad. I outsmarted that one, but many a buck has made a chump out of me.

Like all intelligent animals—and most game has to be intelligent if it would survive—mule deer display a remarkable knowledge of the hunting seasons. The cycle comes so regularly in their lives that they sense its approach, and when they hear the first distant rifle shots which announce the opening of the season, they change their habits at once.

[26]

One fall I knew where a bunch of large bucks was running. During the summer I had seen them a dozen times within a square mile, and always they would run off a little way, then stop and look at me. They watered at a tank a mile or so off the road, then bedded down not far away in a brushy draw. Many times I had got within easy rifle shot, and once I was actually near enough to take a fairly good photograph of one of them. In common parlance I "had them tied up." So when the season opened, my wife and I drove out to look them over before they were disturbed. We were the first hunters in the territory, and no car had come nearer than two miles on the unfrequented road. However, hunters were on a mountainside a couple of miles away. We heard distant shots.

Did we get easy shots at those "tame" deer? We did not. Although we approached the draw cautiously upwind, we saw them going over the ridge a quarter of a mile away. They were hell bent and showed absolutely no curiosity. Man had ceased to be a friend of the deer and for a month would be the deadliest of enemies. They knew it as well as anyone.

In some localities the Rocky Mountain mule deer is called the "jumping deer," and those who have only read about the animals and have never seen them are apt to form the idea that the bound is the only means of locomotion the animals have. Nothing could be farther from the truth. The animals have three gaits beside the walk —the trot, the bound and a dead run. The bound, about which so much has been written, is largely the gait used when the deer is confused and startled. He also uses it going up and down hill, although I have seen big bucks trot clear to the top of a steep slope with all the form of a standard-bred horse. Many times a drowsing deer jumped from his bed will come out bounding, then go into a trot or a run. A badly scared deer will nearly always run in level country. The run is by no means a gallop, but a dead run like that of a quarter horse or an antelope, and it is unbelievably swift. Very rough country with the terrain composed of large sharp rocks, or "mal pais" as it is called in Arizona, will nearly always make a deer bound. Otherwise I believe he more often trots or runs.

I remember shooting at a running buck three hundred yards away across a sagebrush flat in Mexico. I was using an old .30–40 and underestimated his speed. Every one of my five shots went behind him. The memory is a painful one, for the buck was large and fat and my party needed the meat. I also remember surprising a young doe which had been eating mushrooms in a little cove against a thick stand of young spruce. She could not get through the spruce and her only way of exit was past me. While she was making up her mind she bounded into the air. And how she did bound! I'll swear her feet were three feet from the ground. Finally she rushed by me with a startled snort and stretched out across seventy-five yards of open park like an antelope.

What of the mule deer's senses—what of the defenses he uses in his battle for survival? On which does he most depend—his eyes, his nose, or his ears? My guess is that he depends most upon his ears. They seem to me to be the keenest belonging to any American game animal. Nature did not make them large and flexible through any caprice, but because the deer lives for the most part in a country of rocks and stones where the approach of an enemy is often first detected through sound. His nose, too, is very good, and many times I have seen deer move out from a scent that came from a half-mile away. On the other hand, the eyes of the deer cannot compare with those of the antelope or the mountain sheep. They see well in semi-darkness, but like most game animals they cannot pick up an object unless it is moving. On several occasions deer have almost walked over me when the wind was in my favor and I remained stationary. An antelope would have known at once what I was. A sheep would have been suspicious, but the mule deer took not the slightest notice of my presence.

Then, too, mule deer seem to place no great reliance on their eyes. They may see and watch a moving hunter, but unless they have been hunted hard and are very wild they seldom make off until the suspicions of their eyes have been confirmed by either nose or ears. Wise old bucks will run when they see a moving object silhouetted against the skyline, but I doubt if they know what they are running from.

The ears, then, are the first line of defense, the nose the second. Eyes come in handy, of course, but before a mule deer bounds away in his great curving leaps of alarm, leaps which often leave tracks twenty feet apart, he must scent or hear you.

Most mule-deer fawns come into the world in June. A few arrive as early as late May, and many as late as August. The date of the birth depends on several factors. For one thing, the deer of the North and of high altitudes breed earlier than those of the desert lowlands. For another, a great deal depends on the supply of bucks. A doe comes in heat three times during the mating season, but she stays in heat only a couple of hours. If a buck is available during her first heat she conceives, but if none is at hand, she may wait until her third time or not breed at all. The scarcity of bucks in heavily shot-over areas is responsible for most of the "barren does" the hunters like to talk about. Several so-called barren does were killed by scientists in southern Arizona a few years ago and *all* of them were found either to have lost their fawns to predatory animals or never to have had an opportunity to breed. August fawns come of course from does who have not found a buck until their very last opportunity. Except in the lowlands, an August fawn is a misfortune in every respect. He is small, weak, and still nursing when the snows come. He has kept his mother from laying on fat against the cold, and often neither he nor his mother will survive the winter.

Twins are the rule rather than the exception among mule deer, just as they are among antelope and whitetails. Like all deer, they are spotted during the first few months, and for several weeks they hide while their mother browses and goes to water. Those first weeks are dangerous ones for the fawns—the most dangerous in their lives. Coyotes and bobcats are constantly on the prowl for them. Golden eagles patrol the skies hoping to spot a bit of tender venison. Perhaps a third of them perish before they are steady enough on their long spindly legs to go far afield with their mothers. Many times I have heard the panic-stricken bleat of fawns and then found where a coyote or a bobcat has made a meal.

But it isn't long before fawns are running with their mothers and are acquiring wariness and sophistication. In September and early October they shed into their first gray coats, and never again do they wear spots. Throughout the winter they run with their mothers, and often they continue to hang around them the following year. Many times in the fall I have seen family groups of an old doe, a yearling or two, and two fawns of the previous summer.

Oftentimes hunters think the young buck is after the old doe if they see such a family group during the mating season, but I believe it nearly always means that the male has clung to his mother's apron-strings. But during their second fall the young bucks are nearly always chased away by old ones who look upon them as rivals.

By the beginning of his third fall, when the young buck is some-what less than two-and-a-half years old, he is very definitely beginning to be interested in the does. I doubt if he has any great success as a rule, because the world is full of large, determined and ferocious bucks who will brook no rivalry from any little prongs and three-pointers. By the next year he is large and strong enough to challenge the big fellows, and the year after, and for several succeeding years, he is one of the cocks of the walk unless he falls prey to a mountain lion or is killed by the bullet of a hunter.

In northern Arizona, and in most of the colder parts of the range of mule deer, the bucks shed their antlers late in February or early in March. New antlers begin to grow in a couple of weeks, and by the middle of July they are full grown under the velvet, but still soft and tender. They begin to harden in August, and early in September the bucks are horning the bushes. By the first week of October some-what more than half the bucks have antlers polished hard and bright for fighting, but occasionally a buck is killed even after the middle of October with hard horns under full velvet. As a rule, the healthi-est and strongest bucks shed their antlers first and clean the new growth off first. A castrated buck never gets rid of the velvet at all, and grows strange gnarled antlers.

Before the middle of November, in the colder parts of their range, the bucks' necks are beginning to swell and they are starting to run the does. Often four or five bucks will string along after one doe—the ruling four-pointer first, his understudy next, an amorous and hopeful two-year-old last. Often the two strongest bucks will battle over a receptive doe while the younger and weaker bucks take advantage of the situation and cover her.

Battles between bucks, which start before the actual mating season and continue throughout it, are always noisy, sometimes bloody, but seldom fatal unless the antlers become locked. Then it is but a matter of time until both bucks meet a slow death by starvation. The dozens of locked sets of antlers picked up each spring show this fate to be far from uncommon. Usually the smaller and weaker buck, or the older and less agile decadent buck, finds out that he is inferior and makes off. Battles seldom last more than fifteen or twenty minutes and are more pushing contests than anything else. Often the bucks gouge each other's necks and sometimes one of them manages to put out his adversary's eye. I once shot a big buck which had recently lost an eye, and a friend of mine killed one which was totally blind. It had lost one eye years before and the other within a few days. At the time he was shot, curiously enough, he seemed to be managing fairly well and was not particularly thin.

Before the end of November, the mating season in the Rocky Mountains is in full swing, as shown by the fact that the gestation period among mule deer is seven months and most fawns are born early in June. However, particularly in regions where bucks are scarce, the season may swing along for two-and-a-half or three months. The bucks labor under terrific nervous tension. They grow thin and bedraggled, their flesh becomes coarse and rank. They eat little, fight and run. In times of deep snow many of them come out of the rut so exhausted that they die of starvation and exposure, or fall prey to coyotes or mountain lions.

But when the last does have been bred, they go off by themselves once more and forget the females which have caused them all their grief. Presently they shed their antlers and begin growing new ones, slowly at first, but rapidly when the new and nourishing growth of the spring comes along. Throughout the spring and summer, mature bucks tend to run together. Does go off by themselves to raise their fawns, but the big bucks like male companionship. During the antler-growing period it is more common by far to see two bucks in close companionship than to see one alone. Once in early fall in northern Arizona I saw twenty-five big bucks running in the same herd, and often I have seen five or ten. These close friends of the early fall, however, become bitter enemies as soon as a female is involved, just as human beings do.

The layman is inclined to view the sportsman as a far more serious enemy of the deer than he really is. As a matter of fact, he is only a minor menace to the deer population. Year in and year out it takes at least five hunters to kill a buck. On the other hand, a mountain lion will kill from fifty to seventy-five deer a year, or as many deer as 250 hunters. Bobcats, golden eagles and coyotes prey on fawns, and sometimes even black bears turn fawn-killers. Coyotes are a menace to the deer herds, particularly in times of deep snow; and often they don't even need snow, but will gang up on full-grown deer and kill them in open country. The coyote is a bad actor and a far more serious menace to game than many believe. The grizzly and the lobo wolf, great game-destroyers throughout the West at one time, have themselves been practically exterminated.

But even if he escapes hunters and predatory animals, the mule deer still has no easy path, as he is often beset by smaller but no less deadly enemies. Most of us remember the terrible outbreak of hoof-and-mouth disease which took such a toll from the deer herds of California around 1924. Lung worms, round worms and tape worms weaken the deer so they fall easy prey to predatory animals and inclement weather. Wood ticks and bot flies cause much suffering and sometimes death. Much has still to be done in the prevention and cure of the diseases of wild game, for not infrequently an epidemic will mysteriously strike down a large proportion of the deer in a given area.

Sportsmen kill relatively few deer; but meat and market hunters, wherever they are not severely dealt with, make great inroads upon the herds. The sportsman kills his annual buck, brings him home, brags about his skill, and gets soundly cursed by the more sentimental conservationists. A nester who lives on the game, on the other hand, kills twenty or thirty deer annually, says nothing about it, and is considered a romantic child of nature by the same sentimentalist. The hide hunters of the old days were worse enemies to the deer than even the mountain lions.

Still, the big mule deer is not on his way out. He has come through his dark days, and more and more his value is being recognized, in dollars and cents as well as sentimentally. The powers that be are beginning to realize that he deserves his place in the forests, and that one deer is probably of more value than several sheep. He is gradually increasing and even extending his range. He will be with us forever if we want him, and I know we do want him!

CHAPTER III

LOS BUROS

IF an ordinarily observant sportsman, or even a scientist, should see in the same enclosure examples of the three Southwestern species of mule deer, he would probably have a difficult time telling one from another. Particularly in the winter, their coats are much the same; they have the same sort of tails and antlers. However, a closer examination will show that of the three subspecies, the Rocky Mountain deer is darker both in the summer and in the winter. The big burro deer of the Sonora coast is just as large and just as heavily antlered, but much lighter at all seasons. The Mexican mule deer from the arid country of Arizona, New Mexico and West Texas is smaller, more lightly antlered, and in color about halfway between the northern and the coastal deer.

But in habits, these close relatives, the desert and the Rocky Mountain mule deer, are very different creatures, almost as far apart as sheep and antelope. The northern deer are primarily water-drinkers and ordinarily go to a stream or spring two or three times a week. They love rough, semi-open hill and canyon country, and bed down on ridges and at the heads of draws, and whenever they get into trouble they head into the steepest, roughest country they can find. The desert deer can live without tasting water, however, in any country which supports water-bearing cactus. They are animals of the tangled desert flats, of mesquite and ironwood thickets, of cholla patches. When they sense the approach of an enemy, they head into thicker and thornier country instead of taking to the hills.

[35]

Whenever the desert deer are found away from their beloved flats, whenever they take to the hills and mountains, it is always a sign of over-grazing by cattle and much persecution by man.

The range of the desert mule deer of both subspecies is from the eastern edge of California to the Big Bend of Texas, and from central Arizona to the country south of Hermosillo, Sonora. The Mexican mule deer, or *Odocoileus canus*, is far more widely distributed than *Odocoileus eremicus*, as scientists record it as occupying all of this vast range except for a narrow strip running along the Sonora coast from the region south of Tiburon Island past Yuma, Arizona, and extending into California, which is the range of *Odocoileus hemionus eremicus* or the burro deer, a large, light-colored, close-coupled, heavily antlered animal. However, the Mexican mule deer takes many different forms. In parts of the Arizona desert it is almost as large as the deer of northern Arizona and New Mexico: big bucks weigh from 175 to 200 pounds. But in the Big Bend of Texas it is distinctly a small deer. Antler development is poor and the big bucks weigh no more than from 145 to 160. The biggest desert deer I have ever seen come from Tiburon Island, where the wild and primitive Seri Indians make their crude camps, and from the country immediately surrounding it. Indeed, the subspecies was first classified at the foot of Sierra Azul de los Indios, or Blue Indian Mountains, on the mainland not far from Tiburon. However, the range of the so-called burro deer must be narrow indeed, as bucks I have shot within thirty-five miles of the coast are plainly of the Mexican variety, light-colored, true, but long-legged and light-antlered. But the deer just off the coast are definitely different, and even the Mexicans and Indians in that country recognize two kinds of mule deer.

Along the border most American sportsmen call these desert deer "blacktails," continuing that ancient misnomer. The ordinary Sonora Mexican simply calls any desert buck *el buro*, while the more literary town-dwelling Mexican calls him *ciervo reyal*, or royal stag. The name "buro" has led to an amusing mistake which appears in almost all scientific works—that of calling these desert dwellers "burro deer." Now a *buro* and a *burro* in Mexican Spanish are very different things. The *buro* is a mule deer and the *burro* a jackass. American scientists, not being able to detect the difference between the single and double "r," dubbed these animals "jack-asses"—a ludicrous mistake but a natural one.

But whatever the name, they are among the most lordly of animals. They are hard to find and harder to hit, and the sportsman with the head of a fine desert buck in his collection has a trophy he has a right to boast of.

In the Sonoran deserts the big game is very definitely zoned, and seldom does one species invade the domain of another. The open plains and playas have their antelope, the mouths of the canyons and the little foothills their whitetails, the highest, most rugged desert mountains their bighorn sheep, and the flat tangled jungles of cholla, *saguaro*, *pitahaya* and ironwood their mule deer. Sheep often feed down in lowland valleys or even cross open plains on their migrations between ranges, mule deer may climb the little foothills for a look-see, and whitetails, when badly frightened, may temporarily invade sheep country; but for the most part the various species stay put. Each has its own little bailiwick and does not like to leave it. Each group of animals clings to his native terrain like members of some tribe of primitive human beings. Yet—and here is where a curious contradiction appears—when one species is exterminated, or for some reason does not exist in suitable country, another tends to take over its habits and to occupy its land. I can illustrate this but I cannot explain it; and I hope that someone who is a better biologist than I am will solve the problem. Wherever sheep have been killed out, deer of some kind nearly always move into former sheep range and take over many of the habits of sheep. In the Cucurpi Mountains of Sonora, whitetail deer range in what would have been sheep country if it had not been so far from the main path of sheep migration. In many desert ranges of Arizona, where sheep have been exterminated, desert mule deer have forgotten their thickets and plains, and have become bighorns in everything except appearance. They leap from rock to rock with the same reckless speed, and dash down a cliff with the same wild verve of the *cimarrones*. Yet these are the very same animals which never touch foot to a mountain that has sheep on it. Explain it if you will—I can't.

On the other hand, in certain sections of Sonora, sheep are often found in areas where there are no mule deer; and when so found they nearly always range much lower than they otherwise would. In the San Franciscos, for example, they habitually range clear down in the valleys during the winter and not only feed there in the early mornings and late afternoons but actually bed down under the trees both night and day. It is probably a food problem, but on the other hand it has all the earmarks of a mutual non-aggression pact to me.

But for the most part, *el buro* is strictly a creature of the lowland flats and valleys with their almost incredibly thick tangle of thorny vegetation. In them he finds food, water and protection from his foes. When his great sensitive ears—probably the best belonging to any American game animal—warn him of the approach of lion, tigre or man, he slips off as soundlessly as a gray ghost. When eddying currents of air bring him hostile scent close at hand, he goes off in the great flying bounds that carry him twenty feet at a jump.

But the desert jungles that are his home are not the completely hostile places they might appear. As a matter of fact, they support an astonishing variety of wildlife—quail, whitewings, dove, rabbits, javelinas, as well as the great gray deer.

Probably the staple of *el buro*'s diet is the tree called ironwood by Americans and *palo fierro* by the Mexicans. He eats it at all seasons of the year. In the early fall, when mesquite beans are ripe, he devours great quantities of them and grows enormously fat on them, just as the Rocky Mountain mule deer do on the nuts of the piñon. All through the spring and summer he feasts like an epicure on the delicious fruit of the pitahaya, prickly pear and other kinds of cactus. Like the Mexican bighorn, he seldom if ever touches water. When his regular food becomes dry after a prolonged drought, he knocks the head off a *bisnaga*, or barrel cactus, and chews the water-laden pulp. If none is handy, he thinks nothing of girdling a great saguaro or even braving the thorns of a pitahaya. In the winter when the fruit of the cholla is in season he eats it with relish, just as do both sheep and antelope.

The ability of these Mexican deer to survive drought is astonishing. Not only have I found them plentiful in regions where there was absolutely no water within fifty miles, but I have seen them fat and cocky in drought areas where the native desert-raised Mexican cattle were dying like flies. In the winter of 1934 I hunted mule deer between Pitiquito and the Gulf after the worst drought in the history of Sonora. We were in cattle country where thousands of head had perished and drying carcasses lay on every hand. We expected the deer to be thin, too; but every animal we shot and every one we saw was fat and in excellent condition. The fact that they survive as they do is a triumph of adaptability—the proof of thousands of years of evolution, of pushing farther and farther into the deserts away from hunting Indians and water-loving predators.

In Sonora, as everywhere else, the mountain lion is the most serious enemy of the mule deer. I have often heard that lions never go far from water and must drink several times a week, yet I have found lion sign and lion kills wherever there were deer. Near Topopo Mountain on the Sonora coast, forty miles from any permanent water, I found both mule deer and sheep. I also found several lion kills and fresh lion sign. Wherever deer go, lions will follow; they can range far, but occasionally they must return to permanent water.

Whereas lions kill the mature animals, the most serious enemies of the fawns are the smaller predators—bobcats, coyotes and the fearsome golden eagles. All make serious inroads upon the fawn crop, and as a consequence few does are able to raise more than half of the young which they bring into the world. On the other hand, though the predator problem is a serious one, the deer are holding their own and are perhaps slowly increasing, for very few men hunt them successfully. Mexicans have few rifles and little ammunition, and, besides, most of the deer stay far out in the wilderness away from towns and heavily stocked ranch areas.

In Arizona, the big light-gray deer have been hunted hard and have decreased. Thousands were killed for the market in the early days, as all the big centers of population in Arizona are close to desert deer country. Others were killed by the hundreds by cow-punchers, prospectors and homesteaders. Now they are greatly de-pleted near all the large centers of population, as well as on the Pima and Papago Indian reservations, where the combination of year-round hunting, good stalking and modern rifles formed a deadly combination. But most well-informed observers say that at the pres-ent time the deer are increasing. The buck law has done a certain amount of good, and awakened public sentiment which makes ille-gal killing of a deer a serious moral offense, has done even more.

Because they live in a semi-tropical land, these deer follow a somewhat different cycle from that of their mountain relatives. The bucks do not finish cleaning and polishing their antlers until the first week in November, and the rutting season does not get well under way until about the first of the year. Desert bucks retain their antlers longer, too. Few shed them sooner than the middle of March, and I once saw a great six-point buck in all the glory of polished, shining antlers on April 10th. Fawns are born late, too; and on one occasion I found two little fellows not more than a month old hidden in some brush well after the first week in September.

For some reason all the game on the deserts of Sonora grows good heads, and the *buros* are no exception. Some of the finest mule-deer heads I have ever seen have come from animals that never ex-perienced freezing temperatures and never took a drink of water in their lives. The animals found along the Sonora coast from the Altar Valley south to Hermosillo seem especially favored in antler devel-opment. Almost without exception, the heads of mature bucks taken there are wide of spread, very massive and extraordinarily symmet-rical. The very finest area of all for the trophy hunter, though it is hard to get to, is Tiburon Island, home of the most savage and primitive of all American Indians. This is the type habitat of *Odocoileus hemionus eremicus* and the place where he reaches his greatest size and maximum antler development. What is more, the animals are extraordinarily plentiful on the island itself. Coyotes are almost their only enemies. Lions have never swum the straits to follow them there, and the Seri Indians would rather eat rotting fish washed up on the beach than hunt deer. I have seen as many as two hundred deer there in a day, many of them majestic bucks. The largest deer I believe I have ever seen was on the mainland just across from the island. He was in the yellow summer coat typical of *el buro* and his antlers were in full velvet. Though I was not more than seventy-five feet from him when I jumped him, he looked as large as a bull elk. One party taken into that country by Charles C. Ren, the Mexican guide of Ajo, Arizona, brought out three heads with spreads greater than thirty-four inches.

Hunting this great, heavily antlered species of deer is just about as different from most Southwestern hunting as one could imagine. For almost all other kinds of game, except antelope, the sportsman has to climb or ride in rough country and to take long shots. But in hunting *buros* he must steal quietly through tangled jungle, watching the wind, taking every precaution to keep from disturbing so much as a pebble. In mountain hunting it is often not fatal to your chances if the game sees you first, but down in the desert lowlands you must either see *el buro* before he sees you or come back empty-handed.

I learned my lesson early. The first deer I ever hunted were desert bucks. One summer I was spending the vacation with an uncle who owned a cow ranch on the desert. I had a horse all of my own, unlimited time, and access to an arsenal almost big enough to supply a small army. When I found a section where the deer were plentiful, and caught a glimpse of an enormous buck with horns in full velvet, I became a deer hunter as automatically as a bird-dog stiffens into a point at his first whiff of quail. I hunted early in the morning when the desert was cool and the deer were feeding, and in the middle of the day when they were bedded down. I saw tracks by the thousand. I heard deer run. For a month I never saw one. When at last it began to dawn on me that I had to watch the wind, that I had to be more quiet than I had ever been in my eleven years, that following directly on a deer's track was foolishness, I began occasionally to catch glimpses of does and fawns. Then one lovely morning after a rain had made the desert cool and fragrant I got within fifty yards of a big buck feeding on ironwood. To my childish eyes he looked as big as a horse. Helpless and fascinated I watched him for five minutes without firing a shot. Then, when he sensed my presence and ran, I fairly filled the air with lead. I don't suppose I came within five feet of him, yet finding him was a great moral victory. I didn't know it at the time, but that summer's course had made me a fairly good and patient deer hunter. Seeing that old buck was my diploma. Since that time my luck has always been passable.

I don't wish to give the impression that *el buro* is a slick fellow and that the other big-game species of the Southwest are composed of dullards. That would not be true. All of them are well equipped with brains. The desert deer are hard to hunt because of the country they inhabit; and the way they have survived unrestricted hunting is amazing. In southern Arizona where for years the enforcement of game laws was a joke and in many ways still leaves much to be desired, they still exist in considerable numbers, even near large population centers. The tens of thousands of antelope which once shared the range with them have vanished. Sheep are making a last tragic stand, and the whitetails have been driven high into the timbered mountains; but the grand gray desert bucks still run over their ancestral domain, now holding their own almost everywhere, and in some places increasing. In the coastal deserts of Sonora the big mule deer are the most plentiful game animals and always will be.

The deer hunters of the Southwest are a slam-bang crew. The care and stealth so necessary in the heavily wooded East become superfluous for the most part out here, as bucks are usually hunted in thinly wooded country where one can see a long way and get open shots across canyons and from hill to hill. As a consequence the conventionally trained mountain hunter more than meets his match when he tackles the desert bucks.

For one thing, he cannot successfully ride a horse after the desert bucks as he does after the Rocky Mountain mule deer of the canyon country and the little mountain whitetails—and most Southwesterners off horses are like fish out of water. He *can* ride a horse, of course, as there is no law against it, but it doesn't do him much good. The country, especially in the lower elevations, is simply too thick. He may see deer from his horse, but getting them is another thing. By the time he gets off and gets his rifle out of the scabbard, the deer has vanished. Even on foot it is often difficult to get into action soon enough.

In 1934, when I was hunting afoot on the Primavera ranch

some forty miles from the coast in Sonora, I shot two *buros* my first day out. A companion shot another. A week or so later we tried it on horseback. Tracks and sign were just as plentiful, we hunted in exactly the same cholla patches where the deer were feeding on cholla fruit, but in nine hours of hunting we didn't even *see* a deer, much less get a shot at one. On my last trip to the same section, in 1937, I daily passed on horseback through mule-deer country on my way from camp to some whitetail hills. I saw desert bucks, but usually they went bounding away through the brush and were in sight for about two jumps. I did kill one, but I don't think he could have been much of a loss to his race, as he was evidently half-witted. I was riding along almost at dark, about two miles from camp, when that buck bounded out from behind a clump of cholla where he had been feeding. He stood there while I jumped off my horse, took my .257 out of the boot and fired. It was real wilderness country there, and I have no doubt that I was the first human being he had ever seen—surely the first *Americano*.

On the same trip I got a shot at a beautiful buck with a near-record head. I did not get him, and therein lies a tale. I was headed out alone on horseback toward a sheep mountain when I saw that big fellow cross a little opening through the paloverdes and palo-fierros not more than one hundred yards away. He had neither seen me nor heard nor smelled me. I dismounted and took out my rifle. Through the 'scope I could see him browsing on the far side of the tree. The foliage did not look particularly thick so I decided to shoot. At the first shot a whole limb came crashing down. The second sent a shower of twigs into the air, and my big buck decided to move out. Both bullets had been deflected by that relatively thin foliage and did not touch him. Shooting a light 100-grain bullet at 3,000 feet per second, I might as well have saved my powder.

Hunting those desert bucks, you seldom get an open shot, and the best you can do is to crack away through an ironwood or a clump of cactus at a flash of gray-brown hide and shining antlers. As a consequence, the hunter only handicaps himself who uses the fast-moving, easily expanding bullets which are exactly right for mountain game, as they go to pieces like smoke against the branches and twigs which always seem to get in the way. After several sour experiences with light bullets, I always take along heavy soft-points for my .30–'06 or 7mm. when I go into desert mule country with my eye on a good head. With such bullets my luck has improved, and I once killed a big buck stone dead with a bullet that had plowed clear through a four-inch paloverde branch before it hit him. The new .348 Winchester with the 200-grain bullet or the .35 Whelen with the 250-grain ought to be good medicine. So should the heavy soft-pointed bullets for the .30–'06. Any bullet one uses should be heavy enough to shoot clear through and leave a good blood-trail, as you seldom get more than one shot and wounded animals are hard to track.

The hunting experiences which I have just recorded are all Mexican. In parts of their range the Mexican mule deer are found in rolling hills and canyon country; and in such country they can and should be hunted on horseback. This kind of hunting is easier, pleasanter and surer. Parts of the Big Bend of Texas fairly swarm with the small eastern variety of this deer, as they range in the country below the little fantails. In parts of Arizona they are also a horseback proposition.

Yet for the most part they must be hunted on foot, as painstakingly, as carefully and as slyly as if they were Eastern whitetails. And, as I have said before, they are hard to get.

I have been playing hide-and-seek with them since I was old enough to pack a rifle, and there will still be plenty of them to outwit hunters a century from now. In Arizona they are well protected, and in Mexico the greater part of their range is far from the haunts of man and the pastures of domestic stock. They'll get along.

CHAPTER IV

ELF OF THE BRUSH COUNTRY

IF someone should conduct a beauty contest among the game animals of the Southwest, I have no doubt that the Arizona whitetail would win it hands down. A big buck mule deer, with his massive antlers and blocky body, is a magnificent sight. Likewise a great desert ram or a lordly bull elk. An antelope is bizarre, grotesque—ugly almost to the point of beauty, paradoxically. But the Arizona whitetail is an exquisitely lovely thing. He is small, dainty, graceful—cute! I don't particularly like the word *cute*, but it describes very well this Mexican cousin of *Odocoileus virginianus*.

Compared to the big males, the females of elk, mule deer and sheep are homely graceless things, but the little whitetail does are just as lovely as the bucks—just as graceful, just as *cute*. Again I use that feminine word; there is something very feminine about even the largest and lustiest Arizona whitetail buck.

These little deer are essentially Virginia whitetails done in miniature. The bucks have typical whitetail antlers—long brow tines and all points branching off of a main beam. The tail is the same—a rich, reddish brown on top and pure white below. The ears are larger in proportion to the body than those of the Eastern whitetail and so is the tail. Does and young bucks are a smooth, even dove-gray, much bluer than either the mule deer or the Virginia whitetail in winter coat. Old bucks are darker, with a more grizzled, salt-and-pepper effect. Unlike either the mule deer or the Eastern whitetail, the little fellows do not change to a summer coat of red. Instead, the

[49]

adult animals are distinctly gray the year round. They tend to get a tawny tinge, but they are gray nevertheless. The fawns are red spotted with white like those of all North American deer and the yearlings also grow a red summer coat. *But a mature Arizona white-tail is always gray.*

I once wrote a magazine article in which I made the statement that the antlers of a mature Arizona whitetail buck were about the size of a man's two hands outspread in antler shape. I was taken to task for it by about fifty sportsmen who knew something about the species, but I still maintain that I am right. When I spread my hands that way, using the thumbs as the bases of the antlers and putting them about as far apart as a buck's head is wide, the "spread" is a bit over 14 inches. That is about the average for a mature buck under typical conditions. I have seen hundreds of heads and almost without exception the measurements for both spread and main beam on any particular one are about the same. A buck with a 14-inch spread will have approximately a 14-inch main beam, one with a 17-inch spread will have a 17-inch beam, and so on. That rule almost always applies. The heads are extremely symmetrical, as this would tend to prove. There is little individual variation, except in size, and the heads freak much more rarely than those of mule deer. An average mature Eastern whitetail buck is a five-pointer, but the mature Arizona whitetail is a four-pointer. I have seen heads with many more points than that, but they are the exception rather than the rule. A two-year-old buck, instead of growing prongs, will often grow a small, slender set of four-point antlers, so small that occasionally taxidermists with nothing better to do mount such sets on jackrabbits with an effect that is not at all incongruous.

The size of the antlers varies greatly on the deer of different localities. All the bucks which I have seen taken along the Mogollon Rim, the northern limit of their range, have very small heads. Those shot in the Chisos Mountains of the Big Bend of Texas, the eastern limit of their American range, have heads that are even smaller. The largest heads, and incidentally the largest deer that I have ever seen, came from the high Sierra Madres of Mexico and from the Limestones and Chiricahuas of southern Arizona. In all of those localities, I think the heads of mature bucks average 16 inches or better in both spread and beam, as against 14 for the entire range.

Small though the antlers are, the record books are all wrong about them, or at least the last edition of *Records of North American Big Game* was. The largest head listed was only that of a good big average buck. But the "record" did serve to make the nations' head-hunters aware of the species, and many much larger heads have now been measured and sent in to the committee. The new record is now, I believe, close to 20 inches both in beam and spread, and I have seen several which were almost as large. Two heads, both around 18 inches, which have been officially measured, belonged to bucks which died after they got their antlers locked during the mating season. They are now in the possession of a Tucson dentist.

Occasionally an old decadent buck in limestone country will grow a freak set of palmated antlers with a great many points. I have seen a few with as many as a dozen points to a side, but such heads are far rarer than they are among mule deer.

The little whitetail bears many names, and "Arizona whitetail" is not very happily bestowed, as he is primarily a Mexican species which only spills over the border and penetrates less than halfway up the state of Arizona. Sonora whitetail is probably a better name; so is the English translation, Coues' whitetail, of his Latin handle, *Odocoileus couesi*. Oldtimers in Arizona often refer to him as the fantail, because his tail is so large in proportion to his body, and·in the Big Bend of Texas he is usually known by that name. Mexicans always call him *venado* to distinguish him from the desert mule deer, which they call *buro*. I have never heard Mexicans call him *ciervo*, as E. W. Nelson says they do, although literary town-dwelling Mexicans do sometimes refer to mule deer as *ciervo reyal*, or royal stag.

Even in favored localities where the race reaches its maximum development, the *venado* is still distinctly a small deer. An average big buck weighs about 80 pounds dressed and a doe a little over 60. I have seen several extraordinarily big bucks which dressed out at between 110 and 119 pounds, and I have heard of a few which went a bit over 120, but they are very, very rare and are indeed giants among their kind. In some localities, notably the Chisos Mountains of western Texas, I doubt if the average full-grown buck would weigh 70 pounds. They are so small that a husky hunter can put one over his shoulder and walk away with it easily. The carcass of one will not weigh down a horse even in rough country if you put it back of the saddle.

The scientists who have collected and studied the little whitetails have got most of their information from those found in the mountain ranges along the Mexican border in Arizona, Texas and New Mexico. As a consequence, a good deal of their findings as to habits and habitat are faulty. To make an analogy, studying these deer in the United States is something like a sociologist who writes about the habits of Arizonians from his observations of those found working in New York City.

Even in the 'nineties when Nelson studied them they had already been shot at and harried by cowboys, prospectors and market hunters, and as a consequence they had moved into brushier, rougher country than that in which they are found in the natural state, and they had become very wary. In all the border states they are now brush and rough-country animals, but in isolated parts of Mexico they are more often found in relatively open country—so open that an Arizona-trained hunter would not consider it deer country at all. When I was in the Sierra Azuls in 1934, for example, I found the bucks ranging low along the bases of the high mountains in country so open that only the heads of the draws supported live oaks. Unless the deer could put a ridge between us I could often keep them in sight for more than a half-mile.

Most scientists do not realize that the little whitetails are also found in true lower Sonoran deserts, where, like the desert mule deer, the sheep and the antelope, they have learned to do without open water. I have found them all over the Sonora desert, sometimes within fifteen miles of the coast. They still remain hill and mountain animals, however, and they seldom range far away from the bases of the hills, to which they flee when they are frightened. They range over any mountain which has a little cover and soil and not great areas of solid rock on it. I have seen them plentiful around the bases of the Cubabais, the Sierra Viejos, the Californias, the Picus and the Costa Ricas, all far-western Sonora mountains. The most plentiful I have ever seen them was in a low range of hills southwest of the little Sonora placer-mining town of Cienega. These desert whitetails may for all I know possibly be a new subspecies. W. T. Hornaday collected a doe in the Cubabais in 1907 when he was on his famous Sonora sheep hunt, but he was unfamiliar with the species and hence drew no conclusions.

Typical whitetail country is the upper Sonoran zone of rolling hills, clumps of live oaks, occasional alligator-bark junipers, yuccas, piñons and hillsides covered with rich gramma grass. On the other hand, the yellow-pine forests of the Sierra Madres are full of white-tails, as well as turkey and Mearn's quail, and in the high ranges of Arizona and New Mexico, where cowboys and nesters harry them, they are found in the summer and early fall clear up into spruce and fir on the very tops of the mountains. The Mogollon Rim, the north-ern limit of their range, is a country of about 7,000 feet elevation, a land of yellow pines, spruce and fir on the north slopes and decidu-ous Gambel oaks in the canyons.

Much is still to be learned about the species. There are possibly many unclassified races, as deer of the same general description range clear from central Arizona to Panama. There is some slight evidence that the "fantail" of the oldtimers, the mysterious little whitetail of early Montana and Wyoming, was an advance guard of the Arizona whitetail. For evidence on both sides I refer you to the chapter called "The Northern Fantail" in Seton's *Lives of the Game Animals*. When my article on the Arizona whitetail came out in *Field and Stream*, I was deluged with letters from hunters in the Northwest and all of them declared that I had described their mys-terious "fantail."

A similar story, with considerable variation, has long gone the rounds in Arizona—that there is a sub-race of the whitetail in certain sections here which is even smaller than the recognized Arizona whitetail. Cowboys and prospectors tell of mature does with young no bigger than rabbits, of tiny mature bucks. So far most scientists have scoffed at the yarn.

But now I must give my own bit of evidence. The story had always intrigued me, as the mysterious and romantic always does. So, when I heard in 1935 that a tiny deer which the Mexicans called *cavrito*, or little goat, ranged in the southern end of Sonora's Cucurpi Mountains, my wife and I went in to see for ourselves. In a week's hard hunting we saw two deer, a buck and a doe, which our native guide assured us were *cavritos*. Luckily we shot them both. The buck, a four-year-old two-pointer, weighed but forty pounds dressed, the doe, also four years old, but thirty. We skinned them carefully and brought the heads and hides back to Arizona, where A. A. Nichol, University of Arizona game specialist, said they were undoubtedly a new subspecies and corroborated my estimate that they were four years old. Except that they were much smaller and slightly more reddish all over, they looked like ordinary Arizona whitetails.

But my story must end unhappily. Nichol turned the heads and hides over to a colleague, who attempted to tan the hides by immersing them in a solution in a pan on his back porch. Then came a jolly police dog, who ate them up. The skulls are still in the possession of the museum of the university's department of biology. What, if anything, has been done about them as I write this in 1937, I do not know.

But all native Sonora Mexicans recognize a distinctly different and very rare little whitetail deer which they call a *cavrito*. In addition, I have since seen one at the foot of Las Mochis Mountain in

Sonora. Nichol saw two in southwestern Arizona in the late spring of 1937; and Nic is a trained scientist, not a romantic.

The Arizona whitetail breeds occasionally with the desert mule deer, and the cross has given rise to the so-called Crook's blacktail, a strange animal which has characteristics both of the mule deer and the whitetail, a compromise in antlers, tail, metatarsal glands. It more nearly resembles the Columbian blacktail than it does either of its parents. The cross is probably not particularly uncommon, as the range of the whitetails and the desert mule deer overlap in many places. On the west side of the Santa Rita range in southern Arizona, scientists working at the Southwest Range Experiment Station have discovered that the cross is rather an ordinary occurrence. The reason is interesting. Whitetails are regularly shot in season there, and as a consequence there is a great surplus of whitetail does over bucks. On the other hand, the desert mule deer are protected by a closed season and the little two-point bucks are prevented by the big fellows from finding a mate among their own kind. The result is that along the edge of the mountains, where the two species come together, the crosses occur. A little mule deer buck is about the right size for a full-grown whitetail doe.

On the other hand, the same scientists duplicated nature's experiment in their own pens. It was not particularly successful, as the whitetail doe bitterly resented those twin results of her moment of weakness. She would have nothing to do with them and they had to be bottle-raised. At last reports they were doing well, though neither mule deer nor whitetails would associate with them. The only friend they had was an antelope. The way of the half-breed anywhere is difficult; psychologically, if in no other way.

Like the desert mule deer, the little whitetail breeds later than do the northern species. In cold countries, November is traditionally the month of the rut, but in southern Arizona and Sonora the necks of the bucks do not begin to swell until after the middle of December. Most of the running period falls in January. The first fawns are born in July and many come into the world as late as the first week in September. Many times I have seen little fellows still in their spotted red coats as late as the middle of November.

The bucks begin to shed their horns around March 15th and continue to shed clear into the middle of April. I remember seeing one bedraggled old fellow still carrying antlers on May 1st. But the little whitetails seem to grow their new sets much faster than mule deer do, for by the middle of July they are full grown under the velvet, and by early October all I have ever seen have been polished hard and bright.

On a few occasions, usually in the middle of the winter, I have seen large herds of whitetails, ordinarily comprised of does, fawns and young bucks. They are, I am convinced, no more gregarious than mule deer, though some scientists have given them credit for so being. More often than not, the bucks run in pairs. Seven big bucks together is the largest bachelor's club I have ever seen.

The little whitetails are not nearly so migratory as their cousins the mule deer. Because they are often found in abruptly rising ranges, they almost always can get into country comparatively free of snow by going to south slopes or into the canyons, so their winter and summer range are never very far apart. However, in the Mogollons of New Mexico and the Blues of Arizona, where for some reason they are found in what would ordinarily be considered typical

Rocky Mountain mule-deer country,* they move into the cedar and piñon forests when the snows lie deep.

Because of their habit when molested of seeking the wildest, most inaccessible country they can find, whitetails are hard to hunt. In fact, in proportion to their numbers, I should say that they are even harder to hunt than desert bighorn sheep. So in spite of their small size, a pair of whitetail antlers is a trophy to be cherished and bragged about. Show me a man who regularly gets his whitetail, and I'll show you someone who is a good stalker, a patient hunter, and a fast, accurate shot. He has to be, or he has little success with Arizona whitetails.

But hunting these little animals in the border mountains has its compensations. For one thing you will get plenty of exercise; and it is impossible to hunt whitetails without getting into good condition. You do not walk—you climb. Before you get into whitetail country you usually have to go a thousand feet or more above your camp. All day you push uphill and down, out of one canyon into another, across one ridge to a saddle, then up another ridge. All the time you must strive to travel silently, you must watch the wind, you must keep everlastingly on the alert for a vanishing flag, for a sudden thump or rustle which says a deer is near. Then when your efforts have been crowned with success and you have your buck down, you face the problem of getting him to camp. He will be small. Probably he will weigh no more than eighty pounds dressed. But carrying even an eighty-pound buck down from a mountain peak and managing a rifle and perhaps a camera and a canteen at the

---

* The natives of the Big Bend to Texas are convinced that the little whitetails can run mule deer out of any country to which they take a fancy. I am skeptical.

same time is no task for a weakling. If you don't believe me, try it! Then, too, the Arizona whitetail hunter must work on the top of the world with only the buzzards and the incredibly blue sky above him. Below he sees a lovely panorama of mauve and violet desert spotted with silver tanks where cattle water, with brown threads of dry arroyos, and with the distant purple upthrust of other desert ranges like the one which he is hunting. When he pursues the little whitetails he becomes a creature of the upper air like an eagle or a hawk; he almost ceases to be a terrestrial being.

As I look back over twenty years of hunting, my pursuit of these dwarf deer stands out pleasantly. I can remember sweet sunny October and November days alone on the very top of a rugged desert range, poking cautiously along through the chaparral, watching the wind, trying to be quiet, pausing now and then to admire the beauty of the desert below me. I can remember lunches eaten by some tiny mountain spring with the mystery of lofty wilderness all about. Then suddenly the chaparral spouts deer. A couple of bucks, deciding the jig is up, dash for safety. Then comes quick, hot action. The buck is down. For a moment I pause to admire his sleek beauty. I remember, too, long painful scrambles back to camp with a dead deer limp on my shoulder. But these are labors of love. I'd much rather come down a mountain burdened by a trophy than empty-handed.

Usually the hunter who bags an Arizona whitetail earns him; but some, of course, are killed by the sheerest luck—as, for instance, two of the several I have killed.

Once when living in Texas I found a spur of the Chisos range where the very rare Mearn's quail existed in considerable numbers.

Now, wherever you find the Mearn's quail you also stand a good chance of finding the little whitetails. The reverse is also true; and as a matter of fact I had run across the quail while hunting for deer. So, after two days of whitetail hunting during which I had seen nothing but does and fawns, I decided to turn my deer hunt into a quail hunt, and left camp with a 20-gauge double instead of my rifle. After an hour of climbing I was on the high lonely ridge, covered with piñon, cedar and yucca, where I had seen the quail. Before long I had a covey scattered and lying close. Leisurely I tramped around kicking birds out from beneath my feet, waiting until they had flown twenty yards or so, then letting them have the open barrel. I had hunted a half-hour and had got five or six birds when I kicked one up that had hidden under the leaves of a yucca. He flew straight away, and when he was directly over a patch of chaparral I let him have it. He crumpled in mid-air and dropped straight into the brush. The moment he hit, a whitetail buck jumped out of that little brush patch. Despite my astonishment I automatically gave him the full-choke barrel. At twenty yards the charge penetrated to his heart and I came down the mountain that day with the rarest deer and a mess of the rarest game birds in the United States. Such is luck! A quail with one barrel and a deer with the other!

My other "easy" deer came my way while I was a student at the University of Arizona in Tucson. It was the first whitetail I had shot in Arizona, though I previously had killed several in Mexico. When the deer season opened and bucks began to come into Tucson on the sides of automobiles, I was overcome by a strange fever. I could not study, my classes no longer interested me; so I borrowed a rifle and persuaded a girl who owned a car to come deer hunting with me. The young lady was from the East and had never seen a wild deer, but she agreed to furnish transportation. We followed a dim road into one of the canyons on the south slope of the Santa Catalinas, parked the car, and climbed out of the canyon. We had walked about fifty yards when a buck ran out ahead of us and started up the mountain. One shot from the .30–30 I carried clipped his backbone as neatly as if I had done it with an axe.

As we walked up to the animal, my mouth hung open with astonishment. The young lady, however, took the whole business as a matter of course. "This is fun," she said. "Let's run out and shoot another deer one of these days." I did not have the heart to disillusion her.

But these two bucks were rare exceptions. I have killed others in the United States only as a result of long, patient hunting. The little deer know all the tricks of the trade. If they hear you or catch your wind, they sneak quietly away, leaving only their tracks and their warm beds to tell of their presence. If you catch them in an awkward location and they think you do not know they're about, they lie so close you can almost step upon them when they move. Like the quail and the ruffed grouse, they seem to have learned that sudden noise will disconcert the hunter and make his shots go wild.

I am paying all these compliments, understand, to the deer of the American Southwest and not to the citizens of Mexico. South of the line, in isolated sections where they are seldom hunted, I have seen whitetails not a great deal more wary than cattle. Native Mexicans seldom hunt, because ammunition is expensive; and the *politicos* do all they can to discourage the ownership of weapons, for the

stones but producing nothing. When we finished it was about noon and we were hungry, so we stopped and ate our lunch. As we were about to set out for another canyon, I idly tossed a big stone into a patch of thick brush. Instead of hearing the clash of rock upon rock, I heard a hollow thump, and out came a big whitetail buck, flag up, going like a bat out of hell. The buck and I were both surprised, but we managed to cut him down before he topped out.

As far as tactics are concerned, hunting the whitetails on the Mexican deserts is a comparatively simple matter. They usually feed a little way out on the flats, and bed down from one hundred to a thousand feet up on the side of the hill. Unlike their American cousins, they have not learned the virtues of skulking; and when the rank scent of man rises to their sensitive noses, they leave in high gear. Getting them then is simply a matter of shooting fast, straight and often.

But of all the ways to hunt whitetails, my favorite is to hunt on horseback over the rolling oak-clad hills of southern Arizona and northern Sonora. It's a lazy man's sport, perhaps, but it's great sport nevertheless. You go slowly up the ridges, around the heads of the canyons, watching far and wide for the flash of the glittering fan which means a whitetail. Then when you see one, it means piling off and going into action—cutting him down on the dead run before he gets over the ridge. You pass by many deer that way; but, too, you see many—two or three hundred yards away, usually, and moving swiftly.

The one difficulty in such hunting is that because the ranges are long and the bucks' heads are diminutive, it is often difficult to tell the bucks from the does. A big buck will always run with his head up and his antlers back over his shoulders. His sex can thereby be determined even at long range. But the little fellows, in case you simply want a buck, more often run like does. You ought therefore to have a 'scope sight on your rifle, both for the seeing and the hitting. But many does are killed in Arizona annually—far more, I suspect, than even the game wardens ever know.

If I were to pick the game animal best fitted to survive unrestricted hunting, I'd take the Arizona whitetail. His brains, his wariness, the type of country in which he has learned to find refuge when hard pressed—all combine to make him the most difficult of all deer to kill. In addition, the little fellows are prolific, the does having two fawns a season. In Arizona and New Mexico the herds are increasing, and in some localities they are probably as numerous as they ever were. In the southern Arizona mountains they have held their own despite the fact that almost the whole population turns out every fall to hunt them down. With the brush full of hunters and their range narrow and limited, they hardly know which way to turn; and in spite of their brains and craft, many are killed. In fact, almost the surest way to get a buck is to pick a runway and let the other fellow drive one over to you. But I don't hunt that way. I crave action and movement.

Every time I go to southern Arizona I hear this lament: "The bucks are all killed off. All I see are does and fawns." But when my friends tell me that old story I shake my head and chuckle softly to myself. I know these crafty little fellows, and I realize that the wise old bucks are on the highest peaks, in the most inaccessible canyons, and in the thickest brush.

When the madness of the hunters' moon is over, and men once

more leave them alone in their mountains, they will come forth to battle merrily for their does, and to beget young which will continue with their elfin presence to lend mystery and enchantment to the high timbered ranges that rise sharply from the somber desert.

CHAPTER V

LORD OF THE PINNACLES

AMONG the big-game hunters of the Southwest no animal is valued so highly as the desert bighorn. A sportsman may have hunted deer, turkeys, elk and bear for years and with the greatest of success; but until he has taken his sheep, until he has matched his brains, his endurance and his skill with those inhabitants of the rocky peaks, he is still but a sophomore. A big ram head on the wall of his den is the diploma of the graduated big-game hunter.

Sheep are the most valued of all trophies. But why? For one thing, they are rare; and rarity always lends value. The possession of a legally taken head means a long and often expensive trip into Sonora or Lower California. Further, the head of a good ram means heat and thirst; it means climbing over the roughest and most terrible mountains in North America. Whether or not sheep are the most difficult of all Southwestern game to take may be open to argument, but there can be no question that hunting them exposes the sportsman to more downright physical hardship than going after any other species.

But the rarity of the trophy and the difficulty of obtaining it are only part of the sport. To me it is one of the most exciting and romantic games a man can play—exciting because it is spiced with danger, as mountaineering always is, and because it gives glimpses of the rarest and most interesting of American horned game and insight into its life—romantic because it gives me an excuse to climb around in the wildest, roughest, most weirdly beautiful country on the globe. Desert country is at its best seen from above, and, of all the deserts, I know of none more lovely in bird's-eye view than those of the Sonora sheep country . . . the olive-green of paloverde and ironwood forest, the gold of sandy playas, the purple upthrust of distant ranges, vast crawling rivers of solidified lava, dead black against yellow sands, the pale empty blue of the sky merging with the ultramarine of the distant Gulf of California.

For the romantic who likes to combine scenery with his hunting, there is no time like the early spring on those deserts—the last week of March, say, or the first weeks of April. It isn't too hot then and the desert is at its best after the winter rains. Grass and weeds have tinged the yellow playas with a faint and transient green. Brush is new, polished. Paloverdes are masses of glorious yellow bloom, and ironwoods are clad with purple-white blossoms. Ocatillas flaunt scarlet banners and damp places along the bases of the cliffs glow brightly with patches of California poppies.

Up on the peaks and cliffs hummingbirds sucking nectar from ocatilla blooms resent the sheep-hunter's invasion of their domain. They dart at him, singing like bullets. New-born rock squirrels peer from the crevices between the rocks, and the ewes are beginning to bunch once more with their long-legged frisky lambs. One-, two- and three-year-old rams are found now and then still with the ewes, clinging as best they can to mamma's apron strings; but in the spring the old rams are off by themselves, the old grandfathers usually alone, the mature breeding rams in pairs and trios, occasionally in bunches of four or five.

Hunting sheep is romantic, and it is also one of the greatest of gambles. Their rarity, the difficult terrain they inhabit, the ease of making a tactical error that will spell failure in the best-laid campaign, the unpredictability of the rams themselves—all spice the trip with uncertainty. You may hunt for ten days and see a hundred sheep and never get a shot. On the other hand, you may take a fine ram within a mile of camp the first day. I have seen both things happen. A careless step may send you tumbling down a precipice or hurl you into a clump of cholla. In either case you may be put out of action and forced to go home without a trophy.

Many sportsmen think of the bighorns as being almost exclusively inhabitants of high cold country near or above timberline, and the fact that the hot barren deserts of the Southwest and Mexico once formed one of the finest sheep countries in the world may come as a distinct surprise. Yet this is so. Early explorers found bighorns over almost the entire area. The animals ranged wherever the country was rough and free from timber. They may have been as plentiful as the white sheep now are in Alaska. Surely they were found in what now seem incredible numbers. Every desert range had its sheep. So did every mountain peak which went above timberline. Pattie, an early explorer, miner and beaver-trapper, wrote in his diary that the walls of the canyon of the San Francisco River were full of sheep, some of the rams with the largest horns he had ever seen on an animal. The bighorns were canyon-dwellers almost as much as they were creatures of the mountains. They were very plentiful in the canyons of the Indian country of southern Utah and northern Arizona. The prehistoric Indians called "the basket-makers" hunted them 1,500 years ago, and the sites of their ancient homes are filled with their bones and horns. The later cliff-dwellers were sheep-hunters too, and the modern Hopis ate sheep until the animals were killed off by the Navajos within the last few years. Bighorns ranged the length and breadth of the Grand Canyon of the Colorado. They are still found within it from Desert View clear to Boulder Canyon. There is a saying in the canyon country that they were so plentiful in the early days that Bright Angel, the first trail down into those great depths, was built on sheep meat. The Supai Indians who dwell in lovely Havasupai Canyon, which runs into Grand Canyon from the south, still kill an occasional sheep, and the animals are supposed to be most plentiful in Kanab Creek Canyon on the north side and on and around Powell Plateau. A few years ago a big ram wandered out of the canyon itself up to the Kaibab Plateau and showed up at the Ryan ranger station high in the piñon and yellow pine.

Today the sheep are most plentiful in Arizona, and probably in their entire American range, in the mountains and canyons where the Bill Williams River empties into the Colorado. I am constantly astonished at the wide range the animals once occupied. Rough, steep, but not particularly deep canyons throughout northern Arizona contained sheep—Walnut, Oak Creek and the canyon of the Little Colorado. Bighorns were plentiful in all the rough but low desert mountains around Phoenix. They are still found in some of the very highest ranges that surround the Salt River Valley. The last record I have of a ram killed within the valley itself was of an old ram killed on Camelback Mountain around 1898. Camelback is now in the midst of an orange-grove and winter-home section. Old sheep bones are still occasionally found in caves within a few miles of Phoenix.

The first Spaniards to invade the Southwest found wild sheep and at once they fastened the name upon them by which they are known to Mexicans today—*cimarrones*. The word is now obsolete, but at that time it was applied to any wild species similar to a domesticated one. In the Philippines today the wild water buffalo are known as *cimarrones*. No Mexican who lives in sheep country ever calls bighorns *borregos*, as that word is reserved exclusively for domestic sheep. Town-dwelling Mexicans sometimes refer to them as *borregos salvajes*, or wild sheep, just as Americans often do. The natives of the little sheep-hunting town of Sonoyta, Sonora, usually call them *chivos*, or goats.

The desert rams of the Southwest are the advance guard of a great army of sheep which extends across parts of three continents and halfway around the world, and which ranges in North America from the Arctic Circle to the blistering deserts of northern Mexico. The Barbary sheep of northern Africa are on one end, and the desert bighorns on Sierra Azul de los Indios opposite Tiburon Island off the Sonora coast are on the other.

In appearance they differ so little from their relatives, the regular Rocky Mountain bighorns, that it would be difficult to say where one species leaves off and the other begins. They are all of some shade of grayish brown. "Gunmetal-brown" is a word I have coined to fit their typical color. It will do as well as any. Most are distinctly on the brown side, but they tend to be "blacker" in winter and "browner" in summer. But there is great individual variation in sheep, and I have seen bighorns which appeared to be gunmetal gray running with sheep that were a warm rich brown. I once saw an old ewe that was dressed in brown so light it was almost khaki, and in

1936 I saw a big ram which at a distance of about thirty-five feet appeared almost coal black, so dark that his great brown horns seemed almost yellow in contrast to his hide. Other markings of the sheep are a light gray-brown muzzle and a white rump patch divided by a dark line which ends in a tiny twig of a tail which he elevates ridiculously when alarmed, even as the whitetail deer does. This great individual variation in the pelage of desert sheep must account for most of the numerous subspecies; but more of that anon.

Ewes have straight, slightly ridged horns which give them a most goatlike appearance, but the rams have the great brown curling horns which gave them their name "bighorns" and which have made them the most sought-after trophy in America.

A big desert ram which pops up on a ridge above you—strong, brave, fleet and defiant, with those great horns of his cutting circles against the sky—is to me one of the most thrilling sights in nature. He seems part of those fantastically lovely desert mountains, and the merest glimpse of one makes my heart pound and my breath catch in my throat.

The first American wild sheep ever seen by white men were of the desert variety. In 1540 Coronado wrote from the pueblo of Zuni, New Mexico, that the country contained some "sheep as big as horses with large horns and little tails." He said he had seen some of their horns, "the size of which was something to marvel at."

In 1697 Father Salvatierra and Father Piccolo saw sheep in Lower California. Piccolo described them with great exactness and also mentioned the fact that their flesh was delicious, an opinion with which everyone who has ever eaten mountain mutton will agree.

Yet it was not until 1814 that the American bighorns were described scientifically from a specimen taken in the Rocky Mountains a year earlier. Even now, in spite of the fact that white men have seen and shot at them hundreds of years, the desert bighorns are one of the least-known big-game animals on the North American continent. Much of what has been written about them is superficial or downright inaccurate, as most of it has been arrived at through analogy with the better-known northern sheep. They have never been thoroughly studied, and the few people who know much about them have never broken into print.* Few know them except natives and hunters. They were shot out quickly wherever they lived in accessible country close to centers of population, and those that remain occupy barren, desolate wilderness, hard to get to and hard to stay in. Consequently they are almost as little known as if they lived on the moon. They are the most interesting, mysterious and unpredictable of animals.

A few scientists have come in, taken a specimen or two, and left. Nearly all of them have been eager to find new subspecies, and because they have never realized that the animals are highly migratory and that the individual variation within the species is great, they have found them. Just now the books give several subspecies found on the deserts of the Southwest—*gaillardi, nelsoni, sheldoni, cremnobates, texiana* and *mexicanus.* Many are skeptical of the accuracy of the observations.† The late Dr. W. T. Hornaday, who hunted in

* As I revise this in the summer of 1938, my friend, A. A. Nichol, University of Arizona range ecologist, is completing an eighteen-month survey of the Southwestern bighorns for the National Association of Audubon Societies. His findings, of course, will be the last word.

† As a matter of convenience, A. A. Nichol puts the sheep west of the Colorado River into *O. nelsoni* and those to the east into *O. gaillardi.*

the Pinacate Mountains of northwest Sonora in 1907 and who put his experiences into a book, declares the sheep there are *Ovis canadensis*, smaller, thinner-haired and lighter than the northern sheep, but otherwise exactly the same. He was inclined to doubt all other subspecies except *mexicanus*, which is distinguished by large ears, large molar teeth, and a forehead noticeably less concave than that of the parent Rocky Mountain stock. Now it seems to be the fashion, in popular writing at least, to lump all the desert sheep into one subspecies—*nelsoni*. Why, I do not know. Hornaday doubted *nelsoni* in the first place. How they could have been differentiated, particularly in southern Arizona and Sonora is beyond me, as the ranges the various races are supposed to occupy are not far apart and the bighorns are among the most restless and migratory of all game animals.

The bighorns move from range to range following the spotty desert rains, and during the mating season the breeding rams wander widely. A wilderness range may be full of sheep one month and practically empty of them the next. The bands which feed in one group of mountains in the winter may go a hundred miles when the weather begins to get warm. All over their range they are highly migratory, and now and then some adventurous sheep turns up where no sheep has been seen for a score of years.

The last sheep I saw, as I write this, is a case in point. About one o'clock one February morning in 1938, my wife and I started to drive the 125 miles from Tucson to Phoenix. It was cold, clear and bright as only a moonlit night in the Southwest can be. We had crossed the Gila River, when ahead of us I saw an animal on the road, running with the characteristic hobbling gait of a big ram on level ground.

"Eleanor," I shouted, "that looks like a sheep!"

And it was. I slammed on the brakes and edged the car around so I could get the headlights full on him. He was a big migrating ram, headed north, and like most sheep he had chosen a moonlit night for his journey. A big ram with a complete curl, forty miles from any range known to be occupied by sheep! He was probably headed from the Estrelas to the Superstitions, as both are high, very rugged, and known to contain bunches of sheep. He couldn't make the jump in a night, of course. He had probably been traveling since moonrise. His route would take him across paved roads and railroad tracks, through or over barbed-wire fences. When I saw him he had just finished crossing a field of winter wheat planted by the Pima Indians. When the moon went down he would probably select some rocky hill and lie up, resting and feeding. The next night he would complete his journey.

Furthermore, the sheep in the same bunch often show great individual variation, enough surely to account for the subspecies. Desert rams more often than not have close curls. But they also have slightly flaring horns with fairly wide spreads and even in-curved horns. I have seen all types taken on the same hunt in the same area. Their coats vary, too; but more of that later.* I have seen sheep over wide areas in both Arizona and Sonora and I have seen as much variation between members of the same big band as I have seen in sheep all the way from the Grand Canyon to the big ranges opposite Tiburon Island. When they have been studied thoroughly, and when a complete collection from all desert localities has come into existence, I think most subspecies will be declared myths.

* Age and physical condition no doubt contribute to this variation in pelage.

The first Anglo-Saxon American invaders of the Southwest found bighorns in almost every desert range and barren canyon in the entire area. The animals extended from the mountains of Southern California and southern Nevada on the west to the Chisos Mountains of West Texas on the east, from the canyon country of southern Utah on the north to northern Chihuahua and central Sonora and Lower California on the south.

Though they have been wiped out in many places, scattered and constantly dwindling bands exist over much of this whole great area. Armed with American repeating rifles, Navajos and Pi-Utes have killed every sheep in the canyon country of northern Arizona and southern Utah, as well as all the mule deer and all except a handful of antelope on the reservation. I know a Hopi Indian who declares he saw several sheep in Blue Canyon about 1910, and a Pi-Ute is supposed to have killed the last ram on Navajo Mountain sometime during the World War. The last record of sheep in the Indian country is, astonishingly enough, in 1924, when a Hopi sheepherder from the town of Oraibi saw a big ram at a spring in Oraibi Wash about ten miles from the village. It drank with its domestic kin but ran as the herder approached. The Indian returned to the village, where he got horses and other Indians. They chased that old ram until it got away in the rough cliffs of the canyon of the Little Colorado in the neighborhood of Grand Falls. The Indian who told me about it said he heard a Navajo later killed a ram near Moenkopi— evidently the same sheep, the last of his race in what was once excellent bighorn country.

The last surviving sheep often comes in and joins a herd of domestic sheep or goats, by the way, as sheep are gregarious animals.

Along in the middle 'twenties a young ram joined a Mexican's flock of goats in the Tucson Mountains and was driven with them to the outskirts of Tucson. As so often happens, the Mexicans captured him, penned him up in a woodshed, where he proceeded, almost literally, to butt his brains out. The high rugged Chisos Mountains along the Mexican border in the Big Bend of Texas were once great sheep country, and the animals there were probably *mexicanus* or possibly the closely related and somewhat doubtful *texiana*. They were in other ranges, too; notably the Glass Mountains near Alpine, where I once found the weathered old skull and a few bones of a ewe. The last sheep in the Big Bend proper, two pregnant ewes, were shot by a heroic cattleman about 1910. Probably the only sheep now in Texas are part of the herd which ranges in the general region of the Carlsbad Cavern, mostly in New Mexico. The east-of-the-Rockies sheep are almost gone. They are extinct in the type locality of *mexicanus* near Lake Santa Maria in northern Chihuahua, and they exist precariously only in New Mexico.

In 1922 Ernest Thompson Seton estimated the desert sheep of the United States as follows: Arizona 3,500; California 3,500; Nevada 500; New Mexico 550; Utah 1,000. He also estimated that there were around 25,000 in northern Mexico. In other words there were 9,000 sheep of the various desert subspecies in this country and almost three times that many in Sonora and Lower California. Seton seemed optimistic about the chances for the desert sheep to hold their own. Yet in 1936 Capt. E. H. Ober of the patrol force of the State Division of Fish and Game in California estimated that there were but 2,000 sheep left in California. This is a decrease of 1,500 from Seton's estimate. More discouraging yet is the report of A. A.

Nichol, range ecologist, who estimated in 1936 that there were, outside of the Grand Canyon, only 1,200 sheep on all the American deserts. Nichol's report is, I think, somewhat pessimistic, perhaps purposely so in order to arouse authorities to the danger of the situation.* Let us say, then, that there are probably around 5,000 bighorns in the United States, 5,000 in Sonora, and 10,000 in Lower California. Those are just my guesses, but they are possibly as good as any; and the fact remains that sheep have been and still are decreasing, and that they are actually on the verge of extinction. Except on the west coast of Lower California, where they have come but little into contact with men, they are everywhere decreasing.

Native Mexicans do not bother the sheep a great deal over the more isolated part of their Sonora range, as they can kill deer with less effort. However, they do kill sheep of any age or sex whenever they have an opportunity. In mineralized regions where there are no deer, the Mexicans live on sheep as a matter of course. The owners of the Sierra Pinta mine in the northern Sonora range of the same name hired professional hunters, supplied them with arms and ammunition, and told them to keep the miners supplied with mutton. They did, and as a consequence the sheep in the Sierra Pintas and the nearby San Franciscos were pretty well cleaned out.

On the other hand, there are vast areas in Sonora where there are no natives except a few wandering Seri and Papago Indians, and no water except that brought in either by boat or by truck. No one hunts sheep there except an occasional American sportsman, and the flocks should maintain their numbers indefinitely.

* In December, 1938, just before this book went to press, Nichol estimated 700 sheep in Arizona outside of the Grand Canyon herd.

Two classes of Americans hunt sheep in Mexico. One is composed of Eastern "dudes," generally men of money and wide hunting experience who can afford to pay American guides and outfitters from $25 to $50 a day for a trip. The others are border Americans, also with plenty of experience but with little money, who are willing to plunge into a desert wilderness with a few tins of water and perhaps a Papago Indian or a *mozo* hired at two pesos a day to wash dishes and help hunt *los cimarrones*.

On the whole, both classes are trophy-hunters, and trophy-hunters have yet to exterminate a species. There are, however, game hogs among them. Border Americans hunting in all seasons of the year and killing, in the name of sport, everything that jumps up, have thinned the flocks in the Pinacates, once the finest sheep country in Sonora, to the point where it is now hardly worth while to hunt there. Even head-hunters sometimes run amuck and slaughter ewes. But the hogs are the exception, and most Americans shoot only at good rams.

The recent history of the sheep in the United States is a most impressive example of the truth that no species can be protected simply by a law on the statute books. In most Southwestern states they have been "protected" by a closed season for about thirty years. Yet, in all this time, this most magnificent of game animals has been shot for meat and meat alone. Every prospector, every homesteader, most of the cattlemen who go into the mountains have always felt that game was their God-given right.

Mountain sheep are probably the best eating of all big game, and I have never known an oldtimer who did not put them first on the list. Their flesh is fine in texture, light in color and delicate in flavor, and in the days of open market hunting it always commanded a higher price than that of deer or even antelope. As a consequence, the animals have always been hunted hard in the Southwest, and in spite of the fact that the season in Arizona has been closed for more than thirty years and in California for over fifty there is probably not one sheep in the United States against ten at the beginning of the century.

Of all Southwestern big-game animals, sheep alone are not increasing. Mule and whitetail deer are in many places almost as plentiful as they ever were. Where antelope were left at all they have made an astonishing recovery. Though the native Arizona (Merriam) elk were exterminated in the 'nineties, imports from Montana have so increased that there are now open seasons in both Arizona and New Mexico.

The bighorns would seem to be magnificently equipped for survival. Strong and brave and untiring, they occupy economically worthless country. They can bounce down a mountain in two minutes that a sportsman would find difficult to negotiate in an hour. In some ranges they go to water, but where no springs or pot-holes exist they can go entirely without drinking, depending on the moisture they get from their food and upon the sap of water-storing cacti like the saguaro and bisnaga. Unlike their relatives in the Rocky Mountains, they have for the most part never come in contact with domestic sheep and hence have not fallen prey to sheep scab.

Still, they are going. In the first place, the isolation of their range puts them at the mercy of meat-hunters, who can kill them off in box-canyons and at water holes with practically no chance of detection. The meat-hunter finds a water hole used by sheep, hides out and waits. When a flock comes in he cuts loose, killing rams, ewes and lambs with fine impartiality. A couple of years ago a friend of mine found where someone had slaughtered nine Arizona sheep, all ewes and lambs, at a water hole. Several times, when tramping in the desert mountains, I have come across old prospectors' camps that were veritable kitchen-middens of sheep bones. I have been told that in one small mining town in central western Arizona, mountain mutton has actually been sold over the block in the past few years. Lately commercial head-hunters have joined the meat-hunters in the war of extermination. Unscrupulous taxidermists pay from ten to twenty dollars for the horns and scalp of a big ram and then sell them mounted for an enormous profit.

With the closing of the season, legitimate sportsmen, who are by far the best and most realistic friends of the game, lost interest in the sheep. They never go into sheep country and know little about them. As a consequence the sheep have been left to fight their battle for existence alone and unaided. Yet they have made some remarkable stands. There are still about eighty sheep in the Santa Catalina Mountains a few miles north of Tucson, the second largest center of population in Arizona. The Tucson Mountains themselves were famous for their sheep in the 'seventies and 'eighties, and the animals used to water almost within the city limits. A herd of about half a dozen animals is occasionally reported there still, but they are probably immigrants from either the Santa Catalinas or the Coyotes.

Man is, of course, the most persistent enemy of the bighorns; but in addition they are plentifully supplied with natural enemies, too—enemies which have never been thinned because they range in country which is economically worthless—except for the occasional minerals and the production of game. The most deadly of these is the big Mexican golden eagle which raises its young in the same country in which the sheep raise theirs. These terrible birds must get nearly fifty per cent of the lambs each year. Something gets them, surely, for in the late spring when the lambs are running with the flock the average number of young even in good years is about one to every two ewes. On one small range in northern Sonora in the spring of 1935 I found a place where eagles had killed three lambs, and below an old nest I found a great pile of lamb bones.

The fact that the eagles are increasing speaks badly for the sheep. When meat baits were used for coyotes, many of the great birds were caught in traps; but now that scent baits are universally used, the birds go practically unmolested.

In addition to the eagles, the coyotes, universal villains of the Southwest, climb the mountains in lambing time for their quota of mountain mutton. Lions kill many sheep—especially in the winter and early spring when the flocks range down into the lowland deserts to feed on new-sprung grass and weeds. In fact, at that season of the year I think lions take proportionately greater toll of sheep than they do of mule deer, where the two species range in the same locality. I do know that compared with the numbers of sheep one finds an astonishing number of animals which have been killed by lions.*

Mexicans and Papago Indians have told me that the common turkey buzzard sometimes kills new-born lambs, but I have never had a chance to check up on the story.

* To the enemies of bighorn lambs, add the little desert fox. On his survey, Nichol found where foxes had killed two lambs, and he shot one fox with sheep meat and hair in its stomach.

With all these natural enemies in common with that arch-predator, man, the sheep are simply not prolific enough to hold their numbers. Unlike the mule deer and the Arizona whitetails, ewes seem to have but one lamb about as commonly as they have twins; and as they do not mature so quickly, they breed later.

In addition, they are in many ways not difficult animals to hunt. True, the person who goes into the mountains after them must usually prepare to do heart-breaking climbing and to go thirsty under the hot desert sun; but because of the open country they inhabit, the sheep are easily seen.

Their noses are fair, but not remarkable, and I don't think they hear any better than human beings. Surely these senses cannot be compared to the same ones in deer. Like antelope, they depend almost entirely on their wonderful eyes for protection. They have a habit of standing on some rugged pinnacle and staring at an intruder. If the enemy happens to be a lion or a coyote, all is well; but if it is an American hunter with a flat-shooting rifle it is another thing again. Then, too, they seldom look above them, and their eyes are worthless on stationary objects. A big ewe once fed within twenty feet of me while I sat on a rock not only in plain sight but actually against the skyline. She finally decided I was a curious-looking object and stared at me fixedly. She didn't run until I moved and spoke to her.

Old rams are very intelligent and wary, and unless you get a decided tactical advantage on them they are hard to bag. On the other hand, ewes and young rams are often almost incredibly stupid. They stand and gape, even at close range. The ewes are loath to leave their lambs and are easily killed, and young sheep often follow the murderer of their mother home. I know of two young rams that followed an American sportsman who had scorned to shoot at them, to within a quarter-mile of camp, stamping and threatening like foxy little dogs who had run a tramp away from the back steps. As he was a head-hunter, they did not suffer; but if he had been a Mexican, they long since would have been jerky to go with *chile* and *frijoles*.

When sheep, even old rams, are surprised by hunters, they have a habit of milling about. Unless they have seen the hunter, they often run off a little way and pop up on a rock for a better look.

When an unscrupulous hunter gets the jump on a bunch he can do some astonishing execution. I know one American who got above six Mexican sheep in the Pinacates and killed every one of them—five rams and a ewe. I still have a photograph which he proudly gave me as proof of his prowess. Another group of Arizona hunters —I surely cannot call them sportsmen—got the drop on a herd of Mexican sheep and killed thirteen of them. I know the Mexican who guided them and the Papago Indians to whom they gave the carcasses of the ewes.

Two principal factors have contributed to the alarming recent decrease of the bighorns all over the desert. One is the depression. Hundreds of ill-informed prospectors swarmed into the mineralized mountains of the Southwest from 1930 until 1934. Few of them knew much about mining, but all of them had rifles and tried romantically to live off the country. They slaughtered sheep by the hundreds. The increased price of gold is still keeping some of them in the hills.

The second factor is the great drought which unfortunately

coincided with the depression. The sheep might have stood the unrestricted hunting to which they were subjected and they might have maintained their numbers in the face of the drought, but the two things operating simultaneously were too much for them to bear. Great areas of the southern Arizona and Sonora deserts had practically no rain for years. Vegetation died, pot-holes dried up, and much of the water-bearing cactus died, too. I have seen ranges in Mexico where about a fourth of the saguaros, bisnagas and pitahayas were dead, and where the others were in such bad shape through the long-continued loss of moisture that they looked like fat men after a strenuous program of reducing.

During a long-continued drought, the sheep do not replace the members of the herds killed by men and predators. Ewes, because they cannot get moisture themselves, are unable to feed their lambs properly. Just as desert quail do not mate during a drought, many of the ewes probably do not come in heat, and many of those that do, probably miscarry—as the miscarriage is nature's way of saving the mother at the expense of the unborn young. Frankly, I have never seen a miscarriage on the part of a ewe, but I know that desert range cows miscarry in times of drought, and to me this explanation does not seem unreasonable.

In addition to a lowered birth-rate, the sheep become more vulnerable to predatory animals and men in times of drought. In Mexico, they are forced to go to water holes, a thing which they ordinarily do not do, and there fall a prey to lions and to wandering tigres. They bunch up in regions where a transient shower has fallen or where some arroyo with underground water has kept the cactus in good shape. In cases like this herds of from fifty to one hundred sheep are often seen—easy work for the pot-hunter or the hungry mountain lion.

Young sheep have been scarce all over the Southwest for the past few years. In 1935 I saw a herd of ten mature ewes, three young rams and *one* lamb. I imagine the case was fairly typical. On one extended trip the members of my party saw about forty sheep, twenty-seven of which were rams, mostly big ones. Where were the lambs? They either didn't get born or didn't survive.

In addition to their enemies—predatory animals, weather, man —sheep evidently are subject to obscure and little-understood diseases that have never been thoroughly investigated. Desert rats have often told me of finding several sheep dead on one mountain—all from natural causes. Much work remains to be done on the diseases of sheep. Even in Yellowstone Park, where the herd is rigorously protected, the bighorns are barely holding their own.

The desert rams are not nearly so heavy as those found in the Rockies, and a big one will weigh from 175 to 225 pounds dressed as compared to from 250 to 325 for one from Canada. Ewes, and this is only an estimate, as I have never weighed one, look as though they would dress out at from 135 to 160. The sheep are about as heavy as Southwestern mule deer, but their legs are shorter, their hooves are larger, and they are chunkier, more heavily muscled animals.

The unskinned head and cape of a big ram will often weigh forty pounds or more. The heads are larger in proportion to their body weight than are those of other sheep. An average good head will have a 15-inch base and will measure about 30 inches around the curve. I have a big head from an old ram that today, several years after it was killed, still has a base of over 16 inches and a curl of 36. When he was killed the base measured almost 17. The ram was eight years old, but curiously enough the points are both perfect, something very rare in any sheep and particularly rare in those found on the deserts. The record head, I believe, is one taken by C. C. Ren, of Ajo, Arizona, in the Pinacate Mountains of Sonora in 1931. Its measurements today are as follows: base 17½ inches, spread 23¼, length of curve 45. That's a big head for any sheep—even for one of the monsters from Canada.

The horns of an old ram are usually pretty badly battered. Nearly all of them are chipped in front where they bring their heads together when fighting, and most of them are badly broomed at the end. Some believe that the rams knock the tips off so that their horns will be less of a burden. My notion is that the shock of their fighting does the brooming. Anyway, most of them are broomed.

Rams grow both seasonal and annual rings on their horns. The small rings probably record some local shower and quick plant growth, the annual rings tell of the winter rainy season which on the deserts is the time of plenty for sheep, whereas summer is the time of rapid horn growth for northern sheep. To a close observer, the rings are unmistakable.

The ewes have long, slender horns sometimes measuring ten inches or more in length, and the young rams have thicker backward-curved horns. Many an innocent has believed he has seen an ibex because he has run across a ewe or a young ram, and the old American ibex myth reappears almost annually in Arizona, always from a place where there are bighorn sheep. Scientists often solemnly investigate the story. They always come back with the same solution.

Some sheep-killing farmers in southwestern Arizona were recently acquitted from the charge of killing sheep by a sympathetic native jury. They hadn't killed sheep, they claimed: the animals they had were ibexes, on which there was no closed season. The story, which has been denied a thousand times, is still current that Theodore Roosevelt planted ibex in Arizona about 1905. It is ludicrous, but the sillier the story is, the harder it often is to scotch it.

The desert bighorn is the most unpredictable of creatures. He can do stranger things than any animal I know of and he can be found in more unexpected places. I learned that interesting fact early in my sheep-hunting and sheep-observing experience, as one of the first "mountain" sheep I ever saw was a big ram ambling serenely along through a desert forest of mesquite, ironwood and paloverde miles from any mountain. Seeing that big old ram down on the flat made me pretty indignant. He was a "mountain" sheep and he had no right to be there. I felt that I had been misused and taken advantage of. Another time, not expecting sheep, I carelessly thought I was on the track of a big buck mule deer, but it turned out to be a lone lazy ewe bedded down under a paloverde. The tracks of the rams are unmistakable, but those of the ewes greatly resemble those of mule deer if one observes them carelessly as I did that day. A Mexican I know once saw a big ram wade the Sonoyta River in northern Sonora and bed down under a peach tree on the edge of a cornfield. Like all Mexicans, he immediately became filled with an overwhelming desire for *carne* to go with his *chile*, so he walked into town, borrowed an old *escopeta* and one shell, sneaked up and killed it.

[88]

A few years ago, a friend of mine who is a professional guide in Sonora took a party of sportsmen on a sheep hunt to the desert ranges along the coast between Puerto Libertad and Tiburon Island. It was a sheep hunt except that they didn't see any sheep. They found old tracks, dry droppings, and a few weathered heads, but no rams in the flesh whatever, in the valleys, on the peaks, anywhere. It was a week before they solved the problem. The sheep were there, but they were all down on the rocky beaches, keeping cool by the salt spray of the breakers.

During certain seasons of the year these desert mountain sheep are not mountain-dwelling animals at all unless they are forced to the heights by predatory animals or man. When the December and January rains come in the deserts they feed in the lowland valleys on weeds and new-sprung grass, on the fruit of the cholla, and on the fresh leaves of the ironwood. In times of drought they also come down and eat the pulp of the saguaros and bisnagas (giant and barrel cactus) which grow along the arroyos. In 1936, when the great drought was coming to its climax and many parts of the Sonoran desert had hardly seen rain for years, a friend of mine counted sixty mature sheep in one wide desert arroyo. Almost every bisnaga there had been torn open by the frantic animals for the moisture it contained. However, in regions where lions are plentiful or where they are molested by hunters, the sheep feed in the lowlands only in early morning or late afternoon. During the day they bed down high on a mountainside, usually on a point or on a great flat rock, from which they can sweep the country with their keen eyes.

As I have said before, few people realize how highly migratory the sheep of the desert are. Non-hunters are constantly telling me

that they know exactly where a band of sheep ranges. To hear them
talk one would think that they are as permanently located as Broad-
way and Forty-second Street. I usually listen patiently, but I nearly
always laugh, for I know that the sheep they saw last Saturday may
be twenty miles away by now and a hundred miles away next month.
The classification of the subspecies called *Ovis canadensis sheldoni*
is a case in point. The type specimen was shot in El Rosario Mountains near the head of the Gulf of California in northern Sonora.
The Rosarios are separated from the other nearby ranges by several
miles of soft sand dunes, so, not knowing desert sheep, the collector
took it for granted that the sheep there were absolutely isolated.
The ram happened to be a small one and he decided he had a new
subspecies. As much as I dislike to cast doubts on the observations of
an excellent hunter, I must say that he was completely mistaken.
That ram may have been born in the Pinacates, the Gilas, the Growl-
ers, the Cubabais, the Ajos or the San Franciscos. He may have been
a Mexican or an American, and he could have negotiated in a couple
of hours the sand dunes which Sheldon thought so formidable. Many
times I have seen sheep tracks far out in the dunes, twenty miles
from any mountain. I know one American hunter who went into the
Rosarios in October and saw dozens of sheep. He returned in January and found not a one. The reason? A shower had fallen there in
late September. The sheep saw it and drifted in. No more rain fell
and they left.

The region in which sheep live is for the most part one of light
rainfall and scanty foliage. They *must* move if they are to survive.
A scientist friend of mine once went into a desert range in southwestern Arizona to study the animals. He had heard that they were

[90]

there, but for several days he was unable to find any or even see any fresh sign. Then, the afternoon just before he planned to leave in disgust, a shower fell—the only shower in the immediate area. By nightfall he began seeing sheep. In a couple of days they were all over the range. They had seen the shower, they knew it would bring up growth, and so they came.

In the early spring of 1935 the only good rain that fell in northern Sonora happened to hit the San Franciscos, and as a consequence there were at least five hundred sheep there until a rain fell somewhere else. I came in after they had begun to leave, but sheep beds and droppings were literally everywhere, the thickest I have ever seen them. Some sheep were still there when I arrived, but within two weeks all of them had sought greener fields.

Weather as well as feed conditions will make sheep move. In the summer in Sonora they tend to move to the coastal ranges where they can bed down on the ridges and catch the sea-breeze, or even lie on the shore. In the winter they hunt the more sheltered mountains back from the coast. If feed is plentiful everywhere, as it occasionally is even on the desert, they will leave a non-honeycombed mountain during a storm and head for one where caves are plentiful.

Every good well-used sheep range is full of caves, and every cave is deep in old sheep-dung. The sheep, who are almost as comfort-loving as cats, seek them in hot weather and in wet weather. During a rainstorm a deer will bed down under a tree and stay there, dripping and miserable. But that isn't a sheep's idea of a good time. When a storm comes he goes to his cave, holes up, and stays there comfortable and dry. A friend of mine, hunting in hot weather, once dropped off a rock in front of a cave and was knocked down by three big rams rushing out—the only case of "charging" sheep I have ever heard of. Once when I was hunting in Mexico, an Indian showed me the skull and horns of a fine old ram which he claimed he had cornered deep in a big cave and killed with a club.

Because most scientists assume that the breeding habits of the desert bighorns are similar to those of the sheep found in the Rocky Mountains, they usually assume that they mate in November. They are mistaken. The rutting season comes in early September and the lambs are born about the middle of March—some, evidently, as early as February. The young of big-game mammals are usually born in the time of year when food is most plentiful and weather conditions are easiest. In the desert these conditions prevail in the early spring after the winter rains have fallen and the feed has come up; which is the reason for the early rut.

The rams start running with the ewes in late August, and by the first week in September the rut is in full swing. One time during the breeding season I hunted in several sheep ranges in Sonora. Everywhere I went the rams were with the ewes, and I was constantly seeing circular patches of ground, torn up by straining feet and sprinkled with fragments of horn, where great battering heads had met.* The rams we got on that trip all had skinned and swollen noses and freshly broken horns.

After the rut some of the rams leave the ewes and go off to run singly or in pairs until next August. A few, however, will stay with the ewes and young clear through the winter, until the females go off by themselves to give birth to their lambs. Old decadent rams often become solitary. Many of them are so old and jaded that they

* Rams often fight at other seasons of the year, too, but evidently only to keep in practice.

do not bother the ewes even in rutting time. These are the ones with the big heads, as horns continue to grow as long as the sheep lives. When the lambs are strong enough to follow their mothers, the ewes flock up again. It is my experience, however, that rams do not have the same tendency, as one seldom sees big flocks of rams except when climatic conditions have forced them into the same narrow range.

The breeding and lambing seasons of the desert sheep do not string out like those of deer, because rams are relatively more plentiful than ewes—the proportion being about three to two.* Rams are warier, they have a tendency to range higher, they are not handicapped by lambs, and as a consequence the meat-hunters kill more females than males, a condition just the opposite of that existing among deer. Most ewes, I imagine, are bred as soon as they come in heat. During September frantic rams wander widely in search of willing females, and battle desperately with their rivals.

One would think that the big old rams would kill themselves in their fights. They hurl their great horns and their 250 pounds of desperate energy at each other with a crash that can be heard for several hundred yards. One would think that their slender deer-like necks would be broken. But they aren't. They seem to survive with no ill effects except chipped and broomed horns. They may have headaches for all I know. Probably they do.

Many people have been incredulous when desert hunters have told them that in many ranges sheep never go to water. Yet that is the case—it is the case with almost all desert-dwelling game species, and in Sonora some of the best sheep ranges have no open water at

---

* These are my observations on Mexican sheep, which I have studied closely. Nichol finds ewes more plentiful than rams in Arizona.

all. The San Franciscos, once one of the finest of all of them, is composed of porous decomposed granite and there is not a single water hole in the whole range. The Pinacates, where Hornaday first studied the desert bighorns in 1907, contain several more or less permanent water holes but the sheep almost never go near them. As long as a bisnaga or saguaro contains sap the sheep need not worry. Water holes in a range are probably an actual handicap, as open water enables lions to survive and where lions are present they kill many sheep. In the northern parts of their range, though, there are but few water-bearing cactus and there the animals go regularly to the tanks where they fall prey to the heroic meat-hunter and to predatory animals. In times of long and severe drought, too, the cactus shrink and shrivel as they gradually lose their moisture, and then the sheep have to move to water. Again they are exposed to their enemies. In good times they are happy to get along without it, and even where there are permanent tanks I have never seen signs of their being used. I have tracked sheep by them but they don't turn to them.

The type of country in which desert sheep can exist and prosper must be seen to appear creditable. In some ranges it is amazing that anything can live. So long as the mountains afford refuge, so long as they are rough and rugged enough, so long as they contain a little vegetation, are near lusher valleys, and have some water-bearing cactus, the sheep do not seem to mind. Nearly always the ranges look almost completely bare, sun-baked, hostile, deserted. Yet the worse they look the better sheep seem to like them.

So long as they are rough, the ranges do not need to be particularly high. Sheep are often plentiful in mountains that go no more than 1,500 feet above the surrounding country. However, the height of the mountains and the difficulty of climbing them is their first line of defense against human predators, and they are usually killed out of the low mountains, or learn to avoid them.

Usually a frightened ram goes *up*. Nearly always he goes to the roughest country he can find. But in the Pinacates of Sonora, the high peaks are gigantic cinder cones and the rough country is the tumbled lava fields around the bases. So in the Pinacates the frightened sheep go *down*. They hide in the caves and crevices of the lava, and looking for them is something like hunting the traditional needle in the haystack. In cold and rainy weather the Pinacate sheep also go down to the lava beds.

The bighorn is probably the finest rough-country animal in existence, the most daring and skillful mountaineer in the world. The white goat, the only rival to the bighorn in America, is a calm and deliberate beast, able to pull himself up like a monkey. But the sheep is a jumper and bounder. Bouncing from rock to rock, seeming barely to touch, a bighorn can in five minutes go down a steep mountainside that a human mountaineer cannot negotiate in an hour. I once saw a big ram apparently hurl himself over a cliff a couple of hundred feet high when I came from below and surprised him in his bed. We saw each other at about the same instant. I had been pulling myself up the very steep side of a granite mountain hoping to hunt along the comb, when I heard a movement and saw that great ram get up above me, look straight at me for an instant, and jump. He was a beautiful thing poised there in that fragment of a second, his muscles taut with desperation, his great horns light against the gunmetal brown of his sleek hide. And then he was gone over the cliff. I scrambled to the top expecting, even though I knew sheep, to find his broken body lying on the talus slope below. But I did not see him—then. Finally it dawned on me that he had really got away. Making a long circuit, I got to the bottom of the cliff finally and found his plunging tracks in the talus. Then I saw how he had done it. About fifteen feet below his bed there was a ledge not more than six inches wide, below it was another. By leaping from ledge to ledge, touching enough to check his fall, the gallant old ram had got to the bottom. No human being could have got down without a rope. I doubt if even a goat could have done it, yet it was in the day's work for that sheep.

Then as I watched and marveled, I happened to look up. There he was going up another cliff five hundred yards away, jumping from ledge to ledge, bold as a steeplejack, more sure-footed than a mule. At the very top he paused against the skyline and looked at me for fully five minutes. I put my glasses on him, saw the curve of his great horns against the pale blue of the desert sky. He seemed calm and unwinded and when he had satisfied his curiosity about me, he tossed his head, wheeled and disappeared. I didn't get that sheep. I didn't get a ram that entire trip, as a matter of fact; but the experience of seeing what a frightened ram can really do when he wants to, was worth it. Another time I sighted a lone ewe about five hundred yards away and stalked to within fifteen feet of her. Cursing because I had left my camera in camp, I watched her feed for nearly ten minutes. Finally, in spite of the fact that I was "frozen," she became suspicious, and when I spoke she ran, leaping from boulder to boulder like a bouncing rubber ball. I didn't time her, but I'm sure she went down 1,500 feet in not much more than a minute. The whole tribe of wild sheep is bold, daring, reckless and beautiful. No wonder hunters value them above all other game.

His wonderful power to climb and to leap, to negotiate rough country more swiftly than any living thing is, of course, the sheep's first line of defense. On a flat he is relatively slow and clumsy, traveling in a hobbling run. I think a fairly fast man with good wind could overtake one, and sheep caught away from a mountain are easily run down with horses.

In addition to his climbing ability, the sheep has other means of staying out of gunshot. His ears aren't particularly good, but still it behooves the hunter to make as little noise as possible. In the treacherous shifting currents of the mountains his nose is probably of little use, but nevertheless the rancid scent of man will send sheep flying. His telescopic eyes are what he uses. I don't think they are any too good at picking up stationary objects, but try to get into sheep country without moving!

Perhaps some notes on hunting a vanishing species like the bighorn may seem out of place here. On the other hand, the real trophy-hunter takes only the old and decadent males and probably does the race more good than harm. Sheep in both Arizona and California would now undoubtedly be more plentiful and securely established if the season had never been closed on rams at all. To close a season on a game animal often means to abandon it to the poachers and meat-hunters. In Sonora even now the hunting *Americanos* have got the blame for the diminishing sheep, and the season has been closed. The blame, however, must be put squarely upon the doorstep of the pot-hunting native Mexicans and Indians, who care nothing for heads and to whom meat is meat even if it is on a ewe. One group of *sotoleros* (distillers of liquor from the *sotol* plant) went into the Sierra Viejos from Pitiquito a couple of years ago, made many gallons of potent booze, and shot about twenty ewes and lambs for meat. I found their old camp with bones and skulls scattered all about. There are still wary old rams in the Sierra Viejos, but unfortunately mammals are unable to reproduce spontaneously. The Mexican Indian and peon is a good hunter—I must give him credit for that. He can't shoot, but how he can stalk! A couple of hungry greasers in a sheep range with only a box of .30–30 cartridges between them will do more harm to a herd than a dozen legitimate American head-hunters.

But we were talking about hunting. The man who wants his ram must first find where the sheep are—no easy matter, considering the migratory habits of the species. Then he must find where they are feeding and ranging. If they come down into the valleys at night, his best tactic, in the early part of the day anyway, is to hunt along the edge of the mountains, hoping to run a ram up. If he does —and if he is lucky—he can often get a ram without ever touching a foot to the rocks. I have never had that much luck, but I know people who have killed several sheep that way. I even know one man who got a fine Mexican ram when he was out after quail with a shotgun.

If the sheep are ranging low, they seldom go clear to the top of the mountains to bed down. The thing to do, however, is to get high —as high as you can conveniently go. You must get above them, as they seldom look up. They will sweep the lowlands with their telescopic eyes. Now and then they will get up, go to a point, and take a look at everything in sight. If anything moves within miles they see it. But they *don't often look up*. There the hunter stands his chance for success. He must move quietly, watching constantly, pausing every few minutes to inspect the points and the tops of the rocks with his glasses. He must take pains to see the sheep before they see him, since even when he is above them they can jump off a point and be out of sight in an instant.

When the sheep are ranging high, he must go to the very comb of the range and work slowly along, taking care not to display himself against the skyline, as then the sheep can see him miles away and migrate to another range which is not contaminated by the presence of a human being with a rifle. If he wants to look over the opposite side, he must use the greatest care, coming up slowly, looking carefully, and screening his head by brush if he can.

If he sees rams first and starts shooting before they get him located he has a decided advantage. Often they will mill about for several seconds, sometimes they will jump up on a boulder for a better look. Many times they will run up toward the hunter instead of away. Sheep hunting is mostly the ability to climb resolutely and quietly, to keep open, observant eyes, to stand thirst, heat and fatigue, and to shoot quickly and accurately when the time comes. Jumping sheep in a canyon and getting them as they run up the other side is something every hunter prays for, but such a break has always been denied me.

If there are any sheep in a range a hunter will usually see some. But seeing them and getting them are two different things. Big rams will pop up on a ridge from four to five hundred yards away, look you over, toss their heads, stamp their feet and disappear. The beginner is often tempted to risk a long shot, but ranges are hard to determine and usually it is best for him to save his powder. In desperation I used to try 400-yard shots at rams; but I never hit one, so I gave it up. It is good to remember this: silhouetted against the skyline, a ram always looks nearer than he is. That big fellow that seems to be but 300 yards away on the opposite ridge may in reality be 600. On the other hand a sheep high above you always appears farther away than he really is, and you may have a reasonably good shot and not know it.

Following a thoroughly frightened ram is one of the most futile things a hunter can do. When a wise ram sees a hunter, he never skulks in the brush like a deer. Instead he will go clear off the mountain and to another five or six miles away. If you start up the same side of a mountain that rams are on and they see you out of the range, you may as well go elsewhere. They'll go down the other side and onto another peak so fast that they can cover in half an hour territory which you could scarcely negotiate in a day. When a ram disappears over the skyline, swear softly to yourself and give him up. The chances are 10 to 1 that you won't see him again—that day, anyway.

Like antelope, sheep can sometimes be taken by a ruse. Once a large party of hunters was leaving camp to hunt sheep when they spied a lordly ram watching them from the tip of a pinnacle a thousand feet above them. While one of their number slipped around a point and up a canyon, the others stayed in plain sight, laughing, talking and moving about. That fool ram stood there for more than an hour while the one man slipped up the mountain out of sight, got within two hundred yards of him, and killed him with a single shot.

Hunting bighorns is hard work anywhere you try it, but in

North America I think the sport is at its toughest in the barren desert ranges of Sonora. Besides having to do the most difficult climbing you can imagine, you will also suffer heat and plenty of it. Even in December and January the middle of the day is very warm; and as the hunter clambers painfully over those mountains of granite, limestone or basalt, as the case may be, his tongue will swell and he will sweat worse than the fabled brewery horse. To make matters worse, he will often hunt on high ranges close to the Gulf of California, where the salt water lies below him, tantalizingly blue and cool, to torture him as mirages are supposed to torture men dying of thirst.

And in Sonora the sheep hunter must nearly always work out of dry camps, as the best sheep country is nearly always far from permanent water, where water-loving predatory animals and man cannot live. Then the problem is to dash in quickly by plane or automobile, hunt, get your ram, and get out while you still have some water left. If you wait too long you're a gone goose, lost in a hot, waterless desert where a man who is exercising must drink nearly a gallon of water a day in order to survive. If something happens to that last water-can, or if your car breaks down, it is up to you to hike in to the nearest Mexican ranch from fifty to seventy-five miles away, sleeping in the daytime and traveling at night so that the supply of water you carry in your carcass will get you there.

A couple of times I've had trouble with water, but I have been lucky that neither of my experiences was really serious. Once a friend and I went into a lonely desert range in the spring. We had two twenty-five-gallon cans of water with us, but when we finished the first we discovered that thousands of bees had crept through the spout into our second. The stuff smelled like a dead cow. It was either go in or drink that foul water. We drank it—curiously with no ill effects. Yet the sight of a bee still gags me. Another time two hardened old sheep-hunters and I found a hitherto unknown pass between two high ranges and pushed into virgin, unexplored sheep country. No car had ever been there and I'm certain that no white man had ever seen it, except from a boat in the Gulf of California. We were just about to make camp when our fifty-gallon drum of water bounced out of our car and broke. All our precious water disappeared into the desert sand. So there we were, three hard days from fresh water. To the west, across a tide flat, lay the Gulf of California, blue, cool, sparkling under the rays of the sun. It was literally a case of water everywhere but none to drink, except what we had in a couple of canteens.

We soldered up the drum and went bitterly thirsty to bed. But that night a swift storm came up—the first in more than a year in that arid desert. We spread our tarps and set out our cooking pots to catch water. In the morning we saw that fully half that wide tide-flat was covered by muddy water about an inch deep. Desperately we gathered it up before the hot sun sucked it up into the sky again. Using tin cups, we filled cooking pots, and then in turn we filled our repaired drum. What water it was! It was almost half fine silt, it was brackish, it contained bugs and minute shellfish, and the deepest pool contained a dead land-turtle. But we stayed there. We explored the country on that water and we found sheep.

The three of us were hardened desert-rats and none of us were choosey about water so long as it was wet. But that stuff was almost too much for us to bear. The silt was so finely suspended that it never settled; and the turtle, the bugs and the shellfish gave it an exotically putrid taste I hope I never again encounter. But it was wet. It saved our lives, even though it did gag us and clog up our systems. All the time we were hunting, climbing over ragged peaks three thousand feet above that blue tantalizing gulf, I was haunted by voluptuous dreams of water that didn't smell bad. Ten days later, when we finally got back to Pitiquito and started drinking Hermosillo beer, I felt like weeping for joy. That hunt took fifteen pounds off my none-too-corpulent frame; and my two companions, tough old desert-rats that they were, went to the hospital with fine cases of dysentery as soon as we got back to the States. One of them will never hunt sheep again. Yet as I look back on the experience now, I think those four heads we got were worth it.

Unless there is some change which it is now impossible to foresee, the desert bighorns will long survive in the Mexican state of Sonora, as many parts of their range are so waterless and so isolated that the destructive peon with his .30–30 cannot penetrate. On the west coast of Lower California, one of the wildest and most desolate parts of the globe, seemingly they can thrive for a thousand years.

But in the sheep states of the United States their outlook is none too good. Many years ago the legislatures passed perpetual closed seasons, sat back and forgot them. Since that time, every nester, every prospector, every cattleman starving in the desert with his few lean cows, has shot every sheep he saw, with practically no chance of detection. Game departments, which are chronically hard-pressed for money, have ignored them.

Yet the bighorn is the most valuable and sought-after game animal in North America, and protecting sheep could pay big dividends to any state with much sheep range. There are hundreds of men in the United States who would willingly pay $100 for a license which would give him a chance for a shot at a big ram. Only a hundred hunters annually would provide a considerable sum for almost anyone's game department. In addition to license fees, guides and outfitters would profit. From talking to Eastern hunters who have gone to Alaska, Canada and Mexico for bighorns, I am convinced that every ram costs a sportsman from $1,500 to $5,000. It would not take many such hunters within such a state as Arizona to leave considerable money annually in the State and to be a real economic asset to an otherwise poverty-stricken section. With money coming in, the prospectors and ranchers of the region, who otherwise are the sheep-killers, would turn game-protectors, as that would be the side on which their bread would be buttered. With a good plan of game management, barren ranges which now will not support $100 worth of goats could produce bighorns that would bring from $5,000 to $10,000 every year.

All that is needed to start the sheep increasing and flourishing is some real protection, the development of permanent water in ranges where there are no water-bearing cactus, and perhaps a little work on sheep diseases. The possibilities are really tremendous—for preserving the bighorns and at the same time preserving one of the most thrilling and arduous of all field sports.

After many years of gloom, I am beginning to feel that there is a chance to save the bighorns of the Southwest, particularly those of Arizona. The attitude of Arizona's state game department has changed, for one thing. A few years ago I made a report on the illegal killing of sheep, to the man who was then state game warden—evidence I had found myself and stories I had heard. The reply I got was that he thought my report "greatly exaggerated." So far as I could learn, no effort was made to check up, and the sheep ranges of southwestern Arizona continued to be ignored and unpatrolled.

But in the spring of 1936, there were signs in the air of a change of attitude. The Forest Service made a survey of the bighorn herd in the Catalina Mountains, practically in Tucson's back yard, and found that there were about eighty-five sheep ranging there— enough so that with real protection there could be enough sheep in ten years to warrant an open season on rams. They also found something that any sheep hunter could have told them: that the animals are highly migratory and do not stay put.

The most constructive piece of work was the survey of the Arizona sheep country by A. A. Nichol, working under the auspices of the National Association of Audubon Societies. Nichol reported about seven hundred sheep in Arizona, with a few in nearly all the suitable ranges not too close to concentrations of human population.

Now—and this is the best sign of all—Nichol has resigned from the faculty of the University of Arizona to take over the range utilization of southwestern Arizona for the Federal government. Nichol knows more about Arizona sheep than any other living man. He also knows range and game management, and he is working out a plan by which certain areas will be reserved exclusively for sheep, antelope and desert mule deer. Water to carry them through the drought is being developed, and the game in this hot, barren wilderness will be treated as a crop—as all game should be.

Although the sheep have been sadly depleted by the lawless meat-hunters of the area, there is still seed-stock left. Further, sheep will continue to wander in from northern Sonora, where there are

some excellent year-round sheep ranges just across the line. With
the development of water, with protection from pot-hunters, and
with some control of predators, the sheep should be plentiful in from
ten to twenty years. It is still too early to predict, but now for the
first time since a white man killed a bighorn, it is beginning to look
as if *los cimarrones* may be safe for posterity. And if so, the grandest,
toughest of all American big-game hunting will continue to draw
those who love hard work and high places.

CHAPTER VI

SWALLOW OF THE PLAINS

CALLING a fairly large, deer-like mammal a "swallow" may sound like a pretty extravagant figure of speech, yet I know of no other term which so well describes the pronghorn antelope in motion. A herd of fleeing antelope skimming over the plain, wheeling, maneuvering, is like nothing so much as a flock of swallows.

A bundle of nervous energy, a gaudy coat of white, tan and black, a pair of telescopic eyes, and legs that can propel him faster than any other American game animal—that's the antelope.

Mexicans call him *el berendo* (pronounced bay-rain-dough), the frontiersmen dubbed him a goat, and many Americans speak of him as the pronghorn. By any name he is one of the most beautiful and interesting of animals.

The antelope has a reputation of being fast, but it is hard to exaggerate his speed. It is difficult to believe that anything composed of flesh and blood can move so fast. I have clocked whole herds traveling at more than fifty miles per hour, and individuals have cut across in front of me when the speedometer of my car was holding steadily at sixty. A barren doe in good condition and running on smooth hard ground may possibly do as much as seventy, though this is only a guess. The speed of any animal is to some extent an individual matter, just as it is among human beings. Bucks, particularly the old ones with the towering horns that are the pride of the trophy hunter, are far slower than the barren does, and I imagine that most of the old fellows would have to extend themselves to do fifty miles an hour. I remember chasing one huge buck and being able to keep up with him at forty-five, but on the same day a younger one made the car at the same speed look almost as if it were standing still. In any case, antelope are fast, very fast—far faster than most observers realized until they had the opportunity to check them with the relatively accurate speedometers of modern automobiles.

All antelope seem to take great pride in their speed and they love to race. I have seen them race automobiles, trains, horsemen. A retired locomotive engineer told me that in the early days in the Big Bend of Texas they used to race his train regularly, and that on one occasion he ran over the last members of a large herd when they tried to cross in front of him. Even fawns a few weeks old seem to be able to keep up with the herd.

Cold type is a poor medium in which to describe the appearance of the prongbuck; and pictures, curiously enough, never do him justice. He is boldly colored, bizarre, outlandish—the harlequin of the deer-kind in North America. When I saw my first herd of antelope I was a lad of fourteen or fifteen. I had seen many deer and had shot a couple. Naturally I expected to see animals that looked something like deer. What I did see gave me the curious illusion that I was gazing upon some extinct mammal risen out of the Pleistocene, or that I had suddenly been transported to Africa. The prongbuck is like nothing else in America—or in the world, for that matter. He evidently originated in America, as fossil remains found alongside those of camels and horses extinct a good 50,000 years, show his ancestors somewhat smaller than modern forms but much the same.

At a distance a herd of antelope always looks like a collection of tiny spots of pure white, and surely white is their most conspicuous color. The sides and belly of the antelope are white; so is the rump patch, which is composed of erectile hairs and can be "flashed" as a danger signal, just as the deer of the East use their white tails. There are also stripes of white alternating with buff on the necks of the animals. The saddle is buff, and the horns when fresh grown are dead black and come out directly above the eyesockets. The head of a big buck looks like that of some large and grotesque beetle.

I have heard people suggest that nature made a mistake in coloring the antelope so conspicuously. With this I cannot agree. Pronghorns are easy for a trained observer to detect, even at a distance of a mile or more, but one who is not used to looking for them has great difficulty in seeing them. Nearly always he takes a herd for exposed light-colored rocks until the animals start to move. It is possible that predators would make the same mistake, as their eyesight is not so keen as that of man. In any case, the antelope's coloring was devised to protect him from extinct dire-wolves, cave bears and saber-toothed tigers, and not from twentieth-century riflemen with binoculars.

The pronghorn at one time occupied the whole Great Plains and inter-mountain region from the Mississippi to the Pacific Coast and from southern Canada to the northern half of Mexico. Estimates place their numbers in the 'seventies and early 'eighties conservatively at from 40,000,000 to 60,000,000. Almost all observers are agreed that they were more plentiful than the buffalo. Ten years ago there were only 30,000 animals left. Although they occupied a large part of their former range, they were rapidly diminishing in numbers and were in real danger of extinction. Now that danger is happily past. It is estimated that there are 70,000 in the United States, and they seem to be increasing everywhere. One of the largest herds in America is on Anderson Mesa, near Flagstaff, Arizona. It increased from fewer than 100 (Forest Service estimates said 25) in 1924 to about 4,000 in 1934. Since then their numbers have been stationary because of poor range conditions. It would seem that those who went into mourning for the antelope were somewhat premature.

The slaughter of the great antelope herds came later than the killing off of the buffalo by the hide-hunters. For one thing, the antelope did not have nearly so much economic value. They are small, and their hides make very poor buckskin, being weak and spongy in texture. Both Indians and mountain men held that their meat was not nourishing and that a man could not keep in good shape on antelope venison alone. They are a small mark and hard to hit, and cannot be hunted on horseback as the Indians hunted buffalo, for even an antelope fawn could outrun the fastest buffalo horse that ever lived. The market-hunters of the 'eighties were the villains of the piece, but not the only ones. Every fence that was put up reduced the antelope range. Sheep gave them sheep-scab and also helped to starve them out. Hunters shot them by the scores, often from railroad trains, and settlers used them as a winter meat supply to save sheep and cattle.

The favorite habitat of the pronghorn is open grassy plains country, but in Arizona he is found like the mule deer about everywhere he can make an honest living. There are herds on sea-level deserts in Arizona and Mexico and there are also herds in the open park country in the yellow pines 7,000 feet above sea level. At one time the antelope was thought to be a grass-eater exclusively, but modern scientific research has proved that he is not. In northern Arizona he is almost entirely a browser, living mostly, as stomach analyses have conclusively proved, on the scrub juniper. He also eats many weeds, and only occasionally, and then only after rains when the grass is very tender, does he graze at all. In fact, the feeding habits of the antelope are much like those of the mule deer, except that on the winter ranges he is indifferent to the buck brush, or cliff rose, that the mule deer so dearly loves.

There are two kinds of antelope country in the Southwest. The herds of northern Arizona and New Mexico are found on high open plains at from 4,000 to 7,000 feet. So are the *berendos* below the border in Chihuahua. Often the herds near Flagstaff occupy relatively small mountain parks hedged in with forests of yellow pine. They are drinkers of water and go to a pond or spring three or four times a week. I have seen them watering many times.

But the great herd which ranges along the Sonora coast and casually into southwestern Arizona *never* touches open water for the very good reason that there is no water within its range. Like the desert sheep and mule deer, the *berendos* have learned to depend for their moisture on the sap in cholla fruit and in the leaves of the iron-wood, and on the water stored during the times of infrequent rains by the bisnaga and saguaro.

But the antelope, I believe, is naturally a water drinker, and the Sonora herd has simply adapted itself to an existing necessity. Perhaps there is a digression here, but the history of that herd is an interesting example of the adaptability of large mammals. Originally it ranged almost entirely in the southwestern Arizona desert below the Southern Pacific railway. In times of drought the animals could always get water in the Gila River. They had been there as long as there had been Papago Indians and Papago traditions.

But in the early years of this century the Southern Pacific fenced its right-of-way and cut the antelope off from the Gila. In addition the country was settling up to some extent, and prospectors were moving in. The antelope were harried constantly, and great numbers of them were shot for meat. As a consequence they renounced their American citizenship and began to drift into Mexico, where they found refuge along the coast—a country of tall barren sheep ranges, sandy playas, rolling dunes, and valleys filled with ironwood, palo-verde, and fantastic forests of deadly cholla as high as a man on horseback. By following the spotty desert rains and eating the quick growth of grass and weeds that comes up on the dunes, by depending on cactus for their water supply, and on cholla fruit during the hot, grassless summer months, the antelope managed to survive. While they were making their adaptation many of them perished. Now they have fought their environment and won. In 1919 a reasonably accurate check of the herd indicated about 1,200 head. Now there must be somewhere around 20,000 as I have counted more than 1,000 from the top of one dune and at that time there were antelope scattered along the coast for 150 miles.

This Mexican herd has learned to be highly migratory. In the summer most of the animals drift south to the thicker cholla patches, some going clear to Tiburon Island. In the winter they move north near the border, where the rains bring up grass on the dunes. A section may be filled with antelope one week and empty of them the next. Like all desert species, they have to move to live.

Now that the Sonora herd has come back, it seems to be permanently safe, as the *berendo* is the hardest of all Mexican game animals for the peon to kill. Peons and Papagos hunt them earnestly but with small success, because, although they are good stalkers and patient ambushers, they are very poor shots. They can lie in wait for a sheep, and they can muffle their feet in gunny sacks and sneak up on a *buro*, as they call the mule deer; but antelope usually cling to the open, and shooting them is a long-range proposition, usually beyond the capabilities of a .30–30 which hasn't been cleaned in fifteen years, in the hands of a man who never practices and likes to get his game at not much over fifty yards.

The habits of the northern Arizona antelope are changing, too —again in an effort to adapt themselves to new conditions. They are becoming more migratory than they were in the early days, and they are becoming more often rough-country and timber animals. In time they may take more and more to the forests, and learn to depend more on their powers of scent and hearing. In other words, they will become somewhat similar in habit to the Rocky Mountain mule deer. In recent years I have found antelope ranging high on the sides of mountains and in thick timber, sometimes as high as 10,000 feet, where they never ranged in the old days. The herd which ranges north of San Francisco Peak, Arizona's highest mountain, is a case in point. It has taken to the timber now because sheep eat off the weeds and small brush on which it used to subsist, and because the Navajo Indians, the most ruthless and wasteful hunters in the West, habitually come over from the reservation to poach them. At one time the antelope in that locality were easy to see because they were always in the flats, but today they are about as hard to discover as mule deer. In spite of sheep and Navajos they are increasing, although not as fast as their kinsmen on nearby Anderson Mesa.

Since Americans first encountered antelope on the plains of the Missouri, the race has been noted not only for its speed but for its great curiosity. Much has been made of it, and the tales have not suffered in the retelling. According to old-time hunters, all you had to do was to tie a white handkerchief to a stick and wave it. Then, according to the story, all the antelope in sight came flocking up posthaste. Another method was to tie a piece of bright tin or cloth to a bush and then hide in the bush.

On my first antelope hunt in Sonora I tried out both plans. I waved flags until I had cramps. I camped in bushes until ants and flies almost ate me alive. Antelope gathered four and five hundred yards away. They stared at me fixedly by the hour and wondered what the hell I was up to, but their curiosity never got the better of their discretion. In the end I denounced the flag-waving act as an old wives' tale and went out and secured a buck by the time-honored method of stalking. Flag waving may work, for all I know, but I have never seen it used with success.

I think the explanation for the antelope's great curiosity is a simple one. As he is for the most part a plains-dweller, his wonderful eyes are his best method of detecting an enemy and his great speed is the best way to escape him. An unsophisticated antelope feels that so long as he can keep an enemy in sight he can run away from him at the first move which seems too hostile.

Once in Chihuahua I hunted for a whole day a big lone buck that had been driven out of his herd. He seemed to be as anxious to keep me in sight as I was to keep him located. The country was cut up by deep gullies, and little mesas rose here and there. My strategy was to sneak up close enough for a shot by getting out of his sight. His plan was to stay in plain sight in open country as far from a gully or mesa as he could get. I finally got within three hundred yards of him and developed a nice case of buck fever which resulted in my missing my first shot. He ran off until he was about five hundred yards away and stood watching me while I lay down, adjusted my sling, and began to feel for the range. On my nineteenth shot I struck him squarely between the forelegs and killed him. I suppose every other bullet passed within two feet of him, but he seemed to prefer facing known danger than the unknown danger of my prowling around in the gullies trying to surprise him.

The eye of an antelope is truly a marvel of nature. It is at least equal to the human eye aided with 8-power glasses, and the only thing in nature to compare with it are the eyes of mountain sheep and birds of prey. An antelope can see a human head a half-mile away, as I have determined by experiments on Arizona antelope. I once saw a herd watching a coyote so far away that I could barely see it with good 8-power glasses.

On the other hand, antelope are fairly easily stalked in timber and rough country. One summer I took a friend to Anderson Mesa to see the antelope herd. The animals were in summer range where the country has a good growth of scrub juniper. As long as we kept out of sight we found it quite easy to get within fifty or a hundred yards of the animals. I sneaked so close to one drowsing buck that I was able to hit him with a pebble. Another time we crept up within seventy yards of a herd of five fine bucks. Our stalk was by no means silent, but we did keep out of sight.

My own experience would tend to show that the eye of the antelope is the best belonging to any game animal, superior even to that of the bighorn. A stationary object doesn't mean much to a sheep; but moving or still a strange object is quickly apparent to the incredible eyes of *los berendos*. Several times I have come over a ridge to discover a herd of antelope feeding, heads down, a quarter of a mile away. I would stand still, with only my head showing against the skyline. Sheep or deer would not have noticed me until I moved, but one antelope would pick me up in a few seconds, then another. In a minute or two, all the members of the herd would be staring fixedly in my direction. Then they would begin slowly to move off; slowly—if they thought I was out of rifle range.

The antelope has the distinction of being the only hollow-horned ruminant in the world that sheds its horns annually. The horns grow over a core about half the length of the horn, and the core itself is never shed. The horns, though pronged like those of deer, are true horns and are composed of hair; but, unlike deer, the older the buck antelope, the better head he has. The finest head I ever saw was on an Anderson Mesa buck so old that in spite of the fact that it was summer, his ribs showed through his hide, and he was so stiff that he could hardly run. I had been shooting coyotes and had a rifle with me. How I longed to collect that trophy! I didn't—a staunch and rugged fear of the police, I suppose. But I'm sure that the old buck never survived the winter, and I'm equally convinced that his head would have measured well over twenty inches. Although the average doe has little spike horns about three inches long, many are hornless. I once collected for a museum a fat young doe with spikes almost four inches in length.

Like sheep, antelope breed in September. The bucks battle bitterly, and the larger and more agile ones run with large herds of does, from which they drive intruders, with eyes flashing and the reddish manes on their necks bristling like the hair of surly dogs. Bucks often kill each other, as the weapons of the antelope are more lethal than the branched antlers of deer. During the mating season it is common to see bucks with raw wounds on their necks and shoulders. Some have been found disembowelled. In addition there is the occasional danger of their horns' getting locked, and when this happens they die slowly of starvation just as locked buck deer do. In my collection, I have several photographs of two antelope found dead with locked horns in the Chino Valley near Prescott, Arizona.

The mating season past, the bucks shed their horns all through late October and early November, though a sick or wounded buck may retain his almost until Christmas. The new horn pushes the old one off the top, and by the time it appears it is a long curved spike, as yet without the prongs, and covered with hair which drops off when the horn matures. This is the reason why many cattlemen insist antelope *never* shed.

By March, in most sections, the new horns are pronged, full-grown, and jet black, though still somewhat soft and rubbery. Later in the spring and throughout the summer they harden, turning brown and brittle. After they are used for the purpose of deciding which bucks are the rulers of the herds, they split, curl at the bottom, and are finally pushed off. They go to pieces in a few months, and even in good antelope country it is not common to find shed horns unless you happen to find them immediately after they have been dropped.

Really big antelope heads are far more common than the record books would indicate, for the reason that the great slaughter of the animals was accomplished by meat-hunters and not by trophy-collectors. The present record, a buck taken near Oracle, Arizona, in the 'nineties, is somewhat over 20 inches. That is indeed a big head, and I have never actually measured one that was better, though I believe I have seen several that would top it, on old bucks running on Arizona's Anderson Mesa. The best head I ever took was a 16-incher, one that ranks well in the records; but on the day I shot that particular buck I think I saw at least a dozen with better heads, some much better.

On the other hand, a 14-inch head is not a bad one and even some of the massive 12-inchers I have seen have made excellent trophies. The heads of Mexican antelope do not compare with those in the colder regions of the United States, probably because food and water are harder to get on the deserts. But I predict that when the seasons are opened generally on the increasing herds in the United States, some lucky hunter will get a new record; and all the heads in the first ten will measure 18 and 19 inches.

Pronghorns are not large animals. Their conspicuous coloring and their thick stiff hair make them seem larger than they really are. In weight they average about the same as the little Arizona white-tail deer. An average buck weighs about eighty pounds dressed, and the biggest one I have ever seen weighed only a little over a hundred pounds. Does weigh about sixty. Nearly all hunters are disappointed the first time they bring one down. The mountain men and buffalo hunters must have considered them poor game indeed. They called them 'goats' and scorned to shoot them.

A microscope shows that the hair of all deer is tubular. Antelope hair is similar, but it is much coarser, and the fact that it is hollow can be seen with the naked eye. It is incredibly brittle. Every time you touch the carcass of a pronghorn the hair breaks off. Vernon Bailey relates coming across an old camp of Navajo Indians who had been hunting antelope, and says that the hair was a foot deep.

Antelope are among the most nervous of animals. They cannot stand confinement and seem never to get used to it. They will not breed in a small enclosure, and they are very difficult to ship. When they seemed to be facing extinction ten years ago, nearly all of the frantic efforts to start new herds were unsuccessful, as the animals died en route. There is only one way to ship them successfully and that is to catch them new-born, bottle-raise them, and ship them in individual crates. When they are captured their favorite stunt is to rush into a fence or wall and break their necks. Then, too, they can literally be "scared to death." Efforts made a few years ago by the Arizona game department to capture and transport members of the Anderson Mesa herd were a failure. Twenty-eight of the thirty animals captured died before they could be turned loose, and the two survivors were released some three hundred miles short of their objective in order to save their lives.

But curiously enough, this very nervousness often makes the pronghorn one of the most difficult of all animals to kill. He is like a man, with all of a man's imagination and nervousness. An unsuspecting antelope shot from ambush will go down just as a surprised man will; but if one is frightened and starts running, he will continue though almost shot to pieces, just as an excited Malay running amok will absorb the entire contents of a .45 automatic without leaving his feet. A friend of mine once connected with an antelope in Mexico, dropping the whole contents of the animal's abdomen on the ground with a paunch shot and almost tearing a hind leg off. The buck ran more than a mile before it fell. On the same hunt I put three .270 bullets into a buck before he went down. An antelope will run like the wind with a leg shot off, and I once saw a large buck run almost a quarter of a mile with his heart completely blown to pieces. Old-time hunters have told me that antelope were sometimes almost as hard to kill with the .44–40 Winchesters they used as were elk.

The enemies of the present-day pronghorns are mostly the smaller predators—the coyote, the bobcat and the golden eagle. The big timber wolves, probably the worst enemy they ever had with the exception of civilized man, are now pretty well killed off. In the two or three weeks before the young can run with their mothers, great numbers of them must be discovered and killed. One of the most persistent fables in American folklore is that deer and antelope fawns give off no scent and hence cannot be found. That seems to me to be nonsense, pure and simple. In the Kaibab, dogs are trained to hunt out hidden fawns so man can catch and raise them. I have seen coyotes combing antelope range during the season of the drop, hunting out the new-born fawns with all the skill and persistence of a good bird-dog in a briar patch. I have also seen the big golden eagles scouring the country at the same time.

Once the young are running with the herd, they are singularly free from enemies, except in the time of deep snow when coyotes take many victims. When they get into the timber, however, they come into contact with the deadly mountain lion, which must be further decimated if the antelope is really to become a forest-dwelling animal on a large scale.

Antelope are gregarious to a higher degree than any other American big-game animal, and they are most often seen in herds. In fact, most antelope do not seem happy unless another one is close by, a provision of nature, perhaps, as four eyes are better than two, eight better than four, and so on.

The does go off by themselves to give birth to the fawns in the spring, but even then they are often accompanied by their young of the preceding year. When the new twins come, however, the does always run the old ones off. Disconsolate lonely little yearling antelope are always common on the range when the new ones are coming on. As soon as the fawns of that year are able to follow them, the mothers flock together—sometimes two or three does with their young, sometimes thirty, forty, or more. Bucks usually run in pairs and threes during the summer months, and the only ones found singly are the old misanthropes who are so used up and ailing that they can't seem to get along with anyone. The solitary bucks, just like the solitary rams, are usually the ones with the best heads.

Just before the mating season opens early in September, the big bucks begin to collect their harems of does. There nearly always are smaller and weaker bucks hanging around on the outskirts, being continually set upon by the big fellows. Then, when the mating season is over, the bucks continue to stay with the does, just as many desert rams stay with the ewes. The herds come together, and during the winter, particularly in colder climates, great herds numbering a thousand and over are often seen. A few years ago, officials of the Arizona game department decided to make a survey of the Anderson Mesa. They were on horseback and covered much territory, but all during the day they saw only a few small herds. Then, along toward nightfall, they ran into the main herd of almost 4,000 animals. The whole country seemed alive with pronghorns. Many times I have seen herds which I estimate to have contained upwards of 1,500 animals.

Antelope are exasperating creatures to hunt. For one thing, they are not hard to see. They are conspicuously colored, and their white rumps and bellies can often be detected with the naked eye at more than a mile. With glasses, of course, they can be seen much farther. Furthermore, even antelope which have been shot at a lot seem, deceptively, tantalizingly tame. They seem to know to a dot the range of a good rifle in the hands of an average hunter. They have their mental deadline all marked out, and if you don't cross it, they do not seem particularly wild.

Once in Sonora when I was out afoot after antelope, I saw a herd of sixteen bucks bedded down on the side of a sand dune about 450 yards away. About half of them wore excellent heads. They saw me as soon as I saw them. I must admit that I was far more excited than they seemed to be. Sitting down on the sand, I looked them over with my glasses. They returned my scrutiny. A couple of them stood up for a better look, but most of them simply lay there.

Now, in spite of many romantic tales to the contrary, a 450-yard shot is a very long one, and I was reluctant to try it. I went back over the sand dune from which I had seen them, made a laborious circuit, and finally popped up about two hundred yards from where I had first seen them bedded down. But they had moved. They were still 450 yards away, all looking at me with the greatest of interest.

I stalked again, but with the same result. Those bucks never seemed particularly uneasy, but they set great store by their hides. Finally, in desperation, I tried a very long shot and missed. This time they went clear out of the country. I got a buck later in the day, but only by luck. An old fellow was bedded down alone and asleep. He didn't see me until I was less than two hundred yards away, and I shot him as he was getting to his feet.

Your only hope, when antelope are at all wild, is extremely careful stalking. Seeing them is not enough. You must get within range. When you hunt, approach every little rise in the ground with the greatest of caution. Never look until you have succeeded in screening your head behind shrubs or bushes. Then, when you have located the game, figure out a way of approaching them without being seen. Keep down in the arroyos, and don't let your curiosity force you to take a peek until you have reached your objective. Another thing: when you reach your objective and look out, don't be too nonplussed if you don't immediately see your game. They may have lain down in tall grass; they may have moved behind a tree. If you have been careful, you can usually bet that they are still there, so take your time, and use your glasses.

If your first shot misses, stay down. Shoot again. If the animals still haven't located you, you will probably get another shot, and possibly even a third, as they tend to mill about when surprised instead of running off as a deer would.

Experience has convinced me that antelope are the most deceptive-looking of all game animals. They are small, but in spite of their size they nearly always look larger than they are. And seen on bright days, with the sun glittering on their bellies and rumps, they usually seem much nearer than they are. But at dawn and dusk and on cloudy days, they fade and shrink, and appear deceptively far away. Figuring out the range is one of the most difficult feats I have ever undertaken. In addition, the white of the rumps and bellies that makes antelope so easily seen also makes them easy to miss. It is the same principle, I suppose, as shooting away from the sun with a gold-bead front sight.

I have hunted antelope off and on for many years. I have spent many days in the field without a gun, observing them. Still I find it difficult to try to estimate accurately how far away they are.

I remember one occasion, early on a gray morning, I was slipping along in antelope country, when through an opening in the brush I saw a herd feeding sedately along across a sandy open park which the Mexicans call a *playa* or beach. With the glasses I could tell one of them was a whopping big buck. He stopped dead still, staring at something at right angles to where I lay. I had all the time in the world to get him in my scope, wrap myself in the sling, and ease off a perfect shot. Deciding that he was somewhere between 325 and 350 yards off, I held the post just over his back, and fired. Far beyond him, through that vista in the brush, I saw the sand kick up. The buck ran off, astonished but unhit. So I paced the distance from where I had shot to where he had run. It was almost exactly 200 yards. My shot could not have been more perfect, but my judgment of range was sour.

Stalking is not only the best way of getting antelope—it is the only decent one. When Wyoming opened the season on the animals some years ago, many men hunted them from automobiles. Lawless American hunters in Chihuahua and Coahuila still run them, but the practice is a thoroughly bad one. Antelope become very wild. When frightened, they run a long way after they are hit, and are never found; and no man can shoot well enough, even at close objects, from a moving automobile. Many wounded pronghorns have been the result wherever running has been tried. Near Hermosillo some rich Mexican *bravos* tried shooting them from airplanes with sub-machine guns and then sending *mozos* with trucks out to retrieve the slain. Great sportsmanship!

The problem of getting a good antelope head is complicated by the fact that often during the open seasons the scalps are not in the best of condition, as the winter coat is not yet fully grown and the hair is not set and hardened. Even the hair of a winter-killed antelope is brittle enough, but if you want to go slowly demented, get an August-killed head mounted and then watch it shed. The sportsman is faced with the dual problem of getting good horns and a good cape. He should look first for the longest horns, then for the best developed prongs, and next for the brightest, cleanest-looking cape. He should never bang away at the first buck he sees, as deer hunters often do. If a man makes a long trip to Mexico or to the West, he should return with a trophy he can be proud of.

If I were ranking the heads of American big game as trophies, I'd put antelope second only to sheep. Antelope are far from common, even after increasing for the past twenty years. They are strange and lovely creatures; and getting a good buck requires patience, foresight, ability to stalk, and skill with a rifle. If a hunter possesses these qualities to some degree, he ought to be able to bag one.

Not many years ago no state had an open season on antelope, and the grand old sport of plains hunting seemed indefinitely doomed in America. Now, so spectacular has the revival been, that New Mexico, Wyoming, Montana and Idaho had open seasons in 1936. Arizona needs one badly, and Mexico will again open the season on the Sonora herd if and when someone impresses the game department in distant Mexico City that the animals are really plentiful.

The pronghorn has inhabited the West for several hundred thousand years, and he has survived changes far more serious than the coming of the white man. He saw the ice disappear and the country dry up. He remained and multiplied while the saber-toothed tiger, the horse and the ground sloth died out. He isn't as dumb as he is supposed to be, and if we want him with us we have but to give him some free range and a little protection. He can take care of himself.

CHAPTER VII

THE ELK COME BACK

WHEN Cortez and his *conquistadores* first reached the City of Mexico, Montezuma showed them as a curiosity the antlers of enormous stags somewhat similar to those of the European red deer, but far larger. They were the antlers of American elk, or wapiti, the first ever seen by white men. They may possibly have come from the Tulle elk of California, but more likely from the great Merriam elk of the Southwest.

The Merriam elk was once plentiful in the mountains of central and southern New Mexico and in the White Mountains of Arizona. Now, unhappily, it is extinct. According to Vernon Bailey, author of *The Mammals of New Mexico, Cervus merriami* was in size fully equal to the northern elk, but paler and more reddish, with skull and antlers more massive and antlers more erect. The once-great herds melted away so quickly under the onslaught of men with modern rifles that only a few skulls and heads remain in existence.

They were very plentiful throughout their range in the 'eighties, but by the 'nineties they were well on the road to extinction, and by about 1902 they were evidently completely gone. For a few years rumors of existing bands of elk, always in very remote places, continued to filter out. Shed antlers were occasionally found. Now and then a prospector or cowpuncher reported seeing very old beds or dried dung. On rare occasions an excited hunter claimed to have seen a big bull; but the eyes of hunters magnify notoriously, and instead of elk, they probably saw very large buck mule deer.

Then even rumors of their existence died out. Only oldtimers remembered them, and the new generation growing up in Arizona and New Mexico was largely unaware that its native states had ever harbored elk at all. An interesting game animal was gone beyond recall.

Yet now the elk are back: not *Merriami*, but his northern cousin, the elk of the Wyoming and Montana Rockies. Man destroyed and man restored, and the return of the elk to the Southwest is one of the most satisfactory chapters in recent game conservation. Once more the frosty September mornings of the high elevations ring to the thrilling bugle of the great bulls; once more the greatest of all round-horned deer wanders through the spruce and yellow pine, along with the mule deer and the turkey. It is pleasant to imagine that somewhere in the remote mountains a few scattered bands of Merriam's elk were still left to mingle their blood with that of the newcomers, but beyond any doubt this is but a romantic fantasy.

According to an estimate made in 1937 by Elliot S. Barker, New Mexico State game warden, there are now about 3,400 elk in the various New Mexican herds. They are hunted annually on special licenses. Their increase, since they were first introduced in 1911, has been spectacular. Some were brought in by the State game department, others by private ranchers. The animals have proved that with protection from human hunters they can multiply rapidly.

The experience of Arizona has been similar. There are now three firmly established herds within the State. One of the two smaller ones ranges in the White Mountains near Escudilla Mountain, close to the New Mexico boundary, the original range of Merriam's elk. Another is found around the chain of volcanic peaks south of the Grand Canyon: San Francisco, Kendrick and Bill Williams. The third and largest herd has found a congenial home on the Mogollon Rim just above the Tonto Basin, where in the 'nineties those feudists, the Grahams and the Twekesburys, industriously killed each other off for the benefit of later romancers. A herd of about 40 animals introduced from Montana in 1916 has increased to an estimated 4,000, and an open season on special licenses has been held since 1935.

A word now about the Mogollon Rim country. It is the best elk country in Arizona, and one of the best all-around game countries I have ever seen. The rim is the tipped-up edge of a great plateau, and the Tonto Basin below it came from a great fault which has left tremendous cliffs from 1,000 to 1,500 feet high—cliffs which extend for over a hundred miles. In places the rim is almost 8,000 feet above sea level, but the plateau which it forms slants gradually north. All the drainage is to the north.

The top of the rim supports spruce and fir. It is a land of tiny lakes, thick timber, icy trout streams deep in the canyons. Here the elk find their summer home, and the whole country is tracked up by them. As the altitude decreases, the spruce and fir are replaced by yellow pine and Gambel's oak, still lower by the piñon and cedar of the upper Sonoran zone. So here, by moving a few miles, the elk can find ideal summer and winter range.

September, along the rim at almost 8,000 feet, finds the bulls bugling their challenges, and the woods ring with the clash of their towering antlers. The first snows move them north into lower country, and they winter on the cedar flats. As snow melts they move up again, and they have their calves in the pines.

In 1935 I hunted in the yellow-pine country some twenty miles south of the rim, during the first big snow of the season. The amount of game I saw was truly amazing. I found fifteen or twenty great bull elk, a good many cows, and deer literally by the hundreds—all moving before the storm. I don't suppose a day passed without my seeing from two to five hundred deer, as incredible as that may seem. Turkeys are found in the rim country, too, though they have not increased under protection as the elk and mule deer have. The Arizona whitetail range through the Tonto Basin and in the deep canyons which drop south from the rim. Now and then one sees their little heart-shaped tracks a mile or two north in the level spruce forest, but for the most part they seem to prefer the rough rim itself. Black bears are common. Game country? I've never seen a better—not even excepting the primitive areas of the Mexican Sierra Madres.

I am not much of an elk hunter, so it seems to me that I had better let men from Montana and Wyoming tell about those great round-horned stags. But I will venture a few observations. In thick country elk are harder to get than mule deer—at least such is my experience. The elk I have hunted seemed to move on slighter provocation; and for creatures of their bulk they can go with amazing quietness and stealth. In the thick cedars, where in Arizona they are found after the snows, they are as difficult a proposition as one could wish for. Further, those great bulls take a tremendous amount of killing. I found that bullets which are deadly on mule deer and sheep go to pieces too quickly on elk, often failing to penetrate into the chest cavity after a broadside rib shot. That first season many a grand old bull shot with deer loads got away to die. Heavy rifles are surely a part of elk conservation.

But the experience of Arizona and New Mexico proves, I am convinced, that any state which wants elk and which has a big area of wild land, can have them. With any protection at all they will hold their own amazingly, and with fair protection they will increase with astonishing speed. Of all the plants made in Arizona, only one was a failure, and that because the happy natives feasted on the elk almost as soon as the trucks could release them.

Elk once ranged over almost the entire area of the United States, from Pennsylvania to California, and they can come back again—just as they have in Arizona and New Mexico.

CHAPTER VIII

DESERT PIGS

FROM the time of the famous Capt. Mayne Ried, American folklore has had it that the javelina is one of the most dangerous of all native game animals. I have heard dozens of stories of herds attacking men unprovoked or keeping some poor hunter treed overnight with all the ferocity of a pack of Siberian wolves. Some of these tales may be true, for all I know, but my own fairly extensive experience would indicate that they aren't. I have seen some thousands of javelinas in my time, in Arizona, Sonora and Texas, and without a single exception, all of them were convinced that *homo sapiens* was a bad *hombre* and one to be avoided. Javelinas will gang up on coyotes and wildcats, and fight fiercely for themselves and their young, but when a man with a gun enters the picture they hurriedly depart.

I have wounded javelinas out of herds and the others have always got out of the way as fast as they could, convinced that resistance would be futile. Discretion, they seem to believe, is the better part of valor; and if a companion is disabled, that is just his hard luck. Unless cornered by dogs, every one I have seen has been bent on getting away as fast as his short legs would carry him.

But the javelina is surely no coward. Backed up against a cliff or cornered in a cave, he'll fight man or dogs with the courage of despair. Many a dog has been killed and not a few hunters have been wounded, especially poverty-stricken Mexicans who cannot afford rifles, and who habitually kill the animals with clubs. But for that

[133]

matter, even a deer will fight man or dogs if cornered. I have known of several horses being gored by wounded and desperate bucks, and once when hunting in Arizona's Kaibab Forest, I got considerably tossed around when I foolishly laid hands on a big fellow I had down.

If a man happens to be in the way when a javelina is making his dash for freedom that man is apt to get hurt, as a javelina does not submit to death tamely. Hunting in Sonora a few years ago, my wife was "charged" by a big boar which she had wounded and followed up. She dropped it at her feet. But let no one think that the little pigs will whirl and come at the hunter as African lions do. That simply doesn't happen. Shot at, a javelina thinks more of his hide than he does of his integrity.

Javelinas are today found in three border states—Arizona, New Mexico and Texas. They are very rare in New Mexico, but fairly plentiful in Arizona. They are protected in both states. In Texas, where they once existed in swarms, they are not protected at all, in spite of the fact that their numbers seem to be constantly decreasing. Javelinas once ranged as far north as the Red River of Arkansas. Now in one subspecies or another they exist from the Mexican border clear throughout Central and South America; but only two of these subspecies have a precarious foothold in the United States— the Texas javelina, which is found in the Big Bend, in the lower Rio Grande Valley, and possibly in the sand-hill country of western Texas and eastern New Mexico; and the Sonora javelina which ranges in the southern half of Arizona and a small strip of south-western New Mexico. The eastern animals are a somewhat darker gray than the Sonora species, but both are approximately the same size and both have a light gray "collar" which starts under the chin and runs diagonally around the neck to the shoulders. In addition, both have a strip of very dark gray and very coarse erectile bristles along the backbone. Their bodies are round and bulky and very large for their small feet and delicate legs. There is practically no difference in appearance between boars and sows. Full grown adults of either sex weigh from about 40 to 65 or possibly 75 pounds.

Given food and cover, javelinas are among the most adaptable of animals. They were formerly found as far north as Arkansas, and even now they range in Arizona and Sonora from sea-level desert to plateaus and mountains, 7,500 feet in elevation. Although they are desert-dwellers for the most part, a good many range in the Sierra Madres of Sonora and Chihuahua. Even now there are still a few bands north of Arizona's Mogollon Rim, a land where winters are severe and snow often lies deep for several months in the year. In the old days the high rugged mountain ranges of southern Arizona were full of them, and they ranged clear up to spruce and fir in the summertime. I have seen their characteristic little tip-toe tracks and have found caves rank with their musk in areas where I would have sworn there wasn't a javelina within twenty-five miles.

Books usually call the javelina a peccary, and his Latin name is *Pecari angulatus*. He is also called simply a pig over much of his range, and I have even heard him referred to rather grandiosely as a "musk hog" or a "wild boar." However, most Arizonians have adopted the Mexican name *javelina*, with the difference that the Mexican uses *jabelin* (pronounced ha-va-lean) for the singular, and *jabelinas* for the plural. (To an American there is seemingly no practical difference between the Spanish *b* and *v*.)

[135]

El jabelin is the American sportsman's only chance to hunt a genuine New World pig. All the others—the wild boars of the Santa Cruz and Catalina Islands off the California coast, the "Roosians" of the Tennessee and North Carolina mountains, and the razorbacks of the Southern swamps—are imported Europeans who have found the American climate to their liking and have thrived.

Biologically the javelina is one of the most interesting of mammals. He belongs to a unique family, and like the pronghorn antelope, he is a species found only in the New World. Superficially he is akin to a European swine, but important differences show that the relationship is a distant one at best. Both are probably descended from a remote common ancestor, possibly American; and fossil remains show that javelinas have been native to both North and South America since the early Pleistocene.

One of the most interesting features of the little animals is their scent—the characteristic from which they receive one of their names —"musk hog." The gland is in the middle of the back just forward of the rump and the vent is about the size of the hole left by a .30-caliber bullet. The scent itself smells exactly like the odor of a skunk except that it is not quite so potent. It is used not as a protection, but as a warning for their fellows.* Deer achieve the same result with the scent of the metatarsal glands, and antelope issue scent from a gland on the rump as a warning signal.

The little pigs are firm believers in the old adage that in numbers there is strength. They are among the most gregarious of animals; and boars, sows and young are found together in grunting,

---

* Ernest Thompson Seton says their scent may also possibly serve to keep troublesome insects away.

squealing companionship the year round. Bands from thirty-five to fifty are still common, and even a lion or tigre would hesitate to attack them. Man with dogs is the only combination they cannot beat.

I am convinced that a full-grown javelina can whip any animal his size. A bobcat or coyote wouldn't have a chance against one, and even a lobo wolf might find the going tough, as the pigs are lightning fast in their movements and their bite is severe. No ordinary dog can come out on top in a battle with one.

A pet javelina belonging to a man here in southern Arizona got loose last year and set out to see the world. Any creature with as strange an odor as a javelina will of course be set upon by dogs, but that bothered our hero not at all. Before an astonished policeman finally shot it with a pistol, it had killed three dogs and wounded about a dozen. In doing all that damage it had suffered hardly at all.

In the wilds javelinas seem to engage coyotes without hesitation. Once several years ago, while hunting quail on the desert, I paused to eat a lunch under a cliff. Suddenly I heard a rush below me and saw a coyote running as if the devil himself was after it. And the devil was indeed in pursuit—in the shape of three full-grown javelinas! The chase ended several hundred yards down the arroyo with a bleeding and thoroughly frightened coyote still in flight. The pigs turned and trotted triumphantly back to a mesquite and cholla thicket from which they presently emerged with the rest of a herd which contained several young. They talked things over and then trotted up the hill about fifty yards to my left. They were upwind from me most of the time and never saw me, but I could smell their curious skunk-like odor very strongly. Perhaps the coyote had tried to stalk a piglet, or perhaps the sows simply hadn't liked his looks. In any case, they had him on the run.

It is this scent which keeps the full-grown javelina from being good eating. Young ones taste like veal, and I have heard their flesh compared to that of the cottontail rabbit; but old ones are almost impossible to eat. Even in Mexico, where the peon is traditionally a hungry man, the carcasses are thrown away. I have read directions for their preparation and cooking. Remove the scent-sack at once, they say. Soak the meat of the old animals in salt water. I have tried it, but with poor results. The meat looks beautiful—smooth, pink and appetizing—but once you try to cook it, that rank odor begins to steal out of the pot. You gag. Presently you throw it away.

If they are such poor eating, then, why have javelinas been persecuted until they are almost extinct within the borders of the United States? The answer is that, like the buffalo, they have been killed off for their hides. Their case is one of the finest examples of the universal law that a game species is doomed as soon as man discovers that money can be had for any part of the creature. At first the animals were largely ignored by the American settlers, because they are small and hard to hit, and as their flesh is not good. Then, in the early 'nineties, a market developed for hides. Each one brought the magnificent sum of fo' bits, and everyone went javelina hunting.

His hide is the javelina's fatal charm. It is thin, strong, and marked with the bristle-holes so much in demand for "pigskin" jackets and gloves. Arizona stopped the commercial slaughter of the animals a good many years ago, and now the herds may be holding their own. Texas has never protected them and, as a consequence, they are almost extinct in that state; and they are nearing extinction in the few small areas in New Mexico where they still exist.

Until five or six years ago, javelinas were extremely plentiful in Sonora, where they have few if any dangerous natural enemies and were seldom hunted then by the natives. Now, however, the tragic history of the species is being repeated there, and every Mexican with a few dogs and some leisure is hunting them—and dogs and leisure are things almost any Mexican has plenty of. Enterprising Americans went through the state offering to buy hides, and now the death of a javelina means from one to two pesos in the pocket of the killer—in other words, from 28 to 56 cents. That is a paltry sum to an American, but in a land where a man will labor hard from dawn till dusk for a peso, it is real money. Every Mexican in javelina country maintains a pack of scarred and mangy dogs, and hunts constantly. In one month a couple of years ago, 25,000 hides came through Nogales, Arizona, alone. About 85,000 were cleared there in one year. No species can long stand a slaughter like that. The flood of hides is ebbing now, but it means not that the little pigs are being hunted less hard but that they are growing rare. On a trip into Sonora in 1937, in an area where I had previously killed javelinas and where I had seen much sign daily, I saw not a single animal and cut the tracks of but one small herd. I spent three weeks in what was formerly good pig country. I saw mule and whitetail deer and a good many mountain sheep, but not a javelina. The hide-hunters had been there since my last trip. Javelina skulls and bones whitened the flats and the arroyos, but live ones were simply not there.

It is a curious thing that the professional game-savers have paid so little attention to the javelina, that they have ignored this astonishing slaughter—the most amazing thing in recent years. If an American sportsman goes into Sonora and brings out an old decadent bighorn ram with bad teeth and but a couple of years to live, the game-savers bombard Mexico City with indignant telegrams. Yet these same men view without a word of protest the bales of hides coming across the border. Why this is I do not know. Perhaps the little pigs lack the charm and appeal of the other game species.

Even in Arizona, the javelina has never had any real protection, and almost no public sympathy. Men who would no more shoot a deer out of season than they would steal a neighbor's horse, kill javelinas at every opportunity. Somehow the notion that the animals are interesting creatures well worth the protection has never filtered through the Western mind.

I was once the guest of a rancher in Texas who intelligently protected the deer and antelope on his place, allowing only a few bucks to be shot annually. Late one afternoon, however, another of his guests came in and said he had caught a herd of javelinas in a box canyon and had slaughtered nine of them. Was the ranch owner indignant? He was not. Deer were worth protecting. But javelinas —just little old worthless pigs that aren't even good to eat. Of the five hunters on the ranch, I was the only one who wasn't enthusiastic in his congratulations.

I have killed several of the little hogs, and I have had much sport in hunting them. Treated fairly, they are by no means easy. They are exceedingly wary, and though they do not seem to be able to see well, they have keen senses of scent and hearing. The fact that they run in herds means that many pairs of eyes and ears and many noses are on the alert for danger. And once jumped, they are hard to hit.

Their peculiar bobbing run, and the fact that they are built so close to the ground, makes them easy to overshoot. If they were fairly still-hunted, killing them off would be difficult if not impossible.

To hit them with a rifle, the hunter must be a quick and accurate snap-shot, as the speed with which a herd of fifteen or twenty can get out of sight must be seen to be believed. It is almost incredible. For an instant the little pigs will be on every side of you, then there is a rush, a crash of brush—and you are alone. I always speak of having "flushed" a bunch of javelinas, and the word isn't so ill chosen at that. The little devils don't fly, but they seem to; and they can get out of sight with all the speed and dash of a covey of quail driving into a thorny thicket.

Occasionally a hunter will get above a herd in some lonely canyon; now and then he will see several individuals foraging at the edge of some desolate playa; but ordinarily he must take them in the brush or not at all, as they are brush-dwelling animals of almost inflexible habit.

I am by nature a fairly deliberate shot. On any animal accommodating enough to stay in sight for a few seconds, I am really a pretty fair hand. But javelinas are my undoing. When I hunt the little rascals I can, by much slinking and watching the wind, usually find them. Finding them and hitting them are, however, two entirely different propositions. Though I have killed several, I have missed literally dozens. I tell this without shame, for I am not alone. Fairly still-hunted without dogs, the javelina is about the toughest proposition for a rifleman in America.

The javelina is a creature of instant decision. Beside him even the fast-vanishing whitetail deer is a laggard. Many a buck has lost his life because he couldn't resist the temptation to take one last look, but not the javelina. The crack of a twig, the rattle of loose gravel, one whiff of the hated man-scent—and he is gone in the proverbial twinkling of an eye. His legs are short, but how he can move them! If his legs were as long as those of a deer, I'd bet on him to travel at the rate of two hundred miles an hour.

Hunting the javelina has a charm all its own. You stroll leisurely through the fantastic growths of sun-drenched lowland desert—saguaro, paloverde, pitahaya, cholla and prickly pear—watching for their round little tip-toe tracks, listening for sounds of a feeding herd. Often you'll see Gambel's quail and light-gray desert mule deer. Nearly always you'll hear the sweet lilt of a mocking bird, and see the scarlet flash of a cardinal and the swift scurry of cottontails or the lazy lope of an antelope jackrabbit. All of these and more are dwellers in the domain of the javelina. Up on the jagged barren peaks above you there are herds of desert bighorn sheep, but today the warm winter sun has made you feel lazy. It's a stroll through the valleys you want—a stroll which may bring a shot at a little pig. Whether you get one or not, you'll at least see some interesting country and you'll ease legs made weary by sheep hunting.

The pigs are game animals of a very high order. Not only is the fair taking of them an interesting and difficult feat, but the head of a big boar makes a unique trophy. Mounted with their mouths open and their long white teeth gleaming ferociously, their heads make novel additions to any sportsman's collection.

The javelina is well worth protecting, yet of all American game animals, he is the one which has got the rawest deal from civilized man. We have passed laws protecting antelope and deer. We have wept over the alarming decrease of bighorn sheep. We have cherished the remnants of our elk. But the javelina has fought his battle against extermination unaided, and he is now extinct over most of the territory where he was formerly found in the United States.

Hunting javelinas with dogs is, however, a quite different proposition from still-hunting. Like the mountain lion, the javelina though swift is short-winded; and a pack of dogs can usually bring a herd to bay in a few hundred yards. They back up against rock or cactus and stand there with their fierce little eyes gleaming, their hair erect, and their long, white, formidable teeth chattering like castanets. Javelinas at bay are the very epitome of truculent courage, energy and determination.

But killing them is child's play, and a couple of men with repeating rifles can exterminate a whole herd. After a few shots the herd will break and run, of course, but the dogs will bay them again and the slaughter continue.

Once in Sonora I hunted javelinas with a Mexican ranch-manager who pieced out his magnificent salary of 35 pesos (approximately $10) a month by using his spare time to collect hides. He had a pack of half-a-dozen gaunt curs, all scarred by the teeth of the fierce little pigs; and he himself limped on a leg from which a boar had taken a very sizable chunk of flesh. His only weapon was a rusty old .30–30 carbine with which he occasionally shot a deer or lion. He no more thought of using it on a javelina than I would of killing a wasp with a shotgun. Instead he used a very heavy ironwood club about four feet long.

We got six pigs in a morning. I nailed one boar through the shoulder with a full metal-cased .30–'06 bullet as it ran through the brush ahead of the dogs; but because my host was scandalized by my waste of good cartridges, I killed my next with a club. The technique is to wait until a dog has a pig fully engaged, then to slip in and whang away with all your might. My host took a mighty swing just as one pig bolted, and instead of hitting him on the head he landed a glancing blow on the rump. The pig whirled and charged him. He was lucky to escape without a wound, but one of his dogs was so badly crippled he had to be carried home on a horse. But did that disturb the *ranchero?* It did not. The remaining dogs cornered the pig against a granite outcrop about three hundred yards away, and while I gave him my moral support, he edged in and cracked his skull.

I must admit that banging my one javelina on the head gave me something of a thrill. It was hunting such as our caveman ancestors once did, and it was not without danger. Spearing the truculent little beasts on foot would also be exciting, and might become a highly developed pastime. I'd like to see someone have a spear made up and learn to use it.

Like their relatives, the domestic hogs, javelinas are eaters of wide and catholic taste; and like all desert animals, those found in the low country have learned to get along without water. On the desert they eat worms, insects, mesquite beans, snakes, lizards and even carrion; and in higher elevations they eat acorns, cedar berries, the tubers of cocoanut grass and piñon nuts. Like domestic hogs, they are crazy about charcoal, and they are often to be found in caves which were used by prehistoric Indians, rooting for the remains of fires that have been out a thousand years. They will never die off for lack of food, surely.

But unlike domestic swine, they have usually but one and rarely two young a year. They increase only by their ability to take care of themselves, and when they are hard hunted by man, the herds melt away.

Laws alone will not protect javelinas in the United States. Their only hope of escaping extinction is an aroused public opinion which will make the illegal killing of a javelina as serious a moral offense as the slaughter of a deer. Without it, casual slaughter by cowpunchers and deer- and quail-hunters coupled with the illegal traffic in Arizona-killed hides will eventually spell their doom.

The little battlers of the brush are practically gone in both Texas and New Mexico. In Arizona a safe seed-stock remains, and I for one hope it increases and multiplies. *El Javelin* is not much to look at, but he has a stout heart and desperate courage. My hope is that he remains an American citizen.

CHAPTER IX

THANKSGIVING GOBBLERS

THERE may be some argument among riflemen as to which game animal on the North American continent is the finest and the most difficult trophy to obtain, but I am sure few will take issue with me when I say that the wild turkey is the acme of the bird-hunter's dreams.

In size, in beauty and in wariness, the turkey has no equal among the feathered kind of America. A big gobbler will outweigh a Canada goose or even a whistling swan, and the subtle lushness of his bronzy reds, blues and greens, ever changing in the shifting sunlight, makes his relative the Chinese pheasant look like a gaudy exotic designed by someone with a lavish hand for color but little taste. In wariness the turkey stands in a class by himself. By comparison even the crafty deer is a trusting fellow and the goose is a believer in the kindness of humanity.

The often-quoted story of the Indian's explanation of the difference between deer and turkey hunting is one of the truest bits of experience ever to obtain wide circulation: "Deer see Indian," an old chief is supposed to have said. "He say, 'Maybe Indian, maybe not.' He stamp foot and look. Indian shoot him. Turkey see Indian. Turkey go away. Indian no shoot him."

Whether an Indian ever said that or not, I do not know. Out here in Arizona, at least, turkeys are taboo to Apaches, so it isn't a Southwestern story; but it is nevertheless true. The breaking of a twig, a suspicious movement, the rolling of a stone misplaced by a careless boot—all will send a flock of turkeys scurrying away. And once disturbed, the great birds are almost impossible to find again.

The turkey's acuteness of sight and hearing are almost incredible. Their ears are the most delicately tuned, I believe, of all American game, and their ability to detect moving objects is almost incredible. So extraordinary are these two senses that many old-time hunters swear turkeys can smell, too—something scientists declare no bird can do. Often it is difficult to explain the ease with which the great birds evade the stalker, unless one admits they *can* smell. I am willing, however, to credit their extra sight and hearing.

The turkey is, furthermore, with the exception of the ostrich, the swiftest of all ground-dwelling birds. It has never been my privilege to get authentic data on the speed of a turkey by clocking a running bird with the speedometer of an automobile, but from having seen many run, and from having missed many by shooting behind them, I should say they can do at least twenty-five miles an hour.

In addition to being swift, they are astoundingly silent. One big buck, thoroughly scared and earnestly desirous of getting away in a hurry, can make more racket than a troop of cavalry; but a whole flock of turkeys can run pell-mell through dry oak brush with no more noise than so many wind-blown leaves. Many times while hunting turkeys I have heard a warning cluck from a pestiferous old hen or a suspicious gobbler and then the flock has vanished as if by some evil magic. No patter of feet, no rustle of brush—nothing! Fresh scratchings will remain in the pine needles, perhaps feathers and fresh droppings. But no turkeys!

In the East, the Middle West and the South, wild turkeys have fared relatively poorly. In great areas they have been completely exterminated, and whole states, where they were once plentiful, now contain not a single bird.

In the Southwest, however, the grand old birds have survived much better. They are nowhere found in the great flocks the first white explorers of that section describe, but on the other hand they still occupy the greater part of their former range, and have become extinct only on a few isolated mountain ranges where the sort of country they could occupy is small and easily hunted.

In appearance the turkey of the Southwest is similar to the bird of the South and East, and he resembles him in habits. He is, however, a different species. The bird of the East wears the scientific label of *Meleagris gallopavo silvestris*, and the Westerner is called *Meleagris gallopavo merriami*. Both species probably enter the territory of what is now the United States from Mexico, but in historical times, at least, their ranges have never overlapped. The Eastern birds came west along the wooded river bottoms of the plains country, but records show that when the Americans first invaded the region the two species were still separated from each other by some two hundred miles of open foothills and treeless plains.

The principal difference between the two species is that the tail, tail coverts and feathers of the lower rump of the Western bird are a buffish white instead of the rich, dark chestnut found on the Easterners. Even so they are so much alike that I doubt if most hunters would notice any difference.

The range of the Western bird is much smaller than that of his Eastern relative, as he is found only in Arizona, New Mexico, Southern Colorado, Northern Sonora and Chihuahua, and a little strip of West Texas along the New Mexican border. He is almost exclusively a bird of the high mountains and plateaus, and he is never found very far away from the yellow pines and oaks of the transition zone. In late summer and early fall flocks have been known to go up into spruce and fir, and even to timberline. When snow begins to fly, many winter in the piñon and juniper forests where food is more plentiful and snow not so deep. Back in the 'sixties and 'seventies, some were recorded as spending the winters in desert canyons near high ranges, roosting in cottonwoods and sycamores and feeding out in greasewood flats. To most moderns that will sound like a tall tale, but it is no more incredible than the information that the low barren mountains near Phoenix, Arizona, used to be fine mountain-sheep country—and I happen to know that to be the truth.

Nowadays most birds live and die without ever getting out of sight of the pines or going below an elevation of approximately 6,000 feet. They get through the winter, even in time of deep snow, by moving around to the southern exposure of the mountains where the direct sun melts the drifts and makes pine seeds and acorns available.

Unlike their very distant relatives, the quail of the Southwest, turkeys need water and are never found far from it. They drink twice each day, morning and evening; and in late years tanks put in by sheep ranchers and cattlemen for the benefit of their flocks have extended the turkey's range in many parts of the plateau country of northern Arizona, where except for a few springs, practically the only natural water is found in very deep and inaccessible canyons.

Southwestern mule deer get along very well close to human habitation and even near large towns. When accustomed to human contact they become tame and even friendly. Not so the turkey. The adjective "wild" which is always applied to the bird of the Southwest is not given in vain. It is a creature of the wilderness, and if human beings become plentiful, away goes the turkey. I have never seen a "tame" wild turkey, and I don't suppose I ever will.

So the typical turkey country of the Southwest is something like this: It is pine country which contains many oaks—not a few, but many—since the birds depend on acorns when other kinds of food fail them. It is a country of living streams and springs which do not freeze in the winter, and it should have access either to lower and warmer country or to a south exposure, which amounts to the same thing. If you find country which answers to that description and still do not find the birds, you can be sure of one thing: man, hunting in season and out, by fair means or foul, has killed them off.

The hunting of the Southwestern turkey dates from the coming of the Anglo-Saxon American. Before that time the doughty Apaches overran practically the entire turkey area; and for some curious reason, these Indians considered both turkey and trout taboo and never ate them. In those days, domestic sheep and cattle had not destroyed the cover, and the ubiquitous coyote had not invaded the mountains behind bands of sheep, so the birds had few enemies and their numbers must have been incredible. My grandfather, who came to the west shortly after the Civil War, told me he had seen flocks of five hundred birds, and that flocks of more than a hundred were common.

But these halcyon days did not last long. Within a few years the pioneers succeeded in penning up the Apaches, and went about the serious business of cutting the timber, burning off the cover with carelessly started brush fires, introducing sheep and cattle, and turning the game into coin of the realm. Market-hunters shot the birds by the thousands, often raking a watering flock with a withering blast from an 8-gauge shotgun and getting almost every one. Before Thanksgiving and Christmas birds were brought out of the mountains by the wagonload, and it was a poor market indeed that did not have wild turkeys displayed at almost any time of the year.

Before many years the noble birds were on the verge of becoming extinct; but now they seem to be slowly coming back, as game laws are affording considerable protection and under the regime of the Forest Service the cover is increasing. In many places the birds are plentiful and afford excellent hunting, but with the exception of the wilds in the Sierra Madres of Mexico, where the deadly white man has never settled permanently, they are nowhere present in their former numbers.

Like all other game birds, turkeys are subject to great seasonal fluctuation in numbers. A mild winter followed by a good breeding season will make them plentiful everywhere. On the other hand, a couple of long hard winters followed by late snows and cold rains will cut their numbers in half. A year ago the turkeys of Arizona were at the bottom of a cycle. Now they are once more on the upgrade. The fall of 1931 found them plentiful everywhere, and almost every hunter who spent any time in the woods came home with his limit. But the winters of 1931–32 and 1932–33 were exceptionally severe. Snow lay six feet deep over most of the turkey country. Springs were late and cold. As a consequence, very few birds were seen and fewer killed during the hunting season of 1933. After the season was over and disgruntled hunters were loud in their wails that there were no turkeys left in the country, conservationists came forward with suggestions that the season be closed in 1934. It was necessary, they said, if the birds were to be saved. The turkeys themselves proved their friends wrong. The winter of 1933–34 was mild and the spring warm and dry. By early summer reports were coming in that the hatch was good. And it was. The fall of 1934 saw probably five turkeys in the woods for every one of the previous open season. Now everyone is happy, and the turkeys, weather permitting, will continue to increase.

The yearly schedule of turkeys is not greatly different from that of other gallinaceous birds. Early in the spring, while snow still lies deep over most of the range, the hens make their nests, usually seeking out the wildest and most inaccessible parts of the mountains. By the first of June the young flocks are following their mothers, often ten or twelve in a hatch. Now is the critical time. If snow or sleet falls or cold rains come, the young turkeys die by the dozens, as they are extremely delicate during the first few weeks of their lives. By the middle of July the young are about the size of white leghorns, and early in August they are approximately as large as full-grown chickens of the meat variety.

The summer menu of the wild turkey is extremely varied. It includes rose haws, strawberries, manzanita berries, and the fruit of the wild mulberry and prickly pear, as well as insects, of which the grasshopper seems to be the favorite.

By the time the aspens begin to turn in October, the young turkeys are about three-fourths grown and usually very fat. It has been my experience that the turkeys are then eating the last of the insects and are turning to the seeds of yellow pine and of various grasses.

During the winter they exist on acorns, piñon nuts and juniper berries, and if food is plentiful, cold does not bother them. I have never heard of a turkey dying of old age, or of cold either, for the predators get in their deadly work when the birds become weak from hunger and exposure.

If the young turkeys survive the winter, they breed the following spring, usually about the last of March or the first of April. The woods at that time ring with the gobbling of the males. Sometimes they forget their natural wariness and are completely blinded by love. Almost anyone with a good call can kill a gobbler then, and for that reason the open seasons in the Southwest are all in the fall.

But soon the gobblers desert their harems and go off peacefully with their erstwhile enemies. The hens hunt out secluded spots and construct their nests. With the new hatch, the cycle begins once more.

I don't know how long a turkey lives if he escapes his enemies, but a friend of mine who has spent his entire life in the mountains swears the same bunch of gobblers has been running near his ranch for twenty years. The old birds often grow to great size. I have killed one gobbler that weighed almost twenty-five pounds and a hen that weighed eighteen pounds. I have heard of birds that weighed around thirty-five pounds, but I have never seen one. Ordinarily a gobbler will weigh from sixteen to eighteen pounds and a hen from twelve to fourteen. All of these weights are live weights, of course.

That a turkey survives at all is a tribute to his wariness and to the keenness of his senses. His world is full of enemies. The mountain lion loves his venison and his colt meat, yet he is not averse to pouncing on a turkey dinner if one comes his way. Coyotes and bobcats continually prey on the flocks. Skunks and rodents seek the nests. Even the air is full of enemies. Mexican black eagles and horned owls are fond of turkeys and do not hesitate to attack full-grown birds. Cooper and sharp-shinned hawks kill the young. Even men, who would cherish and protect the birds during the closed season, are not averse to potting a savory dinner from passing automobiles. People who would not think of killing a deer out of season slaughter turkeys at every opportunity.

Turkeys can be hunted in many ways. They can be stalked in the same manner that deer are hunted, or they can be tracked in a light snow. These, in my opinion, are the fairest and most sporting ways to take the noble bird. In using them, you are giving old *gallopavo merriami* an even chance. You won't kill many turkeys, but you'll have a lot of fun.

On the other hand, if you want a comparatively sure thing, find a spring or tank where a flock waters, build a blind, or hide behind a log, and wait. If you keep still enough, you can nearly always get a turkey—and with a minimum of trouble. This last is a perfectly legitimate way of killing turkeys, and when I was younger I got many birds thereby. Now, however, I never try it. In the first place, I am constitutionally unable to sit still long. In the second, I dislike sure things. I can always buy a tame turkey in the market.

Ability to use a call skilfully is always a great advantage to the turkey hunter. Once a flock is jumped and scattered, it is not very difficult to call the birds up one by one and finish them off. Young birds especially seem to lose all their natural wariness in their desire to get back to Mother and the family, and come running to the seductive call.

Sometimes their conduct is such as to make the hunter suspicious of their intelligence. Once two companions and I scattered a flock and called up six birds and killed them—this in spite of the fact that all except the caller were in plain view all the time and shots had been echoing and re-echoing through the canyon for almost an hour.

Sometimes, especially at the beginning of the season when the woods are full of hunters, a skilful caller can bring up birds from flocks others have scattered. One time I went with a friend to Barney Pasture, near Williams, Arizona, in the afternoon of the first day of the season. We seated ourselves by a big log and my friend commenced to work his cedar-wood caller. Almost immediately a young gobbler answered from a ridge behind us and before long he jumped over the log, landing almost on the muzzle of my rifle. Within a half-hour two hens came across a park from the other direction, but at about sixty yards they took fright and started to run. My friend dropped his box and knocked one down with a shotgun. I finished it with a rifle.

Many hunters who dwell in the backwoods like to find roosts and then blast the birds off with shotguns as they are outlined against the starlit sky. This is a wasteful and unsporting method, as the birds don't have a chance and the survivors are often gobbled up by predators. Turkeys don't see well at night and always roost as soon as the sun goes down. Afoot in the dark they are nearly helpless.

Trained dogs are extremely useful to the turkey hunter. The ones I have seen are usually plain mutts with a strong mixture of terrier, but in their way they are highly efficient. They are helpful in locating turkeys, especially in thick timber; and they are highly valuable when it comes to breaking up the flocks so they can be called up individually and shot. They are worth their weight in gold when it comes to tracking down and catching wounded birds. If all hunters had dogs almost no wounded birds would escape.

As the ingenuity of man is almost endless, other ways of taking birds as toothsome as turkeys exist. They have been baited, trapped, and even coursed by specially trained wolfhounds. Out here in Arizona the cowboys have a way of riding into flocks of half-grown birds and knocking down "friers" with a doubled-up lariat.

But of all methods, that of tracking the flocks in light fresh-fallen snow is my favorite. The world is then created new and flawless in dazzling white, and the air has a frosty pine-laden freshness as if you were the first man ever to breathe it. The snow is a clean page in which the wild things have written their diaries. Here a mountain lion wandered. Here a couple of old and crafty bucks have crossed the valley headed for the cedars. Now you run across turkey tracks and see where the birds have flown down from a big dead pine on that point over there. You follow the tracks as swiftly and silently as you can, reading as you go their wanderings and their feedings, keeping always alert for the first glimpse of black bodies ahead against the white. You find where the flock has taken wing to evade the rush of a bobcat and note with pleasure that the predator had to seek his breakfast elsewhere. The turkeys cannot be far ahead. Every time you top a rise you expect to see the flock before you.

Then at last you do see the birds. The last of the flock is just crossing the ridge ahead there, headed for a southern exposure where they will sun themselves. You kneel in the snow, place the gold bead on the dark form of a big gobbler, and press the trigger. Before you can shoot again all the birds have vanished—all except the one you shot at. He lies jerking convulsively in the snow, and as you come up to him you regret a little that he is not as you first saw him—free and beautiful and majestically alive.

I have described an ideal turkey hunt—one in which the game is bagged. But successful or not, the hunter is always stimulated and refreshed by a day in the forest at its very best. If he sees turkeys at all, he is a good stalker. If he gets one, he is lucky as well. The chances of the game are what make it interesting.

Most hunters use shotguns on turkeys, but I prefer to use a rifle. In the first place, one nearly always sees deer when turkey hunting; and in the second place, I can be surer of killing the birds I hit. I never worry a great deal about wing shots because turkeys use their powers of flight more as an escape from predatory animals than from men. When the birds do fly, it is no great handicap to the rifleman. Their flight is straight and rather slow, and as they offer a large mark, they are really easier to hit in the air than when they are running. I once killed a big gobbler which flushed like a quail at my feet and sailed out over a mountain valley. Shooting it was surely easier than knocking over a running cottontail.

Many seasoned hunters use No. 2 shot and even BB's on turkeys, but most people report the best luck by using small shot and aiming at the heads. Then a shot or two almost anywhere in the head and neck will result in a bird either killed outright or stunned long enough so he can be retrieved.

The shotgun has its place in turkey hunting—no doubt of it. I have missed too many snap shots with a rifle at birds running through thick brush not to know it. If I had been carrying a shotgun on those occasions, I fancy I should have been successful. One of these days when I'm flush, I'll have an ideal turkey gun built. It will be an over-and-under—a combination of 16-gauge shotgun and a barrel for some medium-weight flat-shooting cartridge. If I'm extra flush I'll get a 'scope, too. Then I'll fare forth into the woods looking for what I may devour. I'll take turkeys running and standing, far and close. In the shotgun barrel I'll use No. 6 shot and in the rifle barrel a full metal-cased blunt-nosed bullet. Spitzers too often keyhole and expanding bullets tear up too much delicious meat.

Ever so often the wail goes up out here in the Southwest that the grand old game of turkey hunting is about over—that before many years the birds will be so rare that hunting them will be a waste of time. With this I cannot agree. Experience has shown that no matter how scarce the birds become, they always come back. It has shown, too, that with good weather and with a little protection from predators, both human and animal, the birds can hold their own.

The days of ruthless slaughter of game and of heedless exploitation of natural resources are over. I look for the birds to increase in the future rather than decrease. Chambers of commerce to the contrary, the population of the Southwest has about reached its high-water mark, and vast mountain areas of both Arizona and New Mexico will never be any more thickly populated than they are now. Turkeys are birds of the wilderness. The wilderness will be with us always, and so will the Merriam turkey—king of Southwestern game birds.

CHAPTER X

DESERT BOMBSHELLS

MY native state of Arizona was at one time blessed with four varieties of quail—the masked bob white, the Mexican blue (cottontop) quail, the Mearn's, or fool quail, and the Gambel's. The masked bob white is gone now—a victim of overgrazing—but the others are still present.

Of the four, I shall now sing of the Gambel. He is my first love. He is beautiful, intelligent, game and courageous. What is more, he is prolific and highly adaptable. No more worthy game bird exists in America and the hunting of him is an art and a science all of its own.

Imagine if you will a quail slightly smaller than the Northern bob white and built on cleaner, racier lines. Above he is blue gray to harmonize with the neutral-colored desert where he lives, and below he is a rich and lovely chestnut. The heads of the cocks are patterned boldly with a deep warm red, as well as black outlined in white, whereas the hens wear only their body gray for a bonnet. Both sexes have a long rakish topknot composed of from five to seven black feathers worn together with the effect of one. That is the Gambel quail—and long may he live and prosper!

Here in Arizona, Gambel quail are found from the deserts to the foothills and mesa country a mile above sea level, and they are far more numerous than any of the three other varieties. In fact they can manage to get along anywhere they find cover, and where the winter snow does not get too deep. Their favorite country, however, is the typical lower Sonoran zone of the Southwest, and outside of it they are never found in great numbers.

To many Easterners the deserts along our Mexican border seem harsh and horrible, but to me, a desert-rat born and raised, they are among the most beautiful portions of the globe. The term "desert" is really a misnomer, as this semi-arid land supports an astonishing variety of plants and animals. Tall gray mountain ranges rise steep from rolling plains cut with sandy arroyos and covered with ironwood, paloverde and mesquite trees. Barrel cactus and giant saguaro grow on flats and ridges and climb the sides of the mountains. A hundred varieties of cholla lurk everywhere to assault the unwary hunter—and, incidentally, to shield the game. Bighorn sheep range in the mountains, and mule deer in the flats and foothills. So do the lions who prey upon them. The lowlands themselves support quail, cottontails and jackrabbits, as well as little gray desert foxes, coyotes, badgers and bobcats. Antelope once ran here, and in some places they still do. Ground squirrels and packrats abound by millions.

So here is the typical breeding ground of the Gambel quail. It has been his country since time immemorial, and it will always remain his own. Some of it has been converted, like the Salt River Valley, to the uses of man. Fat green fields have displaced cactus and greasewood, and the quail have gone along with their cover; but most of it will always remain a wilderness without economic use except as pasture for a few range cattle. Great areas are completely inaccessible by automobile, and many a quail lives and dies without hearing the sound of a gun.

When the Americans came to the Southwest in the 'sixties and 'seventies, Gambel quail were present in great numbers all over the desert. Now they have been thinned out near the larger cities, and wherever the ubiquitous automobile can travel, but they are still plentiful in any section that affords feed and cover. In the early days the trapping and shooting of quail for the market was an important Arizona industry, and did the species great harm until it was finally stopped in the early years of this century. The late Judge Richard E. Sloan, in his book, *Memories of an Arizona Judge*, reports that from one desert station on the Southern Pacific, 35,000 dozen quail were shipped to market in one year. When you stop to remember that each dozen means a covey wiped out, you can at once get an idea of their numbers and of the relentlessness of the pioneer market-hunter, whose one idea seemed to be to exterminate every edible bird and animal. Even the pioneer sportsman was not free from blame. In an old newspaper dated in the early 'nineties, I recently came across an item about a quail hunt. It seems that a party of five had gone into the desert; "but quail were not plentiful, as they returned with only 522 birds."

Happily those days of Gargantuan slaughter are past. The game laws of Arizona now limit the daily bag to twelve birds, and it is my impression that, taken over a course of years, the quail have been slowly increasing over all the back country since about 1915. In good quail years when a dry hatching season is followed by rains that make water accessible and food plentiful, their numbers are astounding.

Throughout the Southwest there are very definite quail cycles, which are brought on, I am convinced, almost entirely by the weather. Predatory animals, hunting by man, hawk migrations—all play their parts, but they are minor ones.

Since I returned to Arizona in 1931, I have seen two excellent quail years. The first was 1932. The rains had been favorable, and quail fairly swarmed over the deserts. Even though I did nearly all of my hunting at the tail end of the long season, I found the coveys both large and plentiful. In one especially favored day I believe I saw nearly 10,000 quail. But 1933 was the first of a succession of poor quail years, and even at the first of the next season the birds were far less numerous than they had been at the end of the previous one. The reason? The little rain that fell came at the wrong time. There was not enough moisture to mature the seed-bearing plants on which the birds largely feed, not enough moisture to bring up the succulent green stuff to nourish baby quail.

The next year was even worse. By the fall of 1934 the entire Southwest was in the grip of a terrible drought. Except along permanent water few young birds were raised. The quail paired early, but the hens did not lay; and gradually coveys went back together. In addition, there was a great migration of Cooper and sharp-shinned hawks which thinned the ranks of the already decimated quail. That year the Arizona Game Commission cut the quail season from six weeks to two and reduced the bag limit from fifteen to twelve birds. The gesture may have done some good.

The middle of November in 1935 found the birds somewhat more numerous, and the season was again lengthened—to thirty days this time instead of the usual six weeks. Rains were spotty, and so was the distribution of quail. In spite of the fact that everyone could tell they were increasing, few birds were killed in 1936, as the entire month of November was windy and coveys lay silent and close. Then came 1937, which will go down in my mem-

[164]

ory as the supreme quail year of all quail years. Rains came at the right time, and vermin seemed to make no great inroads on the birds. As a result the quail seemed to increase tenfold. I hunted about ten days, and every time I took to the field in good quail country I saw birds literally by the thousands. I did most of my gunning on the lower Verde River, in an area which has been hunted hard by Phoenix sportsmen for forty years. One would think the quail had been thinned there, that the area would be shot out. Actually, from the numbers my wife and I saw, I should say that a thousand birds to the square mile was a conservative estimate.

Let's try to picture their numbers for those of you who have never been on the deserts of the Southwest in a good quail year. In driving ten miles through an Indian reservation, I was constantly in sight of quail—tens, hundreds, quail that added up into the thousands—quail walking, flushing, feeding, calling. Out of the reservation it was the same story. Quail everywhere—coveys of from twenty to forty or fifty birds. Quail so plentiful that if a covey called two hundred yards away, I would wait until I saw one fifty yards away rather than hunt the other up. We did most of our hunting near the river when the birds were coming to water, but to be seen in such astounding numbers they must be thick everywhere.

Does legitimate hunting by sportsmen make much difference when birds are so plentiful, when hunters are relatively few, and when there is a vast wilderness area suitable for quail? I don't think so. Arizona could extend the season to two or even three months if it wished, and no one would be able to tell any difference. Bad weather and vermin destroy more quail than all hunters combined.

I am convinced that for the most part—except for the days of market-hunting—the coming of civilized man has been beneficial to the birds, since civilized man is a great destroyer of vermin. The trapper of bobcats, gray foxes and ringtails; the man who shoots hawks—these save quail, and save them by the thousands.

If anyone disagrees with me, I invite him to hunt quail north and south of the Mexican boundary. The country on each side of the line is almost identical. The deserts of Arizona and Sonora both are ideal for the production of the merry Gambel's quail. Yet Arizona has its years of astonishing numbers. Sonora never does. I have hunted in areas in Sonora where men haven't killed a hundred birds since the world began. Yet, except for brush patches close to Mexican villages, I have never seen the birds thick. Many times I have spent weeks hunting deer in country that would seem ideal for the production of quail, and have seen but seven or eight coveys. The birds simply aren't there. Why? Vermin is the answer. The whole country fairly swarms with the predators that attack quail. Mexicans are poor trappers.

No more maligned bird exists in America than the Gambel quail. Easterners who have tarried but briefly among them and who have never really learned how they should be hunted, report that they are really not game birds at all. They say they will not lie for a dog, and that they will not fly but must be shot on the ground. It is true that they will not lie for a dog and that they like to run; but they will fly, and shooting them on the wing is one of the most difficult and exciting sports in America. Even Hornaday, in his book, *Campfires on Desert and Lava*, reports that they must be potted. He saw only the Mexican birds—not their sophisticated American cousins.

To the hunter of bob whites with his dogs and his leisurely walking through a tame and civilized countryside, the taking of the Gambel must seem a mad and bizarre performance. If it is done right it surely is no sport for the weakling. It is as strenuous as deer hunting, as thrilling as sheep stalking, and as exciting as following lion hounds on foot. Of course, like all good sports, it is largely what you make it. If your idea of a good time is to drive slowly along desert roads in an automobile, potting unsuspecting coveys from a car, you can hunt in that fashion. If you lie in wait by a desert water-hole, you can sometimes shoot into a huddled mass of birds as did the early market-hunters. Both methods are in vogue even today, but I do not practice them.

The best time to hunt the little dwellers on the Arizona desert is early in the morning just after the sun comes over the mountains. Then they have flown down from their roosts in the mesquites and paloverdes, and are feeding. Usually they are located by sound in the early morning and late afternoon, as they are among the noisiest of all quail. Except when they are hiding from hunters—wild or civilized—or when they are drowsing under some thorny bush during the middle of the day, they gossip continually. The sound of a covey undisturbed and feeding is liquidly metallic—curiously like the burbling of a small trout-stream running over stones. The hunter must approach as quietly as possible, keeping out of sight. Let us suppose that this covey has not as yet been shot at. Presently you will see them moving and scratching among the bushes. You approach to twenty-five or thirty yards. Now is the time for action. You can shoot into them, bagging a couple on the ground, or you can rush at them yelling like an Apache, shooting only after they have taken to the air. The covey rises with a roar like a squad of tiny airplanes. Now if you have shot, pick up your dead birds and follow as fast as your legs will carry you, marking well the place where they alight. Nearly always, if there is grass on the desert that year, the birds will scatter and hide, although sometimes they will continue to run. So just before you reach the spot where you saw the covey hit the ground, go slowly with your gun at ready. Then a bird will roar up under your feet. From that time on, if the birds are well scattered, the shooting will be fast and furious. Circle the spot where they disappeared, going wider each time, and you may get shots at a dozen or more singles. You must be your own pointer and retriever. You have no dog to warn you when a bird is about to flush, and as a consequence you will often jump a foot when a bird bursts out from under a clump of bunchgrass which you'd swear would not harbor a cricket, much less a game bird the size of a quail. If you get one quail to every two shells you are above the average as a hunter. Sometimes in such shooting I have killed five or six birds without a miss; but just as often, especially when I have been winded from a long hard run, I have scored that many clean misses.

These quail are hard to hit. They fly with great swiftness, and if there is any cover available they always take advantage of it. They are also hard to kill. For their size they can carry more shot than any other game bird I have ever seen, and often in heavily shot-over country I have killed birds with old wounds that would have laid a goose low. And even when they are down they are hard to find, though killed stone dead. Their colors merge perfectly with the desert ground, and if they have a spark of life in them they will run down a rabbit hole or drag themselves into the protection of a cactus or a packrat's nest. When you have a quail down, the only ethical thing to do is abandon everything else until you have found him. Otherwise you will lose at least half the birds you kill.

It is the instinct of every Southwestern animal and ground-dwelling game bird to take to the hills when molested. They seem to know they can get around better in rough country than man, so at the end of a season the hunter who wishes to find quail in great numbers must turn mountaineer. Hunting like this calls for great powers of physical endurance. Many times I have walked fifteen or twenty miles in a day's hunt, spending twelve hours without food and with very little water. In the mountains, quail can see the hunter for great distances, and often they flush at two or three hundred yards. Many times I have seen a dozen coveys without getting a shot, so wild have they been. But sooner or later the hunter can count on breaking up a bunch, and then the fun begins.

On the last day of the season in 1932 I hunted a rugged little range of hills north of Fort McDowell on the lower Verde. The quail were wild. They flushed out of range and did not scatter. At four in the afternoon I had only three birds, a pair of sore feet, and an epic thirst. Dog-tired and discouraged, I sat down under a palo-verde to curse my luck and to rest my weary bones. After I had lit a cigarette and taken a couple of puffs, I heard a large covey talking in the canyon below me. Instantly I came to life, my fatigue forgotten, and sneaked down the hill. Before I had gone twenty yards, a covey flushed below me, sailing across the canyon. I shot and got one. Another covey flushed and I pulled a double. As my second shot echoed through the canyon, bunch after bunch got up, all flying across the canyon and scattering along the opposite slope. What followed will always remain in my memory as one of the never-to-be-forgotten days in my hunting experience. I ran around to the head of the canyon and across to the other side. At once the shooting was good. It was as if the quail had said, "We have played with you all day, oldtimer. Now we'll give you a break." The birds lay close and quiet, flushing singly at from ten to twenty-five yards. In the next few minutes I got nine quail, and I don't think I used more than twelve shots. Five hundred birds must have been scattered along that canyon.

Luck always plays a great part in hunting Arizona quail, and that is one of the fascinating elements of the sport. Here I shall relate one of the most curious incidents of my career. One evening after returning with a few quail from a short stroll out on the desert, I saw a bunch of quail flying from water to roost for all the world like a flock of ducks. They must have traveled a mile, passing out of range to the right of me. No sooner had I got over my astonishment than another covey appeared thirty yards above the ground in exactly the same manner. This time they passed above me and I got two. Another covey appeared flying—and another. Without leaving my tracks I killed my limit. But that is a rare occurrence. I may hunt for a score of years without having it duplicated.

Lest I give a false impression of the Gambel's quail as a game bird, let me say that my lyric outbursts have been concerned with educated birds in country where there is some close ground cover. Mexican coveys that have never in their unsophisticated lives been shot at will run and run and run rather than take wing. So will birds in very isolated parts of the Southwest where the human predator simply is not on their list of enemies. On several occasions I have followed behind fleeing Mexican quail, picking them off one by one with a .22 without ever getting a flush. But even those birds seem to learn. Bedevil them enough, let them get used to the sound of a gun and learn that when one goes off one of their companions falls kicking—and even they will begin to flush.

Often, too, a good quail year will come when there is but little grass, so little that cattle will have trimmed what there is even around the bases of cactus and brush. Then the birds have no place to hide and of necessity must run—and run hard and long. Your confirmed wing-shot will curse long and bitterly then, as the flushes will be few and those at long range. Even the pot-shooter will moan, as the birds learn to a "T" the range of a shotgun and keep at a safe distance. But given a bit of cover to hide in, and a certain degree of sophistication, the desert birds will furnish field sport equal to anything a man can find in America.

Many years of contact with Gambel quail have convinced me that they are among the most intelligent of birds. At the risk of being shouted down, I am going to say they are smarter even than wild turkeys. Given ideal cover, some water, and plenty of food, they simply cannot be exterminated either by vermin or hunters. A case in point are the quail in a fenced mesquite thicket I know of on the upper Verde. The pasture, as it is called, covers about forty acres of level ground thick with greasewood, mesquite and cactus. Enclosing it are rough low hills cut with canyons filled with paloverdes where the birds roost. The pasture harbors at least twenty coveys of from ten to thirty quail apiece. A lot of quail for that amount of ground, you say? Yes, but try to get any! The natives have long since ceased hunting them. They have given it up as a bad job, and the only ones who waste their ammunition there are the visitors. The birds have been hunted for forty years. They are just as plentiful as ever and they grow wiser every year. To encounter them is a liberal education. I consider myself an up-and-coming quail hunter, yet the biggest bag I ever got there was seven.

When the first shot rings out in the pasture, the birds cease talking. If you find them, you do it with eyes alone. Three times out of four they flush behind you after you have walked past and they never fail to fly behind the nearest bush, keeping plenty of sturdy mesquite between themselves and the muzzle of a gun. Their knowledge of psychology is at once remarkable and disconcerting. If a quail is hiding nearby and you light a cigarette, he never fails to take off. If you say to a companion, "Well, they've got away from us!" and put your gun to the ground, you will be sure to hear the roar of wings and to feel a clumsy fool. They know all the tricks other quail know and a few besides. If a covey flies over a ridge, instead of lighting and running ahead in a straight line as well-mannered and respectable quail should do, these Verde quail turn sharply at right angles as soon as they are out of sight of the hunter and sneak swiftly away. Their favorite stunt is to walk quietly out of the path of the clumsy hunter, without talking, without flushing, without giving the slightest indication of their presence.

These little fellows have my greatest respect; if they'd only give me a break now and then, they'd have my love as well.

Every quail hunter should know something of the language of the birds. I have already mentioned their talk when they are feeding and undisturbed. They have other calls too. Their get-together call when they have been scattered sounds like a cross between the call of a mourning dove and that of a bob white. Sonora Mexicans declare they say, "Los Papagos! Los Papagos!" Two sharp *queet-queets* mean danger is present—to fly or run. Their talk when going to roost is a continuous babble—different from the feeding talk, but difficult to describe. Often when flushed singly, they will give a panic-stricken *chirp* as they take off.

The warning cry most often comes from the sentinel which the wary coveys nearly always post to watch for hunters and hawks. Usually the watchman is perched on the swaying tip of an ocatillo, as that gives a fine unrestricted view of the surrounding country; but if no ocatillos are present, boulders, paloverdes—almost anything—will do. When you see a lone quail perched against the skyline, rest assured that there is a covey nearby. But stay out of sight. Once you are seen, the birds will be off.

The quail's year starts in the late winter, when new-sprung weeds and grass nourished by December and January rains come up over the desert. Gradually coveys become larger and larger, until in April, when the pairing season begins, I have often seen them number into the hundreds, perhaps thousands. Quail from a square mile or more will gather into one huge pack. This is the courting time. The cocks fight, the hens look coyly on, and everyone has a good time generally. The ties which have bound the males and females together seem to dissolve now, and if any pair stays together more than a year I think it is an accident. These great gatherings seem to be a provision against inbreeding.

Within a few weeks, the birds have selected their mates, the big coveys break up into pairs, and the mating begins. The laying time is a noisy one in the desert. For a while the pairs go about, constant, devoted as two human newlyweds, always together. Then the hen builds her nest and begins to lay. The cock picks an ocatillo or a paloverde nearby and watches, singing his complicated song of pride and triumph. "I am a cock," he seems to say. "I have won a lovely little hen and I have her in an interesting condition. Oh, what a guy am I!"

The nesting hen and her eggs are beset by dangers. Pack and cotton rats will eat the eggs and kill the mother. So will snakes and Gila monsters. Even the clumsy coyote or the slow-going skunk is a potential menace. The big paw of a wildcat or the sharp teeth of a ringtail has ended the career of many a hen. In his study of the Gambel's quail, D. M. Gorsuch records the sad case of a hen who was attacked by ants and who ate so many of them in self-defense that she died. Even the great feet of unseeing cattle often step on and destroy nests.

But if one nest is destroyed the birds will usually try again. Some will tackle the job the third time, determined to reproduce themselves at all costs. I have seen tiny birds clear up to the last week in August, and many hunters have found half-grown quail in their bags in mid-November.

But the great bulk of the quail come into the world in late May, June, and early July. June is really the principal hatching month. The little quail are tiny, striped creatures not much larger than dimes, but they grow rapidly. The average bird is about half grown toward the last of July and as large as he'll ever be around the first of October.

It is commonly believed that the coveys which the hunters encounter early in the season are simply a cock, a hen and their young.

This I am inclined to doubt. I think the cocks have a tendency to go off by themselves and the hens likewise. I do know that more often than not, I will take only cocks from one covey and only young hens from another. The sexes come together again toward the end of the hunting season. They grow interested in each other and the cycle starts all over again.

Another interesting feature of the Gambel's quail is the apparent surplus of cocks over hens. Why this is, I do not know, yet every hunter I have talked to agrees with me that it is so. I find that I nearly always bring home more males than females, sometimes in a ratio of 2 to 1, seldom less than 3 to 2. So do other hunters. Yet when the mating season is over, there are always disconsolate males crying their hearts out on the desert, bitter and unhappy because they were not strong enough, bright enough or alluring enough to get mates. While other birds nest, begin to raise young, they stick to their ocatillos and lament.

And they are very jealous creatures, filled with the instinct of fatherhood but thwarted by the contrariness of the female. Nearly always they succeed in luring young away from other birds and it is no uncommon sight to see one proud bachelor leading a covey of young birds of all sizes, proud as if he had begotten them himself. And these bachelors make good parents, too. They show their young charges the feed and the water, teach them how to hide, warm and protect them from chilly summer rains. And when they are in a tough spot, they will eagerly feign broken wings to lead the danger away. No living thing has the instinct for fatherhood better developed than does the quail.

I have heard many express the belief that Gambel quail migrate.

To some casual observers that would seem the only explanation for their sudden shrinkage or expansion in numbers. With this theory, however, I do not agree. Experiments with banded quail in New Mexico show that although some birds may live almost a score of years they have never been shot more than a few miles from the places they were banded. Often when they are found adjacent to a steep mountain range they will go clear to pines in the summer and move down again with the first snow of winter. But the average bird lives and dies in a square mile of territory. When quail are scarce it means they have had a bad breeding season. When they are extraordinarily plentiful, it means weather and food have been right. Even at best, they have a tough row to hoe. Although they are keen-witted they are able to maintain themselves only by their astounding ability to multiply. An unseasonable rain will kill thousands of young, skunks and rodents are continually alert for their eggs, and hawks, coyotes, owls and bobcats prey on the adult birds.

So you of other sections can have your ringnecks, your bob whites and your grouse. I am content with my little friend the Gambel. May every pair raise a flock of forty instead of merely twenty!

CHAPTER XI

MESKIN BLUES

MANY times I have heard Gambel and California Valley quail denounced as runners by indignant Easterners. Whenever I do, I always know that these worthy hunters have never encountered the Mexican blue, or scaled quail, who is the real runner of the quail family in America. A hunter who has never matched wind and endurance with this powder-blue fellow has no idea how far a quail can carry the business of abandoning his wings and putting his trust in his legs.

Running is almost as habitual to the Mexican blue as it is to the ostrich. For his size he is probably the fleetest bird in existence, and the fact that he'd rather stay on the ground than take a chance in the natural element of all self-respecting birds upsets orthodox sportsmen.

Just as the Gambel is the typical quail of Arizona, the Mexican blue is the most widely distributed and hunted game bird of New Mexico. The state is its center of abundance in the United States and coveys are found practically everywhere within its borders, except in the highest mountains. The birds are also found in southeastern Arizona, in the Big Bend and the Panhandle of Texas, and clear down the central tablelands of Mexico to the neighborhood of the Valley of Mexico. A few birds are also found in southern Colorado along the New Mexico border, and I have heard that there are a few in southeastern Utah.

The Mexican blue probably comes in contact with more varieties of quail than any other American member of his family. In Texas to the east his range overlaps that of bob white. In parts of southern New Mexico and Arizona he is found in the same country with the Gambel and the masked bob white and all through his American range isolated colonies of the rare Mearn's quail appear. In Mexico he encounters dozens of species of quail, for which, though I have shot several varieties, I have no name, as I have never discovered a book on the birds of Mexico.

Hunters with a scientific turn of mind call the bird the "scaled quail," and I have heard him referred to as the "cottontop"; but in the country where he is most plentiful the natives call him the "Meskin blue." Two varieties of the bird are known, the regular scaled quail (*Callipepla squamata squamata*) and the chestnut-bellied scaled quail (*Callipepla squamata castanogastris*). What terrific names for birds so small! The chestnut-bellied variety is found only in the Rio Grande Valley of Texas.

Compared to the gaudy little Gambel, or even to the bob white, the Mexican blue is a fairly drab fellow. The feathers all over his body are an ash-blue edged with black, which gives him the appearance of wearing scales. His top-knot is gray-brown tipped with white, and cocks and hens do not differ materially in appearance.

But this natural coloring of the Mexican blue is his greatest asset, as it enables him to exist in relatively open country where the more gaudy Gambel and California quail would perish.

The blue quail has often been called a desert bird. Though he is often found on the deserts, his true range is the grassy country of the upper Sonoran zone, where a few scattered cedars, patches of chaparral, and a little catclaw furnish him cover when hard pressed.

He can stand far more cold than the Gambel and he can get along with less cover.

In size the bird is about the same as the bob white, and he is slightly larger and more chunkily built than the Gambel, furnishing about one-fourth more meat.

The sportsman used to the tactics of bob white will find the blue quail a bewildering and disappointing proposition. He won't lie for a dog, he seldom hides, and unless he is caught where the footing is bad he always "chooses to run." Personally, I'd much rather shoot Gambels, but on the occasions that I have found myself in blue-quail country I have hunted them and liked it.

When you go after these birds you must forget everything you know of conventional quail-shooting and make up your mind to do as the natives do. You will kill most of your birds on the ground—I can hear the bob-white hunters moaning—and you will run until your tongue is hanging out a foot and you swear you cannot go another step. By the end of the day you will have some game and you'll have had plenty of exercise—if little wing-shooting.

A few years ago I took a Missourian, a confirmed hunter of bob whites, out with me after blues. Before we got out of the car in a section where the birds were fairly plentiful I told him he'd have to shoot them largely as they ran. "Not me," he said emphatically. "I don't shoot birds on the ground." After an hour's hunting I had six birds, and all but one of them were ground-killed. My friend had none. Then we separated, going after different coveys, and presently, when I tarried on a little knoll for a smoke, I saw my friend shooting—but, alas!—not at flying birds. When we met at the car for lunch he showed me his bag of eight birds. "All shot on the wing?" I asked. "No, mostly on the ground," he admitted sheepishly, "and it isn't any too easy at that. I missed more birds than I hit. When I connect with one I don't get much satisfaction out of it, and when I miss one I feel like a damned fool!"

And hitting running blues indeed is not easy. Their powerful legs carry them at great speed and they are skilful dodgers. Then, too, straight-stocked bird guns too often throw their charges high. About the only way the hunter can make sure of getting them is to aim three or four inches below the bird.

Their instinct to run rather than to fly when in danger is truly astonishing. Many times I have followed behind a covey, killing straggler after straggler, without the birds' ever flushing. In fact, the more they are hunted, the more they keep to the ground and the more they run. About the only times the hunter can count on wing-shooting is at the first of the season when they are relatively unsophisticated, or when they are caught feeding in thick grass where they cannot run. Then they will often hide and flush one at a time like Gambels or bob whites. But here the hunter runs into another snag. The blues are the most difficult of all birds to find after they have been brought down. At the opening of the quail season in Texas one year my wife and I scattered a large covey of blues in high grass. The result was a hot corner which I'll never forget. Every time we took a step a quail bounced up and whirred off. When the smoke cleared away we estimated that we had grassed twenty birds. We found exactly one dozen! The protective coloring that enables the birds to live in relatively open country makes them almost impossible to see unless they are in motion. Many times I have had to hunt for ten minutes to find a dead bird lying in the open.

Compared to the Gambel, the Mexican blue is a dumb-bell. For one thing, he is a relatively unsuspicious bird. Even where he is much hunted he shows no overwhelming fear of man, and where he is little persecuted he is a set-up for the pot-shooter. The hunter first discovers the presence of blues, as a rule, by seeing them running before him, dodging in and out of grass and brush. Now a good fast trot will just about overtake a blue, and if the hunter moves fairly quietly he can nearly always be sure of a shot. Often the birds will flush when they are shot at, but they never fly more than a hundred yards or so. They usually land running and continue in a straight line from that point. When pursued by man they never seem to take cover. As a consequence the blues are easily hunted, and it is no very difficult task to exterminate a whole covey. In other words the blue quail can nearly always be counted on to do the expected. When they do do anything unexpected, it is usually on the stupid rather than on the smart side.

Once when hunting in Texas I came across a dozen blues in a covey. After I had chased them for a quarter of a mile hoping they'd take wing, they all flew up into a scrubby mesquite tree and perched there in a couple of rows, talking quietly to themselves as if to decide just what sort of a creature I was to be tagging around at their heels all day. I walked up within ten yards of the birds, held my gun at ready, and waited for them to fly. I looked them over and they looked me over. Finally they decided I was eccentric but harmless and flew down from the tree to feed at the command of the old hen. I hunted up another bunch.

Another time when I was hunting deer in northern Mexico the blues fairly swarmed around our camp, and I amused myself and

kept my party in breakfast meat by shooting their heads off with a
.22 at a distance of fifteen or twenty yards. Several times I'd get
three or four birds out of one covey before they'd take the hint and
fly or run off. The blues at that time were incredibly plentiful all
through the high semi-arid grasslands of northern Chihuahua. Curiously enough their numbers were due to the work of the Mexican bandit. When the revolution broke out the country was filled
with cattle that had eaten away the cover, but the bandits cleaned
out the longhorns and the quail increased. On our return from that
particular trip one of my companions, an old-time Texas cowman,
decided to get enough quail to supply his friends with a dozen or so
apiece, as the season in Texas had not yet opened. Shooting from the
car he bagged over two hundred of the birds in twenty miles! That
seems like slaughter, I'm free to admit; but at that time the whole
country was literally alive with quail. On a two-week outing we
must have seen a million.

Now and then, of course, the blues really furnish some good
shooting. They will flush occasionally, especially when the hunter is
able to get above them on a hill or on the side of some arroyo, as they
seem to be in terror of anything that comes from above. Now and
then, too, they will scatter and hide. When they do, it is a red-letter
day in the life of the hunter used to more sporting birds, and a painful mystery to those who have never shot them except on the ground.

In Texas once I was driving alone along a lonely ranch road
looking for quail, when I spied a bunch of about fifty birds bathing
in the dust of the road. Instead of stopping, I rushed at them in the
car honking the horn. In their surprise they flushed in all directions,
scattered and hid. I walked about kicking them out and within a

quarter of an hour I had the limit. All of them were shot on the wing—something which I shall claim as a world record for Mexican blues. This was the first and last time I have ever done anything like it, and I have never heard of anyone else running into a streak of luck like that. The explanation is probably that the birds were all young of the season and had not yet outgrown the habit of hiding—necessary to their existence in the early part of their lives.

The Mexican blues are very regular in their habits—a fact which works against them if the hunter is shrewd enough to take advantage of it. When hunting them I always carry a watch and write down in a pocket notebook exactly what time I run across a covey and where. Nine times out of ten I find the birds exactly where I found them before. They feed on the same schedule, water at the same time, and roost in the same place.

A few years ago I had the time-table of three very large coveys that ran a few miles from my home. Any time after work that I wanted to do so I could run out and find my birds. I never hunted more than a half-hour on any trip and I never killed more than six birds, as this number gave my wife and me two apiece for dinner and one apiece for breakfast. I was as sure of the meat as if I had bought it in a butcher-shop. I never took anyone with me and never shared my secret, and at the end of the season plenty of birds were left. That's not very sporting, I'll admit; but it is typical blue-quail hunting.

Vermin and men kill thousands of Mexican blues every year, but they are not their worst enemy. Curiously enough it is the domestic animals which are responsible for their decrease almost everywhere and their extinction in many localities. Nature intended the blues to find most of their cover in brush and weeds and tall grass—in other words the vegetation that is the food of sheep and cattle. The cover on their natural range, then, is not permanent, like the clumps of cactus and mesquite thickets where the Gambels range. After a dry year, when the cattle eat everything off, the adult blues fall easy prey to Cooper and sharp-shinned hawks and their nests are robbed by crows, coyotes and skunks. A succession of dry years means they are practically exterminated except in the areas where permanent cover exists.

A pasture in Texas is a case in point. When I first went there only a few cattle ran on it. Cover was good, and as a consequence it furnished the best blue-quail hunting in the Big Bend. After a couple of years, the owner sold his cattle and overstocked the pasture with sheep. At the opening of the next season I did not find a quail, or even a track. The only signs of the birds I did find were some powder-blue feathers and a few broken-up nests. Nearly all of the Big Bend country contained quail once, but now it is habitually over-grazed and the birds are fairly rare. The same can be said of large portions of Arizona and New Mexico, and about the only places one can be sure of good hunting year in and year out is where permanent cover exists.

It is the misfortune of the birds that most of their natural range in the United States is in that unhappy area called the Public Domain, where there is no regulation of grazing, and sheep and cattle pick off the vegetation like so many locusts.

The life cycle of the Mexican blue is much the same as that of the Gambel. The first young come in May or June in families of from twelve to twenty-four, and often, but not always, a pair of birds will nest twice in a season. If anything happens to the first nest, the birds will always try again. By September the birds are almost grown and shortly thereafter coveys begin to come together. Gambels gather in large packs, but the blues seem to have even a stronger gregarious instinct. By late winter and early spring they come together by the thousands. Several times in Texas I have seen packs that would occupy an acre or more of ground with three or four birds to the square foot. Once in Chihuahua in March or April I came across a pack that covered at least five acres, and made a moving murmuring blanket of gray-blue almost unbelievable in extent.

Unlike many hunters, I have considerable curiosity about the conduct of game out of season, and many times when prowling through springtime deserts I have seen the blue cocks engaged in bitter and no doubt painful battles over the heart and hand of some coy hen. Several times I have watched a dozen battles in progress at once. The love-maddened cocks go at it for all the world like miniature game-roosters, leaping and striking and making feathers fly. At such times the cock is something of a fool, just as anyone in love has lost most of his natural wariness and skepticism. I can remember taking a ringside seat at battles without the contestants showing any sign of fear. The Cooper and sharp-shinned hawks are also aware of the lack of caution of the birds, for they infest quail country at love-making time.

If the hunter must arm himself especially for blues, I think the best medicine is a light twenty, half-choke in the right barrel and full in the left. The full-choke barrel is right for distant ground shots and the more open barrel proper for the rare chances one gets on the wing. A regular bob-white gun is far too open, and most pieces designed for upland game have stocks that are far too straight for the ground shots one has to take if he pursues the Meskin blue. Above all the gun must be light, as shooting birds darting in and out of the brush requires a weapon that can be handled quickly, and carrying a heavy gun all day will wear the hunter out. The best gun for this purpose I ever owned was a high-grade Ithaca twenty that tipped the scales at only five-and-a-half pounds.

Many a time I have cursed the "Meskin blues." I have sworn they were no game birds and I have cheerfully consigned them to hell. But even so they serve their purpose. They are perfectly adapted to the upper Sonoran zone of the Southwest where neither the Gambel nor the bob white is able to survive, and they furnish quail hunting to thousands who would otherwise be without it. In the years to come I look for these hardy little runners to increase. Both the government and the individual ranchers seem to have learned their lesson that over-grazing does not pay, and even now there is a bill in Congress to regulate grazing on the public domain. The birds are hardy and almost incredibly prolific, and when the cover comes back they will increase—faster than most people expect.

CHAPTER XII

MYSTERY QUAIL

IN the mountains of the Southwest and northern Mexico, the Mearn's quail occupy about the same relative position as do the dusky grouse in the woods and mountains of the North. Hunters after large game occasionally pot a few, but almost nowhere are they regularly hunted.

They remain the mystery birds of the Southwest, and if the masked bob white, which are now probably extinct in the United States, is excepted, they are this country's rarest game birds. For years they remained to me, as to most sportsmen, only a part of a sentence on a hunting license: "On Mearn's, or fool quail, no open season."

Among all the varieties of Southwestern quail, the Mearn's is the only one which is not primarily a runner. He behaves exactly as eastern sportsmen fond of their dogs and their close-lying bob whites would have him. His flight is swift and noisy, he lies close and quiet, and he is the best eating by far of any of the birds in the section where he is found.

Yet, paradoxically enough, the Mearn's is practically unknown. Few hunters have ever seen one, and still fewer have ever brought one to bag. Naturalists have long since named them, of course, and most well-informed sportsmen know of their presence; but for the most part they pass their lives outside of the ken of man and live and die unmolested except by the natural enemies.

In spite of the fact that they are almost as fabulous as hoop-snakes or sidehill gougers, they are well supplied with names. The cowboys who run across them occasionally and the prospectors who pot a flock now and then with their rusty old single-barreled shotguns call them fool quail. The Mexicans call them *perdises* (pronounced pear-the-sis), as distinguished from the Gambel quail, which they call *cordonises* (cor-tho-nees-is); and sportsmen of a more or less scientific turn of mind call them Mearn's quail or Massena quail.

The Mearn's quail is about the same length from beak to tail as the bob white, but it is my distinct impression that it weighs a bit more. The adults of both sexes are so round as to be almost comical in appearance and when they walk they look like little animated balloons. The cock is one of the most beautiful of quail. He is streaked on the upper part of his body with feathers of black, red and yellow, and spotted below with pale brownish lavender. The back of the bird reminds me curiously of the colors in a peacock's tail. Both sexes have a hardly noticeable crest of dark feathers, and the heads of the cocks are curiously marked with brown and black circles which gives them a most clown-like appearance.

The hens are on the whole similar, but much more drab, and the lush coloring of the adult cocks is completely lacking in the immature, which are nondescript creatures of reddish brown barred with black.

These beautiful and interesting birds have remained a mystery simply because of their chosen habitat. In the United States they are found in numbers only in the highest and most rugged of the desert ranges which rise along the Mexican border in Arizona, New Mexico and the Big Bend of Texas. Like the Arizona whitetail deer they are a Mexican species which spills across the border, and between the deer and the birds there seems to be some strange affinity. Never have I found the quail where I didn't find the deer, and the northern limits of their range coincide exactly—in Texas, in Arizona and in New Mexico. The explanation of this remains for some future biologist to work out. I have never seen them below 5,000 feet and I have heard of their being encountered as high as 10,000. Undoubtedly they range to the top of the mountains in summer and descend when snow begins to fly.

They are most plentiful in the high steep Sierra Madres of western Chihuahua and eastern Sonora in Mexico. That is their type country and was probably the point of origin from which they spread across the border—long before there was a border, of course—into the mountains of the Southwest.

Their way of life seems to demand a country that is largely up and down, as it enables them to choose their food and their climate. When it gets hot, up they go into the cool thin air of the peaks. When snow falls, a short flight will take them into some warm canyon or barranca three or four thousand feet below, where snow is unknown. In high, flat country such as the great Mogollon Plateau of central and northern Arizona they have never been plentiful except along the rim, where they can get to the lowlands in a hurry.

Snow seems to be their Nemesis everywhere except in straight-up-and-down mountains. Many places on the Mogollon Plateau I have heard the same story: "Yes, there used to be lots of fool quail around here, but came a big snow in such-and-such a year and wiped 'em out. Haven't seen one since." Even along the rim a big snow, such as the one that fell over the mountains of the Southwest during

[189]

the winter of 1931–32, will exterminate the species unless the rim breaks off into real desert.

In the late spring of 1934 a few coveys were reported on the Mogollon Plateau, where I lived, but they are so rare that I did not see a bird in three years of prowling through the woods after deer and turkey.

If he escapes hawks and skunks and ring-tailed cats, the average Mearn's quail lives and dies without seeing a man with a shotgun. The few hunters he does run across are usually invading his haunts after the little Arizona whitetail deer and are armed with high-powered rifles, about the poorest weapons imaginable for quail shooting. As a consequence, the few hunters who run across a covey usually watch the birds for a few minutes, wish devoutly for a .22 and go about their business.

The fact that he is practically never hunted makes the Mearn's quail about the stupidest bird that lives when it comes to man. Human beings are simply not on his list of enemies, and when he encounters one he shows little fear. Southwestern hunters who are used to the quick take-off of suspicious Gambel or the running of the blue consider him the dumb-bell of the quail family. But this is no sign that the quail lacks intelligence. Fear of man is not instinctive; it is the fruit of bitter experience. In the wilds of Mexico I have got close enough to whitetail deer to hit them with rocks—and no one has ever accused the whitetail of lacking gray matter.

One fall down in the Big Bend of Texas I was hunting deer on a series of piñon-covered ridges in a small but steep range known as the Glass Mountains, when I heard a covey of Mearn's quail feeding near me. I looked around but I was not able to see them, but I was sure they were near, as I was familiar with their talk. Sitting down on the trunk of a fallen piñon, I waited. Presently they came into sight—a covey of at least twenty, all busily scratching for insects and gobbling the piñon nuts with which the ground was covered. In a few minutes the birds were all around me. Presently a hen—probably the mother of the brood—stopped feeding, approached within a couple of feet, and gave me a curious looking-over. She evidently decided I was a very queer specimen, for she gave a soft chirping noise. Instantly every bird stopped feeding and regarded me with bright friendly eyes. After a minute of this close solemn scrutiny, during which I began to feel self-conscious, the birds began to feed once more. A cock approached and started to eat piñon nuts by one of my boots, so I reached down and picked him up. I examined him carefully for a couple of minutes and then put him down. As soon as he felt he was free, he moved off with a couple of backward hops, looking at me belligerently and fluffing his feathers as if to say, "Don't get familiar, stranger, or you'll regret it!"

A few minutes later a big soaring hawk floated by a couple of hundred feet in the air. A hen spoke softly and the covey vanished as if the earth had swallowed it. Only by looking closely could I see them squatting on the ground as immobile as the stones they lay among. The hawk passed by and once again the birds began to move and feed. After a half-hour or so I got up, walked carefully away, and resumed my quest for deer.

Lest you get the idea that all the hunter needs to take Mearn's quail is a pair of hands, I must tell you now that occasion was the only one where I actually picked a bird up. Several times, however, I have got within three or four feet of feeding coveys.

No wonder the ranchers who encounter them occasionally while riding range call them "fool quail"!

But these buttery little fellows have the makings of fine game birds. All they need is education to offer sport second to none.

One December several years ago I was hunting little Arizona whitetail deer in the Chisos Mountains on the Mexican border in Texas. The Chisos is an astonishing range. It rises out of desert a few hundred feet above sea-level to about 9,000 feet. Desert mule deer run along its lower slopes and the whitetails keep to the chaparral and timber of the high peaks and ridges. There are bear and lions here, and javelinas in the desert canyons.

On the first two days of my hunt I saw no whitetail bucks, but I did see fool quail by the hundreds. The piñon crop had been good the previous fall. Sign showed that deer and bear had been eating the nuts some time before, and now the quail were gleaning. For two days I walked in and out of unsuspicious coveys, wishing for a shot-gun or even a .22 pistol. The third day I decided to turn my deer hunt into a quail hunt, so I climbed 4,000 feet straight up to a piñon-covered ridge with a light 20-gauge instead of my Springfield.

What followed was the most unusual quail-hunt in my experience. Imagine a gradually rising ridge not more than a hundred yards wide, timbered with a forest of piñon trees that looks like a gnarled and neglected orchard. Imagine prickly pear and yucca and dry bunchgrass growing among the piñons. On either side of the ridge are great canyons almost half a mile deep and beyond are timbered peaks.

I was literally on top of the world. Below me I could see thousands of square miles of desert and mountain in Texas and Chihuahua, all in the delicate pastel shades distance always gives an arid country.

Almost as soon as I topped out I encountered a covey. I watched the birds for a minute or two until I had regained my wind, then I picked up a handful of small stones and threw them in their midst, hoping to make them flush. They flushed! They made about twice as much noise as flying bob whites or Gambels, and in my surprise I touched off both barrels without getting so much as a feather. But I marked the covey down and trotted up the ridge behind them. When I had gone perhaps fifty yards a bird burst out at my feet with a roar such as might be made by a ruffed grouse. He had been hiding on open ground, but if he had not flown I would never have seen him. More from surprise than anything else, I folded him up. Twenty yards further on another bird got up with a like result.

From then on the shooting was all that could be desired. I broke up covey after covey as I gradually worked up the ridge. The birds were no easy marks, and as they flushed into quick noisy flight among the piñons I missed probably more often than I connected. For the most part, the flight of the birds I missed was short, not more than about a hundred yards. But now and then a covey would take off over some deep and dizzy canyon, flying as much as a quarter of a mile before they would dive into a patch of chaparral and disappear.

When I had six or eight birds and my mind was completely on quail hunting, I kicked a cock out from under the leaves of a yucca. He flew straight away across a patch of oak chaparral. I waited him out, then let him have it. Just as the fun went off a whitetail buck bounced out of the chaparral, and I rolled him over—the first, last and only deer I have ever killed with a shotgun. When I had the deer dressed and hung up, I finished getting the Texas limit of quail, which, if I remember correctly, is twelve.

The next morning we fried quail for breakfast and baked them in a Dutch oven for supper. Never have I tasted anything better. Their breasts were perfectly white and all of them were very fat. Even when fried they were much more moist and tender than blues or Gambels, and their flesh retained an indescribably delicate flavor of the food they love best—piñon nuts and the tubers of cocoanut grass.

During the past hunting season, I have twice encountered Mearn's quail. Once while hunting whitetails in the Chiricahuas, I stumbled onto a small covey which thundered up at my feet before I was aware of its presence, and sailed away across a deep canyon. Another time on Sierra Azul, a western extension of the Sierra Madres in northern Sonora, I ran into a large covey and shot a couple. When I quit hunting them, the birds had scattered and were lying close all around me. If I had had a dog and it had not been so late I could have killed ten or more.

Anyone with a good eye, a good ear and a stout pair of legs can do very well on blue quail or Gambels without the aid of a dog. Mearn's quail are, however, another proposition. They live where they can find cover and plenty of it. Very seldom are they found in the open and semi-arid country other Southwestern quail prefer. Unlike the bold and noisy Gambels, they are singularly quiet, shy and furtive. To find them, except by accident, a dog is necessary. I have never hunted them with a dog, but an acquaintance of mine, a retiring and philosophical American mining man who has dwelt on the Rio Yaqui in Sonora for a score of years, maintains a brace of pointers for that purpose and he tells me he envies no bob-white hunter who ever lived.

The sportsman who desires to add these rare birds to his bag will find by far the best shooting in Mexico. The birds there are plentiful and fairly easy of access. In the border states they are rare and found only in scattered localities. New Mexico has an open season on them, believing correctly that hunters play an extremely small part in their lives. The game department of Texas pays no attention to their existence, ranking both them and the blues with the bob whites as far as seasons go.

On the other hand, Arizona protects the birds at all seasons, hoping wistfully that some miracle will bring them back. But they are not increasing. Any bird or animal has a hard time getting by when it inhabits the extreme limits of the range of its species, and the farther away from the Mexican border you go, the scarcer the birds become. At the present time the birds are extinct in wide areas in central and northern Arizona where they were once fairly common. In knocking around over the Mogollon Plateau last summer I traced down every rumor of the birds' presence. I talked to woodcutters, forest rangers and cowboys. But I did not find a single bird, though I did see tracks and feathers of a small covey near Heyser Spring, south of Flagstaff.

The Western habit of grazing domestic sheep and cattle clear to the tops of mountains is largely responsible for the disappearance of the fool quail. Like bob whites, which they resemble in many of their habits, they roost on the ground, and when their cover is gone all the protection in the world will not save them from night-prowling coyotes, skunks and ring-tail cats. In the daytime the swift and ruthless Cooper and sharp-shinned hawks patrol the lonely peaks and ridges after them. Then, too, domestic animals are just as fond of piñon nuts as are the quail. In the winter when the insects are dead and the manzanita berries are gone, the birds seem to depend on the rich little nuts. If other foragers make away with the crop, they starve.

My hope is that some day before my joints get so rusty I can no longer climb mountains, these plump, fast-flying birds will be brought back in such numbers that the bold quail-hunter, not afraid of hard climbing and heartbreaking work for small rewards, can add them to his bag. Hunting them is a scatter-gun experience that can be compared only to the taking of ptarmigan, and eating them is an epicure's delight.

CHAPTER XIII

VISITOR FROM THE TROPICS

LIKE many of the other game birds and animals which make life for the sportsman worth living in Arizona, the white-wing dove is a Mexican. Hot tropical and semi-tropical Mexico is his homeland, and he crosses the American border regularly in only two places—southwestern Arizona and the lower Rio Grande Valley of Texas. The whitewing likes heat and plenty of it. Even southern New Mexico, though surely no summer resort, is too cool for him, as most of it is above 3,000 feet in elevation.

But on the two localities hot and low enough to suit his majesty, the whitewing confers a priceless boon—a summer shooting season. Because of this beautiful bird, gunners may go afield a full six weeks before their brother sportsmen in other states have anything to shoot at legally.

Each year the middle of July finds the birds through with their nesting season and most of the young already strong and powerful flyers. In Arizona all of them are fat on June-ripened wheat, sleek and lovely. The season continues to September first when the dove season formerly opened, but by that time most of the whitewings have left Arizona and have begun their long trek back to tropical Mexico where, like the rich, they winter hundreds of miles away from even a hint of snow and cold.

Hunting whitewings is hot work. The open season comes at the warmest period of the summer and the birds are found nowhere in Arizona except in the lowest and most blistering deserts. As a consequence, jugs full of ice water and even cases of chilled beer are almost as much standard equipment for the whitewing hunter as shells and guns. In those sections where the birds are hunted, the whitewing shoot is a custom of long standing. When stores and offices close, gunners go afield in the hot late afternoon with food and drink. They set themselves at some "tank" where the birds water or on some flyway used by the flocks on their way to water or to roost. It is a leisurely sport, for the birds come to the hunter rather than the hunter coming to the birds, and high swift flocks and singles enable the wildfowler to polish his technique against the more serious business of the fall and winter months.

Then as the sun goes down, the shooting ceases. Bags are counted, and while the evening breeze brings relief from the fierce heat of the desert day, the hunters eat, think up alibis, and brag about their good shots. Somewhere a quail calls, a mosquito drones, and bullbats swoop erratically against the darkening sky.

The whitewing is a close relative of the mourning dove and in appearance he is much like him. Perched, the birds look much the same. Both are long, narrow, streamlined, "dove-gray" birds with the slender heads and necks of most of the dove family. In flight, however, they are so different that a practiced observer can distinguish between them at great distances. The white, which only edges the folded wing when the bird is at rest, now appears as a conspicuous lateral band, and it is apparent that the lower wing feathers are a much darker gray than is the case with the dove. In fact this white band is the most noticeable thing about the bird, and in contrast to it he looks darker all over.

In addition the whitewing is ordinarily a slower and more leisurely flyer than the dove and his wings have always appeared to me to be set at a slightly different angle. Why this should be I do not know, for I have examined dead birds of both species side by side. Yet it is so, and I can tell them apart when they are no more than specks in the sky.

The two species are about the same length, but the whitewing is a somewhat chunkier bird. He is also better eating, as his breast is lighter and lacks the wild somewhat "ducky" taste of the dove. A whitewing pot-pie with onions, green peppers, pimentos and dumplings, is truly food for the gods.

In Arizona the whitewing is almost never called a "whitewing dove." Instead he is nearly always referred to simply as a whitewing —or sometimes as a whitewing pigeon. In Mexico the natives call the birds *palomas de pitahaya* (cactus doves) or *pitahayeras* (literally "cactusers") because they are so inordinately fond of the ripe fruit of the pitahaya or organ cactus. Indeed, there must be some vital connection between the pitahaya and the whitewing. In the spring and summer the birds are plentiful on the Sonoran deserts wherever the cactus is found—and they are plentiful nowhere else. When a crop is on they seem to eat almost nothing but the luscious red fruit, and at that time their droppings are as red as blood. They do not assimilate the tiny hard pitahaya seeds, and as a consequence they must have played a large part in extending the range of the cactus.

The whitewing is also fond of wheat and other grains. Twenty or twenty-five years ago birds swarmed to the wheatfields of the Salt River Valley of Arizona, where I grew up, to feed in the fields. Hunting them at that time was the principal summer sport and the one thing which made the long hot days bearable and even pleasant.

Natives turned out by the hundreds, and through the summer after-noons the popping of guns could always be heard. In addition, wealthy sportsmen from the Pacific Coast and even from the East arrived, established luxurious camps, and shot daily for weeks. Bags of seventy-five and even one hundred birds to each gun were common. The first money I ever earned came from acting as a retriever for a portly Los Angeles banker. My maternal grandfather was a confirmed whitewing-hunter and a crack shot. I followed him afield almost from the time I could toddle, and I killed my first bird in 1908 when I was so small I had to rest the gun on a fence post and the recoil gave me a nose-bleed.

Thousands of birds were shipped to the markets in Los Angeles and San Francisco before the passage of the Migratory Bird Act, and other thousands were fried or made into pot-pies by honest Arizon-ians. Strangely enough, however, I don't think this Gargantuan slaughter did the species any great harm. The grain fields of the valley drew birds from all over Mexico and Central America, but the millions which were killed were but a drop in the bucket to the untold millions which never heard a shotgun fired. Only the ex-treme northern vanguard was ever really hunted and shot, and the birds are scarce in most parts of Arizona now not because they were overshot but because in the early war years farmers found the rais-ing of long-staple cotton more profitable than the raising of grains. The birds found little to eat and hence most of them now stay away. Even now they find what grainfields are left. On the Indian reser-vations, where much wheat is still raised, they are plentiful. In recent years I have heard some Arizonians wail that the birds are nearing extinction and should be protected in the United States. No one who has been in Mexico as much as I have can agree with that opinion. Last June I shot whitewings near Sonoyta, Sonora, where the birds came to the wheatfields in clouds which would have reminded an oldtimer of the fabled abundance of the passenger pigeons. On a recent sheep hunt into Sonora I was in continual sight of the birds for three hundred miles south. They were so plentiful that I should hesitate to hazard a guess at how many I saw. Whenever Arizona farmers see fit once more to plant wheat, the flocks will be back in their former numbers as soon as the good news spreads among them.

The call of the whitewing is very different from that of a dove. I have heard it compared to that of an owl, but in reality there is little similarity. It sounds much like the note of the big bandtailed pigeon of the mountains in that it is deep and melodious, but it is unmistakable, and once heard it is never forgotten. Not only is it lower pitched than that of the dove but it is also more complicated. When the birds are mating it runs almost the entire scale, and is a thing of beauty. Once in early May I was scouting for sheep in the San Francisco Mountains of Sonora. It was late afternoon. The hot air of midday had cooled considerably, and the desert was swimming in the purple haze of evening as the sun sank behind the jagged Pinacate range to the west. A flock of rams had left a high mountain that day, and by circling I hoped to cut their tracks in the soft sand and find where they had gone. On the whole walk of three or four miles a whitewing was my herald and my guide. He flew just ahead of me, alighting on saguaro and pitahaya, and every time he paused he would give his mating call, low, sweet, melodious, clear as a bell. It is at once a call and a song and a thing of moving beauty. I shouldn't blame any female for losing her head when wooed like that.

The mating season for the whitewing begins far south in Mexico and probably as early as February. The pairs work north, nesting as they go, and they raise from three to five broods a season, ending with the June nest in northern Sonora or southern Arizona. The young mature quickly and birds born in February probably mate by June when they have followed their parents on the long flight north. Like the mourning doves, the whitewings lay but two eggs at a time and also like the doves, they build a sloppy, poorly constructed nest in low trees, in cactus, and even on the ground, as egg-heavy females of both species aren't particular when their time comes. Each pair of whitewings is responsible for from six to twelve young birds in a season. On a few occasions I have seen young in nests at the opening of the season in Arizona, but the great majority of birds are through with their mating for the year. Their long trek north has reached its high-water mark, and within a few weeks the birds begin to wing their way back to the tropics. By the first of November, when the last crop of pitahaya fruit has matured and been eaten, the birds desert salubrious northern Sonora, and their place is taken by great flocks of mourning doves, which have spent the summer in the United States. The flocks winter from the Yaqui River country of southern Sonora throughout Sinaloa and even to Panama. By the first of February, Mexicans tell me, the mating season is in full swing and they are preparing to follow the sun north, where wheat is growing for their delight and ripening pitahayas await them.

Most Arizona gunners agree that the mourning dove is a swifter flyer than the whitewing, but there are those who differ. There is no doubt, however, but that the dove appears to be faster. In appearance the *paloma* is the very epitome of speed. My own notion is that the top speed of both birds is about the same, although the whitewing usually flies somewhat more slowly and with a slower wing beat. As becomes a dweller in the tropics he is lazier and he is inclined to coast along on set wings—something the dove never does. Once when I was hunting sheep in the Cubabais in northern Sonora I disturbed a whitewing roosting in a dwarfed *sangrengrado* tree at the head of an incredibly steep canyon. The bird fairly fell out of the tree and plummeted thirty or forty yards straight down. It set its wings and volplaned with gathering speed along the course of the canyon until it reached the bottom; then it darted swiftly upward, for all the world like a ski-jumper, and came to rest on top of a saguaro. All this time it had not moved its wings. No dove that ever lived could duplicate that performance.

When a whitewing is shaken loose from his tropic calm and really makes up his mind to go places, he is as fast as any dove, and when he has been much shot at, he can dive and dodge and twist as skilfully as his northern cousin. Like the dove, too, he's a daredevil and prefers running a barrage to going around it. Birds shot from a blind when they are full of wheat and going back to roost require little lead, but veterans who are used to being shelled daily when they come to some tank for the water they must have, fly as though the devil were after them. The sight of a man or the gleam of a gun barrel will make them twist and dodge until hitting them requires both skill and inspiration. Many a time I have had flocks pass so close to me and so fast that I could hear them cut the air like 75 mm. shells.

[203]

The birds which never leave Mexico and are almost never shot at are as unsophisticated as so many grouse of the tall timber, and great sport may be had by picking them off the tops of saguaros and pitahayas with a .22 rifle. On big-game hunts in the spring and early fall I have varied the diet of my party by this means. Mexicans never try wing shooting on any birds and think any one who does is a fit subject for an asylum. A Mexican *ranchero* I once met boasted proudly of having killed fifty-two whitewings with one shot when they were clustered thick around a water hole, and told me I was *muy loco* because I wasted time and shells by shooting at *las pitahay-eras* before they lit. "All Americans are both rich and crazy," he told me after watching me use up a box of shells to get a measly dozen birds. That same box would have supplied him with white-wings for months, and to buy them he would have had to hire him-self out for a week. No wonder he thought I was demented.

To be perfectly armed for whitewings, the gunner needs two guns. When he shoots from a blind at a water hole, with the birds coming in fast and close, a light open-bored 16 or 20-gauge is ex-actly right. On the other hand, for flight shooting he should have close-shooting 12-gauge. Like pass shooting at ducks this type of work is truly the billiards of shotgun work, and it requires the best of weapons and accurate and delicate holding. Few satisfactions of life are equal to the pleasure derived from knocking down some swift-flying bird high in the sky and fifty yards away. With a full-choked gun and an ounce and a quarter of shot, kills can be made regularly at fifty-five or sixty yards, and I believe that if a gunner had the strength and patience to carry one of the new super 10's he could get birds at up to seventy or seventy-five yards. At any rate,

I'd like to try it. Whitewings are not difficult birds to kill. A couple of shot almost anywhere in their bodies will bring them down, and the heights at which they fly coupled with their speed makes their fall severe. Many times they are stunned when they hit the ground and often they are killed by the impact. Many times I have seen the craws of fresh-fed birds burst wide open.

If you wish, you can walk up to birds feeding in wheat stubble, or you can flush them out of trees and shoot as their whistling wings carry them swiftly away. Few hunters here try it, however. At the time of day the birds are feeding or perched it is simply too darned hot. The thing to do is to sit down with a canteen by your side and let the birds come to you.

Many localities in Arizona still furnish good whitewing shooting, but the sportsman who wants to add this exotic species to his bag ought to try them in northern Sonora in June. The birds are present then in incredible numbers, the full blast of the summer's heat has not yet been turned on, and shooting is altogether a pleasant experience. The wheatfields near the little town of Sonoyta are alive with the birds, and late in the evening flocks swarm to water holes on the Sonoyta River and to tanks in the neighboring desert. And in Sonoyta, too, there is a hunting lodge conducted by an American, where one can stay pleasantly and cheaply.

CHAPTER XIV

SPEEDSTER OF THE UPPER AIR

THOSE hunters who live in the North with its frosty autumns and cold winters miss one of the finest of all scatter-gun sports—shooting at the mourning dove.

I say "shooting at" purposely, for attempting to hit a mourning dove in full flight is about the most exacting and difficult feat possible. The dove is one of the swiftest and most agile birds that flies. He is built for speed. His head is small, his body long and narrow. Even his tail is streamlined. His long, narrow, powerful wings not only drive him at great speeds, but they can send him into astonishing and lightning-like gyrations when he sights danger in the form of a hunter or a hawk.

I have no idea how fast a dove can fly when it has a wind behind it and is overcome by the desire to go places. I only know that I have clocked the birds at forty-five and fifty miles an hour with the speedometer of an automobile. I know, too, that when doves are really opening up I must lead them approximately as much as I lead teal.

It has been my experience that doves are, for most hunters, the hardest of all birds to hit consistently. (I have never shot woodcock or ruffed grouse, so perhaps I'm taking in too much territory.) I do know, however, that I can bring home about twice as many ducks for each box of shells as I can doves. Quail are another and much different proposition.

Doves are confusing, for one thing, because of their change of pace. They can float gently along at twenty miles an hour, or they can split the air at fifty. They can fly as straight as a duck or they can dip, twist, swerve and dive as though the devil himself possessed them. No two doves will fly at exactly the same speed or act alike when they see the hunter.

I have been shooting doves for twenty years, and I consider myself a fair shot; but often when the birds are wild and wary and coming in with the wind, I miss at least three for every one I knock down. Under difficult circumstances I have seen men who passed for fair-to-middling duck shots use a whole box of cartridges and get but one or two doves.

Many times I have been taken to task by kind old ladies for shooting doves. "What?" they say. "Shoot those pretty, innocent little creatures which perch so demurely in the peach tree or on the back fence and mourn so gently? You're a wicked fellow, and you ought to be in jail!"

Yet the dove is a game bird and a fine one. He is good to eat and hard to hit, and in his own country he is prolific enough to hold his own against natural enemies and man. If that isn't the definition of a game bird, I don't know what is!

The Southwestern mourning doves are by far the most numerous of the dove and pigeon family. Their range overlaps that of the big bandtailed pigeons, which are found only in the cool timbered mountains, and that of the whitewings, which are solely creatures of the deserts. I should hesitate to venture an estimate of the number of doves in Arizona in the summer, but there must be millions. Every square mile, from deserts not far above sea level to mountains and plateaus 7,000 and sometimes 8,000 feet high, contains its quota of doves, from a dozen or so up to hundreds. The only sections where doves are completely absent are the tops of the highest mountains, where even in summer the thermometer often drops near freezing and snows are not uncommon. The birds often nest in backyard trees in towns as large as Tucson and Phoenix, flying to suburban fields for food and watering from irrigated front lawns.

Their centers of abundance in the Southwest are the big irrigated valleys such as the Rio Grande, the Gila and the Salt. Here they find weed-seeds and waste grains for food, and water to drink in the ditches. Their numbers are simply incredible, and often a hunter will see thousands in a single afternoon.

But the birds are everywhere. I have seen them in every section of the Southwest, and in most places they are by far the commonest summer bird. Indeed, the low mournful cooing of the dove is the voice of the warm sunny Southwestern summer. It is music soft and tender, gentle and sad; and its low pulsing rhythm becomes a part of the life of everyone who lives long in the Southwest.

By May the birds are nesting in the lower elevations and by the middle of June the season is in full swing all over the Southwest. The nest, like that of all doves and pigeons, is a frail, shabbily built platform of twigs and straw, in trees, in bushes, and even on the ground. One of the largest aggregations of nesting doves I have ever seen was along the lava bank of the canyon of the Little Colorado in the treeless Navajo country of northern Arizona. The nests were all built in depressions in the lava and all contained young and eggs.

The birds lay two eggs at a time, but the young mature quickly; and the old pairs bring off three and sometimes even four broods in a season. Even during the first week in September, when the season opens here, I have shot an occasional female with eggs almost ready to be laid. The first young of the season nearly always mate before the summer is over, so the theoretical productivity of one pair of doves is large, in spite of the small number of eggs laid at a time.

If there ever was a fair-weather bird, it is the dove. Cloudy days depress the flocks and their flights are noticeably smaller. When it rains they mope in trees or under bushes, miserably trying to keep dry, and going hungry rather than venturing out. They flee from frosts and cold weather as from the devil himself. Almost every year the first frost comes on Arizona's Mogollon Plateau shortly after September first, and with it the good shooting is over. The only ones to remain are the few pairs which still have young in the nest and the fledgling birds which do not have the strength to make the migration. Some birds remain throughout the winter in the lowland deserts, but the majority leave for Mexico with the first chilly days of late October or early November. By Christmas not more than one in twenty is still using its old roost.

Doves can be shot in many ways. The duck hunter is at home picking them off from a blind built in the path of a flight. A habitual quail hunter can almost duplicate his sport by jump-shooting birds feeding in a weed patch or stubble field. As a youngster I sniped many a bird out of treetops with a .22. Some game hogs slaughter them with shotguns as they perch on telephone wires or in trees, but no sportsman should consider such a thing. If he does, he is not a sportsman.

In desert areas the birds are most commonly shot as they come to water at some isolated "tank" or water hole in the evening. Because of the dry nature of their food the birds must have water, and they will fly from ten to twenty miles for it. If the sportsman can locate a favored hole, he will have sport galore. As the shadows lengthen and the pastel shades of evening gather, hundreds of birds sweep in, some singly and some in flocks. When the time is right the shooting is fast and furious. During the three years I lived at Flagstaff, Arizona, I had a favorite tank on the edge of the yellow pines where the birds used to gather from miles around. From where I stood to shoot I could see mile upon mile of rolling cedar and piñon forest and beyond that the deep rose and smoky blue of the Painted Desert. I remember the keen cool air of the pines, the pleasant acrid smell of burning nitro, the doves swift and black against the kindling sky. It is such things a sportsman likes to recall rather than the actual killing itself.

Water-hole shooting, though surely not easy, is a long way from being the most difficult way of taking doves. As the birds fly in, they usually circle the tank and check their flight just before they pitch down to water. One who is skilled at judging their flight can usually get them then with almost no lead. He must shoot, however, at exactly the right instant.

The most sporting of all is flight shooting. Doves seem to have aerial highways, from roost to feed, from feed to water, and from water to roost. If you post yourself on one where doves are plentiful and if you are present at the right time, you can have sport beyond your wildest dreams.

Two or three miles from Tempe, Arizona, there is an eighty-acre field which because of the rising water-level was abandoned forty years ago. It is now grown up to sage and a forest of mesquite trees twenty and thirty feet high. In late summer and early fall doves by the thousand roost in the thorny sanctuary of the trees, flying away to feed and water and returning to roost during the hot hours of midday and during the night.

I have shot there ever since I was a barefoot youngster in knickerbockers and as far as I can tell the birds are as plentiful as ever. Nearly always—if my ammunition holds out—I can get the limit of fifteen without leaving my tracks.

Several years ago a power transmission line approximately seventy-five feet high was built along the south end of the field. As the birds come in, they always rise to fly over it, then dip swiftly toward the trees. Sometimes twenty or thirty birds are in range at one time. Taking up a stand behind a shoulder-high mesquite, I can get almost every variety of shot possible. Some come over flying high and straight as ducks, others streak in losing altitude and flash over my head like racing airplanes. Now and then I whirl and shoot at one flying straight away from me. Often their gyrations are so difficult to follow that I don't even shoot, but stand cursing and impotent watching them pitch down to roost in the distance.

Sometimes when I'm right—and also very careful about picking my shots—I can make very pretty runs on doves. I remember one such occasion. I went out rather late one morning to the field and the birds were coming in high and slow, full-fed and lazy. What's more it was the beginning of the season, and many of them were birds of the year which had never been shot at. I killed eight in ten shots—and all of them were at least forty-five yards away. By that time it was looking too easy, so I knocked off and went home, resolving to return late in the afternoon for the other seven I was allowed that day.

I did, but in the afternoon I was off—and badly off. I missed five straight birds and used twenty-five shells in getting seven.

The toughest and at the same time the most thrilling dove shoot I have ever been on came this last winter far into the interior of Mexico, where I had gone to hunt sheep, javelinas and deer. We had been driving all day, and about sundown, when we were anxious to burn some powder, we ran across an aerial highway used by thousands of doves. The birds were flying with a twenty-mile wind behind them.

We got out, formed a skirmish line, and went into action. Now, it has never been my privilege to observe bats emerging from hell, but if they come faster than those doves they are indeed traveling. It was a matter of "here they come—there they go." What is more, the birds were all veterans that had been shelled the length and breadth of Arizona before they went south for the winter. How they did dive and dip and spin when they saw us! Some flashed by two hundred feet in the air. Others came in so low over our heads we could hear them whiz. All dived and side-slipped the moment they saw us. Sometimes whole platoons of birds drove in so fast and trickily that we didn't even shoot, but instead stood waving our guns futilely in the air. For thirty minutes it must have sounded as though a new revolution had come to plague Sonora, yet when the smoke of battle cleared we had less than thirty birds.

Doves are small when the feathers are off, but they are fine eating if they are prepared properly. The unimaginative fry them long and earnestly, and in doing so they ruin them. A thoroughly fried dove has all the flavor and succulence of an Egyptian mummy. A bird dusted lightly with flour and fried on a very hot fire only long enough to brown the flour is good eating, though still somewhat dry.

Doves are best of all when they are made into a stew with dumplings, peas, carrots and onions, or when they are fried first, then put into a pie and cooked in their own gravy. So prepared they are food for the gods.

The best dove dish I have ever eaten, however, came purely by accident—an invention by my resourceful wife.

On the opening day of dove season several years ago, we were en route from St. Johns, Arizona, to the pueblo of Zuni in New Mexico to see a rain dance. Late in the afternoon we found a weed patch in the cedars where several hundred doves were feeding. My wife got out the only shotgun we had with us, and while I acted as retriever, she walked up to the feeding birds and shot them as they angled swiftly away on whistling wings. When we had eight, we called it a day and drove on to Zuni, and there I picked and cleaned the birds by firelight on the little mesa where we camped above the village.

The next day while we were waiting for the dance to start, my wife made the doves into the most voluptuous stew I have ever eaten. Here is how she did it: First she fried several pieces of bacon, then she floured the birds and fried them lightly in the grease. Next she put flour into the grease that was left and browned it, then she put in a can of tomatoes, sliced onions, salt and pepper and let the mixture simmer with the doves in it for about a half hour. When the doves were getting tender, she put in broken-up spaghetti, the crumbled bacon and grated cheese. My mouth waters as I write.

The dove is a curious bird. Whether he is a fool or a daredevil I do not know, but I am inclined to classify him as the latter. If a flock of ducks sees a line of gunners in its path they will fly higher or aside. Sometimes they even turn back. But not the doves. Knowing that a leaden hail awaits them, they prefer to trust to their great speed and their ability to dodge. Often they will slant aside a bit, but never will they turn back. As gallantly as the Light Brigade itself they open up to the last notch and drive ahead—and in the majority of instances they will run the barrage.

Yet no warier bird lives than a perching or feeding dove that has been shot at. Nearly always he will flush at extreme range and make off on whistling wings while your charge patters futilely around him. Still the same bird will nest in your back yard and coo contentedly just outside your window during long hot summer afternoons. Once a-wing, this "tame" town-raised bird is as fleet and wild as his companions of the deserts.

Recent arrivals from the East often ask me what the best dove gun is. My answer is always that there is no such thing. For walking up the birds a bob-white gun is exactly right. The same sort of gun serves excellently where the birds come in low and fast and trickily. On the other hand, a full-choked twelve shooting maximum loads will knock down passing birds at fifty-five and sometimes sixty yards. In that case, your duck gun is the thing and you are really doing waterfowl shooting at doves.

But the big heavy twelves are clumsy things to twirl around trying to put on some dodging little devil coming in with the wind at sixty miles an hour. Then a light sixteen or twenty is the ticket. For most of my own dove shooting, I leave my big twelve at home and take instead a racy-looking twenty with which I do 90 per cent of my shooting anyway, whether at doves, quail or ducks.

Every now and then some windy oldtimer tells me that "there ain't one dove now to a hundred there used to be," but I remain skeptical. In my opinion the birds are as plentiful now as they were back in 1908, when I first started following my grandfather afield. They are not subject to the same fluctuations as quail. Droughts bother them but little. They can always find irrigated land in which to feed and they don't mind flying twenty or even thirty miles to the water they must have at least once a day.

What is more, they are not really hunted hard. The first couple of weeks of dove season the guns pop merrily; but after that the birds are not molested greatly. After quail season opens no one out here thinks of shooting doves unless they happen along.

I consider the fact that the season on my aerial speedsters has been moved back three weeks in the Southern tier of states as a real break. On the first of September, when the birds could formerly be taken, many pairs had not brought their last broods from the nest, and thousands of immature young were shot. Now that the gunners of Arizona, California, Texas and other Southern states cannot get into action until September 21st, an appreciable number will be conserved. The birds were never in any danger of extinction as it was, but the new and wise seasons will make their grip on existence ever firmer and assure my children and my grandchildren practice on the swiftest, trickiest, and most shifting targets a scatter-gun enthusiast could ask for.

CHAPTER XV

BLACKS AND GRIZZLIES

OF all the game animals which have received a raw deal from American civilization—and most of them have—the black bear has probably got the worst. He is for the most part a little fellow and a harmless one, yet a curious series of circumstances has made him a whipping boy and the villain of countless stories.

Folk lore and tradition have much to do with the black bear's unsavory reputation. People are afraid of bears, just as they are afraid of snakes, no matter how harmless. The tale of Goldilocks and the three bears does *Ursus americanus* no good, for example. Papa Bear, Mamma Bear and Little Bear did Goldilocks no harm, even though she was guilty of housebreaking and burglary, but the inference is that they *would* have. The sympathy is always with that pretty little juvenile delinquent instead of with the bears. She leapt from a window in terror, as I remember the story, and her fear of bears of all kinds has gone over into the subconscious minds of tens of thousands of children ever since. It is curious, but to most Americans the bear is a fearsome creature. Perhaps it is partly an ancient racial fear inherited from the time our hairy ancestors used to argue the ownership of warm caves with the bears of Pleistocene Europe.

Then, too, the black bear has had to suffer for the sins of larger relatives. The Alaskan brownie is a terrible beast calculated to strike fear in the heart of anyone. The grizzly was the lord of the plains and mountains, a carnivorous animal who could lick anything that walked and knew it.

[217]

On the other hand, the common black bear is shy, timid and inoffensive. It wants nothing more than to be left alone. It is omniverous but for the most part it lives on mast, berries and insects, sometimes even on grass. Most of the meat it devours comes from game or domestic animals killed by lions or coyotes, or from those that have died of disease.

Nevertheless the black bear's vague reputation as a bad *hombre* persists, and he continues to be the scapegoat for the transgressions of others. Superficially there may seem to be some reason. Coyotes kill a few domestic sheep, then bears come and finish what the little prairie wolves have left. There is bear sign all about and the bears get the blame. An indignant rancher gets out his dogs, harries every bear within twenty square miles and the newspapers carry stories from rural correspondents about the death of old One-Toe the sheep-killer. Actually sheep-killers are very rare among black bears; that is, bears who actually go out, run down sheep and slaughter them. I have followed up several such stories, and with one exception it was very patent that the sheep, the colts and the calves had been killed by something else or had simply died, and that the bears had acted only as scavengers.

Until a few years ago, the black bear was classed as vermin in most Western states because of the influence of the sheep men's lobby in the state legislatures. Bears got no protection whatever. Even in states where there was a closed season, any one wanting to go on a bear hunt had only to go to the state game department and swear that he wanted a special permit to take a stock-killing bear and it was granted to him without question. I know of several instances where ranchers wanting to take dudes out to hunt bears for a good fee would do that. Once I saw two of those "sheep-killing" bears which had been slaughtered to make a New Yorker's holiday. Both were year-old cubs. Mamma had got away.

But now the public seems to be awakening to the fact that the black bear is worth saving and that he has been sinned against far out of proportion to his own sinning. As a consequence, most states of the West now treat him as a game animal and allow him to be hunted only in the regular fall big-game season. Under such treatment little *Ursus americanus* seems to be coming back, and for this I am profoundly grateful.

I do not wish to paint the whole tribe lily-white. There are bad black bears. Now and again there are genuine sheep-killers among them, usually enormous lazy old males who have learned that they can make their living that way very easily. Such criminals often appear among the Navajos of northern Arizona, as those hunting Indians have sheep and are afraid to shoot bears. More of that later.

Bears can often become a real nuisance. They love pork, for example, and many ranchers in bear country find that they either have to kill off the bears or quit raising pigs. They are also fond of honey, and the bee-raiser in bear country has a tough time of it. But the bear usually learns his lesson when he is shot at a few times. He is perfectly willing to leave man alone if he can be left alone in turn.

Of all the creatures that range in the woods, the black bear is the hardest to see. It is my experience that he is even more difficult for the still-hunter to run across than the mountain lion, and the only bears that I have ever encountered unaided by dogs are the ones in the wild Navajo country where the states of Arizona, New Mexico, Utah and Colorado come together. The bears there have seen

[219]

only Navajos, to whom they are taboo, and as a consequence they entertain practically no fear of man. But I have spent much time in the pine and piñon woods below the Mogollon Rim in Arizona, the country which is reputed to be the best bear range in the state. I have seen much bear sign but never a bear. They are simply too wary. All bears have poor eyesight, but they compensate for this lack with their hearing and their sense of smell. The moment a bear receives his first warning of man, he stops, finds out where the man is, and leaves the country as a black, silent streak.

Where bears are wild and relatively scarce, still-hunting them is out of the question. They are simply too gifted for the man with the gun and with his limited sensory equipment. As a consequence they are most often hunted with dogs. And even hunting them with a pack is far from easy.

The mountain lion is a cowardly and short-winded beast. When dogs come close he soon tires and takes to a tree. Not the black bear. Unless he is very fat, he can run the dogs ragged, with those long hind legs of his propelling him at surprising speeds. He doesn't tree as easily as a lion. Instead, he often stops by a rock or cliff to have it out with his tormentors. For that reason the pack of bear dogs usually differs greatly in composition from the pack of lion dogs. The keen-nosed hounds which are necessary for lions are not primarily fighters, though they do make a lot of noise about it. They are not quick, and unless they are reinforced by mongrels with a strong terrier strain—real scrappers, these—an indignant bear will make hash out of them. Some bear hunters use Airedales exclusively, as an Airedale has a fairly good nose, is a fast runner and a quick and resourceful fighter.

For my part I don't care for the sport of hunting bears with dogs. To me it seems like taking an unfair advantage of an interesting and harmless animal that needs every chance if he is to increase and prosper. If enlightened state legislatures would pass laws making hunting with dogs illegal for ten years and if the state game departments would really enforce them, the black bear would come back surprisingly.

For all his reputation as a large and fearsome beast, the black bear is a rather small animal. He stands but little more than two feet high at the shoulders and on an average dresses out at not much more than 250 or 300 pounds. But the blacks vary greatly in size. Bears have been killed which weighed rough-dressed more than 500 pounds. One, an old male sheep-killer which was taken by M. E. Musgrave of the Biological Survey on the Hopi Indian reservation of northern Arizona, weighed 900 pounds—a monster larger than most grizzlies.

Not only do the black bears vary in size but they also vary greatly in color, ranging all the way from a deep glossy black to very light brown, almost a blond. Little blonds and brunettes are often found in the same litter, and the so-called cinnamon bear is simply a common color-phase of the black. Throughout the Rocky Mountains, indeed, the light-colored bears are more common than the blacks, and when I was hunting in the Navajo country a good many years ago, every single bear my companion and I saw was a cinnamon, some almost as light as the hair of a bleached blonde. They were big fellows, those bears, and I have often wondered if they were not an unclassified subspecies.

Throughout most of its range the black bear is usually a creature of damp, thick forests, where there is much water and plentiful mast. However, since most of the Southwest is relatively arid, they are found in surprising places. The Navajo country, where they still exist in considerable numbers, is dry for the most part, but it does have water in the deep canyons. The piñons and cedars furnish mast. The carcasses of Navajo sheep make up the meat portion of their diet, along with the small rodents which they seek out and devour. Black bears were once common and still exist in the semi-arid Davis Mountains of western Texas and below the line, in the Carmen Mountains across the Rio Grande, they are astonishingly plentiful, so plentiful in fact that they can successfully be hunted without dogs. In the Sierra Madres of Sonora and Chihuahua they are found in great numbers, and they range clear down into the cedars, oaks and piñons of the foothills.

Bears hibernate only in the colder portions of the Southwest, in regions where there are large areas above 6,000 feet and deep snows are common. In the lower portions of their range they stay out all winter, for they find little difficulty in securing food. They are highly migratory within limits. Find where there is a good piñon-nut or berry crop, and there you'll find the bears. Find where sheep have died in numbers, and there the bears will be. In places where they live on steep mountains they tend, like many other game ani-mals, to work high up in the summer and come down again when it becomes cold.

The bear's habit of hibernation makes him the world's prize escapist. Confronted with the problem of cold and lack of food, he simply finds himself a den of some sort and goes to sleep, to awake in the spring when times are better. The ripening nuts and fruit of fall have made him very fat, and all winter he lies in a state of suspended animation, barely breathing, his whole alimentary canal empty. Hibernating bears dug out of their dens after they are firmly asleep appear to be as oblivious to the world as a man under an anaesthetic, and may be killed without their regaining consciousness.

The young are born while the mother is in her torpor. They are naked at first and no larger than rats. They nurse, feed, snuggle in their drowsy mother's long hair. By the time they emerge from the den they are recognizable cubs about the size of rabbits, and they grow rapidly throughout the summer.

Bears come out of their dens in the spring, not thin as one would suppose, but about as fat as they were when they went in. Their coats are long, glossy, and unused, as the hair has continued to grow slowly all through their winter nap. The hide is then in better condition than it is at any other time of the year. Many states have a spring bear season. It is the best and almost only time to still-hunt them. They are dazed and stupid when they come out and they move about restlessly, showing up dark against the snow that still remains. For a week or so they eat but little. They become thin rapidly, as their unaccustomed exercise seems to melt the soft fat from their bodies. They soon snag off that glossy hibernation coat.

The black bear is a comical fellow, given to doing many gay and curious things, in the wild state as well as in captivity. The cubs particularly are almost human in some of their actions, and wherever they are confined they are a source of delight to spectators. Like the half-tame bears of the Yellowstone, they soon lose their fear of human beings and become familiar almost to the point of being contemptuous.

I am tempted here to tell something about the one bear with which I was intimately acquainted, although this is a book about wild animals and this bear happened to be tame.

He was for a time the mascot of the battleship *Arkansas*, on which, many years ago, I served. If he had a name I do not know it, for the entire ship's company referred to him simply as "that damned bear." He had been given to the ship, if I remember correctly, by the citizens of Juneau, Alaska, as a cute little cub. But he grew. The ship was his world, the sailors his only companions, and crew's chow his food. He came and went at will.

I made his acquaintance the first night I was on the ship. I arrived late, and as there was no one to assign me to my hammock hooks, I spread my hammock on the deck. About 4 A.M. when the early morning air of San Francisco harbor was chilly, I became dimly aware that I had a bedfellow—and further that this bedfellow was large, warm and very hairy. I drowsily put a hand on him and he woofed at me in a friendly fashion. Instead of accepting his advances, I let out a yell and went rapidly below, believing I was the victim of some strangely realistic nightmare. When the seamen went on the topside a couple of hours later to wash down, they found the bear in possession of my bedding.

I could tell many tales about the bear. From the time he was a tiny cub, the sailors had wrestled with him, but as he grew he became far more powerful than any man on the ship. However, he still loved to wrestle and seemed to feel deeply hurt as his strength grew and his popularity waned.

He never seemed able to adjust himself as he grew up. Instead, he could not understand why the sailors did not love him as they had when he was younger. He became furtive and sly. He took to hiding around corners of the passageways, then leaping out to wrestle with his old friends. But a 200-pound black bear *vs.* even a husky sailor is simply no contest. The bear always won, often tearing the clothes from the gobs' backs.

The examining room of the sick bay contained a leather couch. During the bear's period of popularity, it had been his favorite bed, and even when he was almost full grown he could not understand why he wasn't welcome. He used to lurk in the passageway until someone opened the door and then he would come leaping in and make a dive for the couch, for his eyes, like the eyes of all bears, were poor. All sailors looked alike to him, and if the couch happened to contain a dignified gold-striper complaining to the doctor about his sciatica it made no difference. The bear knocked him off and took possession anyway. The hospital corpsmen used to dislodge him by such subterfuges as shooting nitrous ether at him. He didn't like it.

He finally ended in a zoo—and this is how it happened. One of his particular friends was a lieutenant of marines, who liked to wrestle with him and feed him ice cream and candy bars. That officer lived to regret it.

One day when the Pacific fleet was at San Pedro an admiral inspected the ship's company, and the lieutenant was on the topside in dress uniform, standing straight and dignified in front of his leathernecks. Suddenly the bear came around a gun-turret, saw his friend the marine and became possessed of a desire to wrestle. In a moment an astonished admiral, full of dignity, trailed by obsequious subordinates, saw a red-faced and embarrassed marine officer flat on the deck being mauled by a large and ferocious-looking black bear.

"My God!" he shouted. "What is this—a circus?"

For several months the bear's unpopularity had been preying on his mind. The situation confused him, so he rose on hind legs and made a pass at the admiral. That sealed his fate. The last time I saw him, he was sitting aft in a motor-sailer, headed for the shore and a zoo, gazing wistfully back at the battleship which had been the only home he had ever known. He had received that thing which every seafaring man wants to avoid—an undesirable discharge.

I liked that bear, in spite of the fact that he often tore my pants off when I wrestled with him. He was so darned human. His reactions, once his popularity began to wane, were so very much like those of a human being whose best friends won't tell him!

I have shot a few black bears since then. But, call me a sentimentalist if you wish, I have never seen one treed by dogs without thinking of my old friend the neurotic bear of the battleship *Arkansas*.

The grizzly and the black are far different creatures. The black bear is shy and timid, but the grizzly, in the early days in any case, was the king-pin of the West, the largest, fiercest, most truculent creature of the mountains. He even carries his reputation in his name. "Grizzly" is a corruption of "grisly," meaning "horrible." His Latin name is *Ursus horribilis*, or the horrible bear. The early settlers referred to him as the "grisly." "Grizzly" is a perfectly understandable corruption, as his hide is grizzled. Theodore Roosevelt in his writings always refers to him as the "grisly."

The early American explorers of the Southwest found the grizzly absolutely unafraid of man, even contemptuous. Indians with their feeble arrows and lances fled from them in terror, and even the first beaver-trapping mountain men with their Kentucky rifles which had about the power of a modern .32–20 didn't care to have it out with them.

"There are two kinds of bears in the Rockies," one of the earliest explorers wrote: "the black bears and the red ones. The reddish bears are mischievous creatures, for they fall fiercely on the huntsman, whereas the black ones fly from 'em. The former sort are less, and more nimble than the latter."

Undoubtedly his "red bears" were grizzlies, though "red" is not a particularly good adjective with which to describe the grizzled yellowish coat of the typical grizzly. The nimbleness of the black bears no doubt refers to its ability to climb trees, something which an old grizzly cannot do.

The grizzly's lack of fear of man is something which all of those first explorers noted. A few of them were killed by the big bears, many had narrow escapes. Pattie, an early copper-miner, explorer and beaver-trapper, writes of a journey in 1827:

"We saw plenty of bears, deer and antelope. Some of the first we killed, because we needed their flesh, and others we killed for the same reason that we were often obliged to kill Indians, that is, to mend their rude manners in fiercely making at us and to show them we were not Spaniards, to give them the high sport of seeing us run."

Those same explorers called the grizzlies "gray bears," "white bears" and "red bears," though they also referred to the common cinnamon variety of the black bear as "red bears" also. They were agreed that the grizzly was an extraordinarily large brute, and indeed they are, as many of them weigh upwards of 1,000 pounds, perhaps more.

We now think of the grizzly as an inhabitant of the highest, wildest mountains close to timberline. Those which remain are. But in the old days of the Southwest, the grizzlies ranged in the chaparral-covered foothills and down into the desert valleys where they fed on mesquite beans, just as deer and cattle still do. Pattie tells of killing a grizzly in a cave in the desert country of the Rio Grande River below Socorro, New Mexico. There were grizzlies in the Santa Cruz Valley of southern Arizona, as several oldtimers have informed me. A Mexican ancient in the old Papago oasis of Pitiquito in the Sonora desert told me a few years ago that when he was a child there seventy years ago there were still a few grizzlies in the bottoms of the Altar River. There were wild turkeys there, too, he says—something which seems incredible to me, since Pitiquito is at least fifty miles from what I would consider typical turkey country.

The grizzly merited his reputation as a scrapper. He was in his day the only really dangerous big-game animal ever to inhabit the United States. The mountain lion is a notorious coward, and even the fierce-looking jaguar would rather run than fight. The big fellows were not long in learning that they were overmatched when they met a white man with a repeating rifle, but a wounded grizzly or a she-bear with cubs which she thinks are threatened will put up a desperate battle. In the old days they mauled many hunters and they still do in the regions where they exist.

When their mountains and valleys began to be put to civilized uses, the grizzlies were bound to go. They became great cattle-killers, taking full-grown cows, steers and bulls in their stride. They were shot, hunted, poisoned and trapped. A grizzly would kill a cow, then cover it with dirt to show he intended to come back, just as a lion covers his with twigs. Then the irate cowman would come and fill the carcass full of strychnine and there would be one less bear to contend with.

The scientists have listed many subspecies of Southwestern grizzlies. In his book, *The Mammals of New Mexico*, Vernon Bailey records seven. The number for a relatively small area seems high to me, and as most of the classifications were made from but one or two skulls, I am inclined to think that the scientists have mistaken individual variations for sub-specific differences.

But that is a question which will never be settled, as the grizzly is now practically extinct throughout the Southwest. I am convinced that there is not a single grizzly in all western Texas, where they were once abundant in the Davis Mountains and the adjacent foothills. There still may be a few in the higher and wilder ranges of New Mexico, and a dozen or so are reported annually by the Forest Service. There still may be some in Arizona's wild White Mountains. Their presence is a possibility at any rate. There are some in the Sierra Madres of Chihuahua and Sonora, but they are not plentiful, in spite of optimistic reports by some American guides and outfitters who take dudes to Mexico and who would gladly outfit a hunter to go after saber-tooth tigers or dodo birds if there was a few hundred dollars in it.

So, it is farewell to the Southwestern grizzly. He had his shortcomings, true! But he was a gallant fighter and a bold buccaneer. In spite of his sins, I mourn for him, and I wish that I could really believe that somewhere in my Southwest they still existed. But I honestly believe the last is gone. Any grizzlies which will be reported in the future will simply be, I think, very large black bears. Old

Ursus horribilis has, in the Southwest anyway, killed his last cow, frightened the wits out of his last hunter!

CHAPTER XVI

EL TIGRE

EVERY year dozens of American sportsmen go to Africa for lions or to India or Cambodia for tigers, yet few hunt the jaguars of Mexico. To me it is one of the most curious anomalies of American field sport. The jaguar is as fine a trophy as any tiger; taking one can furnish even more hair-raising thrills; and the trip costs but a fraction of what it takes to make a jaunt to India. The only logical explanation of the neglect of the jaguar, perhaps, is that he is the least known of American predatory animals.

The skin of a full-grown jaguar is a beautiful and gaudy thing and one of which any sportsman can well be proud. It makes even the hide of an African lion look pale and drab, and to my notion it is just as beautiful as the skin of a Bengal tiger. Compared to the jaguar, the mountain lion, the only other great American cat, comes off a very poor second best when it comes to looks. The jaguar is a massive, powerful, solidly built cat, deep orange-yellow marked with black rosettes. His under parts fade to pale buffy white, but his dominant impression is of a huge cat of orange marked with black. In length the largest jaguars measure about the same as big mountain lions, yet the jaguar is usually the heavier beast, for his tail is shorter and he is compactly built, while the lion is lean and lanky. For comparison, let us say that the lion is built like a coyote, but the jaguar has the enormous strength and solid powerful lines of the timber wolf.

Superficially the jaguar is more nearly like the African leopard than he is like his other relatives among the world's great cats, but he is heavier. Only the African lion and the Asiatic tiger are larger, and in South America the giant light-colored jaguars are as large as female lions and tigers. The jaguars of the northern half of Mexico, however, run smaller than their South American kindred. Usually they weigh about the same as mountain lions; that is, the very largest will weigh about 200 pounds.

The original range of the jaguar was from the southern portion of the United States to the southern tip of South America. Many subspecies are found within that vast area, but only one, *Felis onca hernandessi*, which is the most northern form, has ever ranged in the United States. The animals are still common over most of their range, and even in this country they are still occasionally killed along the Mexican border.

I have heard that in some parts of Mexico, the natives refer to the animals as *oncas*,* but throughout northern Mexico they simply call them *tigres*, Spanish for tigers, just as both Mexicans and Americans call the puma a lion. Nearly all border Americans use the same name, and henceforth I shall use it instead of the more literary term "jaguar."

The animals are quite plentiful in most parts of northern Mexico even now, and they can be taken in almost any section where there is cover enough for them to lie up in and game or range cattle

---

* The famous lion-hunting Lee brothers, who probably know more about the great American cats than any other persons, claim that the Mexicans of Sinaloa give the name *onca* to a lion-like cat that is distinctly not *felis concolor*, but somewhat more grayish, with longer legs, smaller feet and an entirely different skull form. They have taken one, and I have a photograph of it dead. It surely does look like a new species, but I have seen neither hide nor skull. I do know that the zoology of Mexico has been only superficially studied; and the Lees, who have killed hundreds of great cats, ought to be pretty well qualified observers.

for them to devour. In almost all the Mexican mountains and foot-hills where I have been the natives report tigres as being fairly plen-tiful—far too plentiful, in their opinion, as they are great destroyers of domestic stock.

On the whole, they seem less adaptable than lions, and they are usually found in warmer, more heavily wooded country. They are far wanderers, however, and may turn up anywhere from the water-less deserts of the Sonora coast to the spruce and fir of northern Ari-zona. A couple of years ago a lone male tigre invaded a little range of desert mountains called Las Mochis north of Hermosillo in So-nora and took terrible toll of the bighorn sheep and whitetail deer there. A Mexican *vaquero* of my acquaintance ran across it and killed it. He was brought up in that country and this tigre was the first he had ever seen. One tigre has been killed on the south rim of the Grand Canyon not far from the El Tovar Hotel, and several have been taken in the high cool mountains of New Mexico. In the brush country of southern Texas, the animals were at one time in-digenous and very plentiful, and they still cross the Rio Grande from Mexico. Here in southern Arizona one is killed every year or so. Several have been taken from the Catalina Mountains just north of Tucson. I know of one shot in the low barren Tortillita Moun-tains, and a few from almost every range in the area. One of the prize exhibits of the Arizona State Museum in Tucson is the beauti-ful hide of a huge tigre killed in the Chiricahuas. Only last year a hunter trailed a tigre for several days, thinking it was a lion, and lost two dogs before he discovered his mistake.

There may possibly have been some tigres in California when white men first arrived there, as records of early Spanish explorers speak of "California lions and tigers." One of these vague early "records" is as far north as San Francisco! Be that as it may, there is one fairly authentic record of a tigre's having been seen in one of the high barren ranges that surrounds the Imperial Valley. It was a female with young, and when seen it had been living on mountain sheep. As the animals wander widely, there is no reason why it could not have crossed the Colorado River and invaded California. The animals have been seen in southwestern Arizona, not far away, where they were killing mountain sheep and desert mule deer.

Hunting tigres in southern Arizona would be like seeking a needle in the proverbial haystack, but as soon as you cross the Mexican boundary you begin to run into spots of tigre country. I saw their big round tracks, bigger than those of any lion, when I was hunting whitetails in the Sierra Azuls, only sixty miles below Nogales. In the Cucurpis, a hundred miles below the border in Sonora, the Mexicans told me they were more plentiful than lions and killed thirty or forty cows and horses annually as well as hundreds of whitetail deer. However, the real tigre country of northern Mexico is the foothill and jungle country of southern Sonora and Sinaloa. A party of Americans went to Soyopa on the Yaqui River of southern Sonora a few years ago, spent about a month, and returned with half a dozen tigres; and almost every American who goes into that section with a real tigre-hunter as a guide comes out with a trophy. I know one border American who still-hunts the animals and usually has good success.

Like the lion, the tigre of northern Mexico is primarily a killer of deer, although he is an eater of small discrimination he will kill anything he takes a fancy to—javelinas, bighorn sheep, armadillos, and in South America, tapirs. In the few places where the range of the tigre overlaps with that of the desert bighorns, they prey on sheep with gusto. West of Hermosillo, where there are a few tigres as well as sheep and mule deer, they kill either species as well as the little Sonora whitetail that forms the main article in their diet. They also kill range cattle and horses, and like the lion they are fond of colts when they can get them.

The tigres of the Rio Yaqui country of Sonora are deer-killers, but in Sinaloa, north of Mazatlan, they live almost entirely on range cattle, killing even the largest longhorn bulls with ease. The tremendous toll they take on the cattle industry can be seen when one realizes that the big cats kill at least once a week. At American prices, this would mean that each tigre would cost Sinaloa's ranchers around $1,500 annually—at Mexican beef prices, about 2,500 pesos. At any rate, the beautiful tigre is a real burden on any ranch country.

Like the lion, the tigre often but not always covers his kill with brush, and on various occasions in Mexico I have had natives show me kills which they assured me were made by *el tigre* and not by *el leon*. They showed me the tracks, too—big round tracks, round of pad and toe marks—not, like those of the lion, triangular of pad and long of toe. As I write this, the last tigre sign I saw was down near the Sonora coast in wild, beautiful desert country, where a tigre was killing range stock and deer. He had wandered in from farther south and the frantic Mexican ranchers were trying to do away with him but they were having scant success.

One of the most interesting tales about the tigre is the one which holds that he and the mountain lion are implacable enemies and fight every time they meet. And, according to the same stories, the

[235]

tigre, in spite of the fact that he is stronger and heavier, usually comes off second best. How much truth there is to them I do not know. I have questioned many Mexicans about them, but none of them have ever seen such a fight. One placer-miner in the Cucurpis, who had killed several tigres, one of them, he claimed, with a club, told me he once killed a big male which had been badly mauled and scratched. He could easily have been chewed up by one of his own kind over some love affair, as Mexicans tell me that the males stage terrible brawls during the mating season.

The habits of the lion and the tigre are very different, in spite of the fact that they are approximately the same size and are often found in the same range. The lion is a quiet and furtive creature—so quiet that backwoodsmen often argue as to whether or not he ever makes a noise at all—who goes about his business of killing deer, calves and colts as silently as a shadow. But the bold tigre? He is one of the noisiest creatures in the jungle. He roars and coughs and grunts almost nightly. No matter where you've been or how much you have hunted, your hair will crawl on your neck the first time you hear the roar of this monarch of the semi-tropical forest.

A cornered lion will turn on his pursuers, but for the most part he is a coward who will flee from dogs—even a single dog. But not the tigre! He will fight men and dogs. He is hard to tree and hard to corner, and he will charge—not just occasionally, but almost every time. The lion has great speed for a hundred yards or so, but he is a short-winded creature of little "bottom"; but the tigre can run long, far, and fast. The lion trees soon after the dogs draw near, the tigre only as a last resort.

I know of only one authentic instance of an unprovoked attack by a mountain lion on a human being—a case of a lion's killing and partially eating a child in Oregon some years ago. But the tigre becomes a man-killer fairly often. According to Ernest Lee, the tigre hunter, an old male that lives near the town of Las Mochis, on the Sinaloa coast, is credited with having killed one woman and seven children at various times. Mexicans have hunted it often, but so far as I know it is still alive. Farther south in the same Mexican state, a tigre made an unprovoked attack on a peon carrying a *machete*. Other peons found the two some hours later—the tigre dead, the peon horribly mauled. The desperate Mexican had somehow managed to penetrate the great cat's brain with his heavy weapon, but he died a couple of weeks later from infection in his wounds.

All through Sinaloa, where tigres are plentiful and are not very successfully hunted, they are the cocks of the walk. The natives are poorly armed and afraid of them, and most of them have tales of how they ran into a tigre on a jungle path and how they—not the tigre—gave ground. In that part of Mexico, the natives pester the big cats a great deal with packs of cowardly, poorly trained dogs. They seldom kill one, and their hunting serves only to keep the cats short-tempered and self-confident.

I doubt if the tigre ever becomes a habitual man-eater, but he will kill men if he is cornered or, evidently, simply if he happens to feel like it. There is an old Spanish tale to the effect that in 1825 a tigre entered a convent in Santa Fe, New Mexico, where it killed four human beings without provocation before it was finally killed in turn. The explanation was that it was driven there by high water. Vernon Bailey repeats the story in his *Mammals of New Mexico* and so does Seton in *Lives of Game Animals*. Bailey is inclined to scoff at it and Seton to credit it. Such a thing might happen. Possibly the animal had rabies. However, it surely is not a normal pattern of conduct, as thousands of unarmed and practically defenseless Mexicans live in tigre country with perfect safety. Those who are killed are the exceptions. The South American animals may be dangerous. I do not know.

The mating season among tigres seems to be in the late winter, and the young—one, two and occasionally three—are born in the spring. Like their parents, they are spotted, but their hair is longer and woolier. Perhaps the fact that the young mountain lions are spotted as are tigres shows both species are descended from a common spotted ancestor. Papa tigre seems to be a permanent member of the family, whereas the male lion is not, and occupies the family lair. I have read that the animals breed annually, but the fact that Mexicans tell me that they have seen young almost full grown running with their parents would tend to show that they breed only every two or possibly three years. If they bred oftener, it would seem that they would increase faster than their supply of deer and javelinas. As a matter of fact, very little is known of the tigre in the wild state.

Just why the tigre roars, no one seems to know. Since he roars at all times of the year, his roar is not a mating call. Possibly the noise he makes frightens his prey into moving. Possibly it's simply the nature of the beast, without any particular significance, and he roars to express a sense of well-being and to let his fellows know he is out hunting. Both sexes roar, and the roars of males and females are indistinguishable.

Since few Americans have ever heard the roar of a tigre, I will describe it. It starts with short coughing roars which are not unlike those which I have heard African circus lions utter. Until about the fifth they increase in volume, then they gradually decrease until the cry ends in a series of grunting growls. The very ground seems to vibrate with the intensity and volume of the sound. Often though he is almost a mile away, the great cat will seem to be right on top of you. The growls at the end, however, do not have the carrying power of the roars, and it is by them that the direction and the distance of the cat can be estimated.

I am no tigre hunter, though I have ambitions in that direction. I have been in tigre country. I have heard them roar, and I have seen their tracks and their kills—often. Tigres can be still-hunted somewhat more successfully than mountain lions, but since they are nocturnal they must be still-hunted at dawn and dusk. A friend of mine who lives on the border and who hunts in Mexico often has killed four tigres by still-hunting. He once walked up on a big roaring male at dusk on the Rio Yaqui and shot it. A couple of Cleveland sportsmen hunting whitetail deer in the same country in 1937 saw a cave in a rimrock high above them and investigated it to see if it was an old Indian camp. Instead of arrowheads, they found tigres —three of them. They killed them all. Taking on a tigre with dogs is exciting enough, but tackling one without help would be even more pulse-quickening, as I know no animal better calculated to inspire awe and respect in the human being than a tigre on the loose.

Once, many years ago, I was hunting deer in Mexico. I was cold, empty, weary from having slept in a Mexican *jacal* heavily infested with little prowling animals which forage on human hide by night, and what is more, I was very much alone. I had crept through a mile or so of scrubby trees and brush thinking more of the breakfast of *tortillas* and eggs and coffee I hoped to promote later than I was of the whitetails I was hunting. I came to a canyon perhaps three hundred feet deep and paused in hope of seeing a browsing deer. Suddenly a tigre walked out of the brush a few hundred yards away on my side of the canyon, crossed, and disappeared on the other side. Even in the gray dawn he was bright orange, a wild, beautiful, terrible thing gliding along through the chill dusk of that lonely canyon. He was the evil hunting spirit of the wilderness, a truculent creature of enormous power. He was in sight perhaps three or four seconds. I do not know. I had a rifle in my hand, yet I made no attempt to use it. I was astonished and enormously impressed. I hate to admit it, but I must have been afraid as well. I do know that cold sweat broke out on my forehead, and that when I remembered I had a rifle my hand was trembling. It was buck fever, but in a particularly virulent and deadly form. I forgot deer and went back for my Mexican host and his dogs. We found the big round tracks, but the dogs lost the trail in about half an hour. We never saw that particular tigre again. If you think you're immune to thrills, just run across a tigre alone in the wilderness. He's quite a different creature from one seen securely behind iron bars. You may know he won't hurt you, but you won't believe it.

One of the most sporting and thrilling methods of hunting tigres would be calling, a method used by the Mayo and Yaqui Indians. Strange as it may seem, the great cats can be decoyed by imitating their call just as moose are called. The method is this: The Indians pick a bright moonlit night in a section where a tigre is roaring. Then the hunter places himself between the caller and his cat. When the animal approaches the caller with his horn, the hunter kills it with buckshot. It sounds simple, but I'll guarantee that it would pack a thrill comparable to that furnished even by lions and tigers.

Another method I have heard of takes advantage of the great curiosity of the tigre—a curiosity even bolder than that of the lion. The hunters build very bright fires, hide away from them in the brush, and then shoot the tigres as they come up to investigate. Again a heavy shotgun loaded with buckshot is the favored weapon. Fire hunting is favored by many of the Yaquis, the real tigre-hunters of northern Mexico.

The most reliable way to take the great cats is with the aid of trained dogs, but the dogs must be good ones, as the many Americans who have depended on pick-up Mexican packs have discovered. Most Mexican dogs are very poor—sight-trailers used to running javelinas and deer. Occasionally they tree a lion they jump, but for the most part the tigres beat them off badly mauled.

Arizona's famous family of cat-hunting Lees has worked out a method of tigre-hunting which seems to work far more reliably than any other. It is their own invention, and is a combination of calling and running with dogs.

They camp in tigre country, and at night they "roar" for them with callers made of the horn of a range steer. They cut a hole toward the tip of the horn, and with the mouth close to the ground, so that the sound will carry, they imitate the great cat's call. Tigres, they say, will often answer from five miles or so away through the tropical night, roaring, coughing and grunting. Often they will come close to camp, in spite of the clamoring of the dogs. The animals seem almost powerless to resist the call, and they can be brought up again and again. A group of Mexicans in Sinaloa called up the same tigre and shot at him every night for five nights, wounded him the third, and killed him the fifth.

But the Lees get the tigres close to camp, then quit calling, and when dawn comes they put their dogs on the trail. When they unravel its circlings and wanderings they are off. Superficially this might seem much like the hunting of mountain lions. Actually it isn't. Lion hunting is 90 per cent cold trailing, 10 per cent from the jump to the kill. In tigre hunting the proportion is just the opposite —10 per cent cold trailing and 90 per cent handling the tigre.

The tigre is a creature of great stamina, courage and determination. Once jumped by the dogs he will head for some favorite cave or tree, and he will fight until he gets there. In fact, a tigre chase consists mostly of a running fight, with the dogs trying to slow him down until the hunter comes up. Further, unlike the lion, the tigre does not seem greatly afraid of dogs. An old one has probably whipped a dozen packs of Mexican curs and has plenty of self-confidence.

So in the last analysis, the whole success of a tigre hunt depends on the courage, the agility, the perseverance of the dogs. They must not turn and run at the tigre's first snarl; they must not flee at the first scratch. They must keep crowding him, pestering him, nipping him, *hurting* him until in desperation he seeks a tree or backs up in a cave or against a bluff to stand them off. And even when he is treed or cornered the hunt is not yet ended, for the tigre is a creature of scant patience and much intestinal fortitude. Lions will often stay in a tree for hours on end. Not the tigre. In a little while he gets bored and out he comes, to maul the dogs, and to make another running fight of it.

The hunter of the great cats is not due for a leisurely ride. He must stay as close to his pack as possible so he can encourage them and back them up. When the Lees take parties out, one of them always goes on foot behind the dogs, as a hunted tigre often takes short cuts where no horse can follow. Then he tries to hold the animals until the sportsmen ride up. Sometimes he can't, however. When a tigre charges, and it is either a Lee or a tigre, they shoot.

Dale Lee was in an amusing and exciting mix-up with a tigre last year—one which proves the tigre is no animal to be trifled with. He and the dogs had treed it, and he sent a Mexican to bring over the party of sportsmen. The tigre seemed patient and comfortable up there in the tree, so Dale, being chilly, started to build a fire. He had put down his rifle and was gathering wood when the tigre jumped from the tree and charged him. He ran for his gun, and got to it only because the dogs rushed in and slowed the big cat up. His first shot hit the animal in the loins, a wound serious enough to slow him down but not to disable him completely. His dander up, the tigre decided to fight it out. He took refuge in tall grass, charged both Dale and the dogs. When the sportsmen rode up he was willing to take them on, too; but they killed him when he charged.

That's but one exciting little mix-up. The Lees have had plenty of them. In Sonora, for instance, the animals nearly always run for caves instead of trees. They are not as fierce, they say, as the Sinaloa tigres, which are used to being pestered by men and dogs, but they fight when they are aroused, and if you are looking for the ultimate in thrills, just crawl into a dim cave with one.

You call the dogs off and go in there *alone*—alone, that is, except for your rifle and your flashlight. A few minutes before, it was noisy down there in the river canyon. After a half-hour running fight, the big cat had finally taken refuge in this cave. The dogs were bellowing, the tigre snarling and roaring. But now from the darkness of that cave comes only an ominous silence. You take your rifle in one hand, your flashlight in the other, swallow hard a few times, and go on in, *alone*, to kill a big tough cat powerful enough to slay a range bull with a blow. But in you go, teeth chattering a little, maybe, heart pounding, impelled by the universal human instinct to prove yourself unafraid when you really are.

The beam of that flashlight seems a feeble thing as you cast it around trying to locate the big cat, and unless you shine his eyes, even a 200-pound jaguar is often surprisingly hard to see. Perhaps you hear first his harsh breathing, then put the light on him as he lies above you on a ledge. Then comes the booming roar of your rifle, and the big cat falls limp almost on top of you.

Triumphant, you drag the great cat out into hot, bright, semitropical sunshine. The dogs greet you with bellows of excitement and your guide grins. It's a great world after all, and you're a little ashamed now that you were scared. But a couple of days later, when you do it again, you get just as big a thrill as the first time.

Here's a hint, the Lees say, just on the remote chance that you ever get mixed up with a charging tigre—and that is SHOOT, even though you know you will miss. Good dogs are used to charging in to the shot. They will hold the creature long enough for you to get another in.

It is the dogs themselves that are the answer to a successful tigre hunt. They must be fast, keen-nosed and courageous. They must be willing to fight, ready to take punishment, and agile enough so that the tigre cannot easily kill them. Even so, however, any tigre-hunter is bound to lose many good dogs. A tigre is a better and more deadly fighter than a bear, and there is no comparison between the big Mexican cats and mountain lions.

Tigre hunting *is* dangerous; and loyal, courageous dogs are the hunter's best protection. I am tempted to record here another of Dale Lee's experiences. He was hunting in Sinaloa. Ernest Lee was with their sportsman and Dale was right behind the dogs. The big cat finally turned to make a fight of it under a rimrock on the side of a canyon. When Dale got there the cat was putting up a defensive fight, as tigres will, batting the dogs as they came close. Then as Dale came up, he went berserk and charged him. Dale wanted to wait for the sportsman, so he dodged. A dog dived in and slowed up the cat, but the tigre knocked him off the bluff, charged again. Two dogs nailed him by the ears this time. He clawed one off and seized the other by the head. Hound and cat locked jaws. The tigre bit through the hound's skull, but the hound chewed the big cat so hard he broke off one of his teeth. Dale, afraid the cat would kill his hound, jumped in and began beating it over the head with his .30–30. Then the hound that had been knocked over the bluff scrambled back and tied in. So did the others.

Then somehow—Dale has never figured out just how it happened—the whole mass—a man, a tigre and four dogs—rolled over the cliff and down to the feet of the astonished sportsman, who missed the cat with his first shot, killed him with the second. They had told him that tigres are tough. He believes it. Curiously, the dog which was so badly bitten survived. Within ten days he was hunting again—and he wasn't afraid of tigres.

Hunting the mountain lion comes about as near being 100 per cent safe as going after any big predatory animal can be. Tigre hunting *always* is spiced with danger. However, a few simple rules make it a less dangerous business, the tigre-hunting Lees say. Animals that charge the hunter are always those fighting the dogs and made courageous by their excitement and rage. If a man will wait until the cat has cooled off a bit he can come close safely.

As thrilling as it is, going into a cave to shoot a tigre, is not, the Lee brothers are convinced, as dangerous as it might seem—*if* the hunter calls the dogs off and waits for the tigre to cool off and calm down. Clell and Dale Lee can both tell of the time they went into a cave after a tigre, couldn't find him for several minutes, and then discovered him behind a boulder within three feet of them. He had seen them, even though they had not seen him, and if he had wanted to kill them he would have had a wonderful opportunity.

For another thing, they say, really *bad* tigres will not stay in a cave. Instead they come charging out to scatter dogs and hunters as soon as they get their wind back.

He is a great animal, this tigre, and hunting him must be one of the most thrilling sports in the world, but for my part I am content to let him remain a Mexican citizen and shed no tears because he is only a casual raider across the line. The animals are simply too destructive. In Mexico, with its millions of whitetail deer, they are a beautiful and interesting addition to the native game; but in the United States with its lions and its hunters, it would be just another drain on a none too plentiful deer supply. So, old *tigre*, I salute you, but I hope you stay on your own reservation!

CHAPTER XVII

THE MOUNTAIN LION

NO other animal in North America appeals so powerfully to the imagination of the man on the street as does the mountain lion. No other creature, in this country at least, has been the inspiration for so many tall tales, most of them completely without foundation. Almost everyone I meet has some foolish and ridiculous story to tell about lions. Fiction, motion pictures and folklore have all fed the growing stream of unfounded nonsense about old *Felis concolor*.

Though lions were at one time found all over the United States and are still common throughout the West, all of Mexico, and a great part of Canada, few people have ever seen one outside of a zoo and still fewer have ever had a glimpse of one which was not put up by dogs. There is no doubt that the lion is the most cautious, furtive and secretive of all animals hunted by man. I know men who have spent their entire lives in lion country without ever seeing one of the predators.

In spite of the fact that half of the people you meet tell you how a lion sprang at Uncle Edgar one night when he was walking through the woods, no number of stories can make the lion anything but the most arrant of cowards. His psychology is typically that of a coward. He will chase anything that runs from him and he will run from anything that chases him. Lions have been known to stalk and kill dogs in the woods, but I don't suppose there is a case on record of a lion which didn't run from a dog which went after it.

I know of one instance where a big male lion was treed by a white poodle weighing about twenty pounds, and shot by a picnicker with a pearl-handled .22 revolver.

The lion is a formidable beast—there is no doubt of that. A big male will weigh around 200 pounds live weight and he is equipped with terrible claws and teeth. He prefers the smaller animals like deer and sheep for a diet, but in a pinch he can kill any herbivorous animal either wild or tame found in America—even full-grown stallions, cattle, elk and moose. Yet lions are not dangerous to man and they never molested even Indians armed only with spears and primitive bows and arrows. Treed lions making a last desperate dash for freedom have knocked hunters down by accident, but I have never heard of a case where the animals, provoked though they were, actually made an attack.

In Oregon several years ago a starving lion attacked, killed and partially ate a young boy; but so far as I know this is the only authentic instance of its kind on record.

Lions probably have more names than any other large mammal found in America. At various times and in different places, they have been called panthers, painters, varmints, catamounts, cougars, pumas, lions and mountain lions; but in the West they are called only by the last two names. I have even heard barber-shop biologists discourse learnedly on panthers and lions and find mythical differences. There are none.

Lions are beautiful creatures after a curiously evil and slinking fashion. Their bodies are deep but very narrow, their legs are short and powerful, and their long necks and flat, small, snake-like heads give them the appearance of swift malevolent power. All subspecies of lions, whether found from British Columbia to Tierra del Fuego at the tip of South America, are almost identical in appearance. They vary from a rufous gray to a light reddish tan and all of them have a dark red-brown streak down the center of their backs. Here in the Southwest the mountain animals run larger and darker than do the desert species, and like the mule deer upon which they prey, they tend to be grayer in the winter and more reddish in the summer.

The great predators are found all over the Southwest from the thick dark forests of spruce and fir near timberline on the highest mountains, to the burning cactus-studded deserts. Any country which contains deer also has its quota of lions, as deer are the natural food of the beasts. Heat, cold, thorns and rocks seem to mean nothing to them so long as they can be assured of a plentiful supply of venison. Lions also prey on domestic animals, however, and they are especially fond of colt-meat. As a consequence they have been hunted hard and have now been driven back into the wildest, roughest and most inaccessible country where cliffs and canyons enable them to escape from dogs.

Lions are by far the most serious natural enemies of the larger game animals. They prefer deer to all other game, but if the opportunity offers they will kill antelope, mountain sheep, turkeys and even porcupines. Each lion kills at least one deer a week, and though the animals have been greatly reduced in numbers all over the West they still probably take a greater annual toll of game than do all hunters put together. Joseph S. Dixon estimates in his excellent monograph on California mule deer that the 600 lions still remaining in California kill at least 30,000 deer annually—about as many as are taken by the more than 100,000 hunters who go afield after them. In most Western states the predator's share would run even higher. In many sections of Arizona I believe lion-killed deer run from 3 to 1 to 5 to 1 over those taken by hunters.

Because of this tremendous carnage each lion must make in order to live, the animals have never been plentiful in the same sense other game is. If they ever had been they would long since have exterminated the game. In the old days there must have been great fluctuations in the game population. As lions grew plentiful deer decreased until the predators starved or moved away. Then deer increased and the lions came back. This seems to me to be a fairly logical explanation of the deer cycles noted by white trappers and Indians before the settlement of the country.

Most people think of a lion making his kill by springing from a rock or a tree down on the back of an unsuspecting buck. That surely would be both picturesque and dramatic, but it doesn't happen to be true. Lions kill deer and animals of similar size by knocking them off their feet with their powerful shoulders and forelegs after a short swift rush, and then either disemboweling them or biting them at the base of the skull or through the neck.

Their favorite method of attack is exactly like that of a blocking back in football who knocks down opposing tacklers with the force of impact. They no doubt kill larger animals like horses and cattle by leaping on them and then biting their necks, but unless very hungry they prefer to confine themselves to colts and calves, in other words, to deer-sized animals.

Lions are short-winded beasts. Their first rush is incredibly swift, but it is of short duration, seldom extending over a hundred yards, and for that reason they prefer to stalk to within from twenty-five to seventy-five feet of their prey. Not every rush is successful, and if the deer escapes them the first time they seldom try to follow it. Instead, they hunt up a new deer and try again.

With their prey dead, lions first suck the blood and eat the lungs, heart and viscera. After they have appeased their first hunger they nearly always bury the kill under leaves and twigs. Often they come back for another meal or two. Sometimes they don't, and as a consequence most of the deer hair and venison found in the stomachs of black bears comes from these old lion kills.

The beasts are skillful and patient hunters, and when driven by hunger they will range over many square miles until they have made a kill and satisfied themselves.

Almost everyone who has spent much time in the wilds has at some time been trailed by a lion, and it is this habit of the animals which has given rise to most of the stories of their potential danger to human beings. But the lions mean no harm; they are merely curious. On one occasion a big lion followed my wife down a forest trail for a quarter of a mile, slinking along behind her and no doubt peering at her through the brush. When she turned to come back along the same path it sprang into the brush and slunk away. The animal had written the entire story in the dust with its big round tracks and in some instances they overlapped those of my wife. But that animal was not dangerous—he only wondered what that strange creature was up to. Another time when my wife and I were picnicking with a group of friends, a lion watched us from a point about a quarter of a mile away. One of the members of the party happened to discover it with glasses and we took turns watching it for a half-hour. When my mother was a little girl in pioneer Colorado, a lion once trotted behind her in plain sight when she was returning from a berry-picking expedition. It made, of course, no move to attack her. Many times when camping out I have found where lions sneaked up and watched us in the darkness within fifty yards, and Pattie, an early Southwestern explorer and beaver-trapper, reports in his diary that a lion once walked calmly into their camp to see what was going on. For this reason many Indian tribes believe lions are friendly to man and actually watch over them and guard them when they are in the woods.

With the possible exception of the black bear, old *Felis concolor* is the shyest and most furtive of animals and the hardest to see. I have killed a couple of lions and I have seen quite a few shot, but always they have been treed by dogs. On the rare occasions when I have encountered them alone I have been unarmed. On the other hand, I can tell some instances of surprising luck. Last year a sixteen-year-old high-school boy on his first deer hunt encountered and killed a lion in broad daylight in the Rincon Mountains near Tucson. A friend of mine who lives in Flagstaff, Arizona, was sitting one morning in a corral, rifle in hand, waiting for a horse to be caught for him, when a big lion jumped over the fence and almost on top of him. It would be hard to say which was more surprised— the man or the lion. However, the hunter recovered from his astonishment in time to shoot the beast.

A few years ago some of the sporting magazines were filled with a controversy as to whether lions screamed or not. I have never heard one, and the fact that many people who have lived in the woods all their lives haven't either, would tend to prove that they do it rarely. However, they undoubtedly do make a noise of some sort. I have heard it described as sounding like the cry of a baby, as the shriek of a woman in distress, and as simply the yowl of a big cat—all by people of undoubted veracity. What does it sound like? Maybe like all three. *Quien sabe?*

The hunter needs a good pack of dogs, three or four at least, as the more noise they make the more frightened the lion becomes. The pack should include a good cold-trailer or two. Many hunters in the Southwest are now using especially trained bloodhounds, but I have heard of some who swear by Airedales, which are ordinarily not thought of as trailers at all. Jack Butler who hunts in the Kaibab and who a couple of times a year takes along Clark Gable, the motion-picture actor, uses bloodhounds exclusively. In most country the hunters ride horses, but when it is especially rough they have to follow on foot. In any case it is a wild and exciting experience and something not soon to be forgotten. When the lion finally comes to bay on a rock or in a tree, it is all over. He can be shot as easily as skunk in a trap and shooting him affords about as much thrill. But the first glimpse of the lion running like a tawny streak before the clamoring dogs or perched in a tree spitting and hissing like a snake is a sight never to be forgotten. Many hunters vary the sport and add thrill to it by taking the animals alive by climbing into trees and lassoing them. I have never seen it done, though I hope to.

Treed lions are usually shot in the brain or spine, so they can be killed instantly. Two hundred pounds of wounded lion landing in a pack of expensive dogs is bad medicine, and fumbling dudes who fail to kill the animals outright are bitterly denounced by the wranglers. For that reason they frown on shots at lions running before dogs after they have jumped out of a tree and are trying to escape.

Lions are not particularly tenacious of life and when they are treed it is no great trick to kill them neatly. Almost any kind of a bullet will do it. Hundreds have been dispatched with .22's, and full-jacketed bullets are a good idea as they don't tear the hides. I know of one Eastern hunter who made an expensive lion hunt and blasted five animals out of trees with high-velocity .30–'06 bullets. Some of the hides carried holes as big as dinner plates.

It is a fortunate circumstance for the deer tribe of America that lions are no more prolific than they are. Females breed only every other year. They have from one to three kittens with the average perhaps a little above two. The young surprisingly enough are spotted, showing the influence, I suppose, of some remote spotted ancestor. Even the young are killers incarnate and there are instances on record of kittens only four or five months old killing young deer on their own initiative.

Male lions are polygamous and far-wanderers, but the females settle down to some rough country of cliffs and canyons where deer are plentiful, and raise their families, killing a deer or two each week. A female with young hunting a fairly small area hard will often make it into a gameless wilderness, killing or driving away all the deer. On a couple of occasions I have had it happen to favorite hunting spots of mine.

There is no doubt that the lion is an undesirable citizen and should be killed at every opportunity. In spite of his slinking evil beauty, he is a villain without a redeeming feature. What is more, he is completely unnecessary at the present time. Before the coming of the white man lions served a useful purpose, as they served to keep the deer within the bounds of their food supply and hence saved the forests. But now man, the greatest predator of them all, has taken over the work of the lion. Lion and man compete at every turn.

Many sentimentalists claim lions are necessary in that they tend to kill the aged and diseased members of the deer herds. This, I think, is nonsense, as nearly all the lion kills I have seen have been young and vigorous animals. Indeed, like man, the lions kill mostly bucks, as bucks are usually in better condition than does.

Lions are not easy animals to exterminate. No successful scent bait has ever been worked out for them, as they prefer to kill their own meat. Few are ever trapped. They can be taken by only one means—a well-trained and skillful pack of dogs. But state and federal hunters and private individuals working under the bounty system are slowly killing them off. It may be a century or two before they are extinct, but eventually they must go. It is written. They compete with man at every turn and in doing so they have signed their own death warrant.

I for one will not regret their passing—if I am still alive when that happens. Each lion killed means at least five hundred more deer for the sportsmen of America, so surely each death should be celebrated and the hunter of lions should have an honorable place among sportsmen.

CHAPTER XVIII

THE COYOTE: DESERT RACKETEER

A HUNDRED years ago, when Americans first began to invade the Southwest, anyone who predicted the coyote would one day be the most serious enemy of the game would have been laughed at. The great, swift prairie and timber wolves would probably have been voted Public Enemy No. 1. After them in close order would be the mountain lion and the grizzly bear.

Surely the coyote would not be taken seriously. He was then a furtive, harmless creature which lived solely on the plains and deserts. He ate rodents and even grasshoppers, and his most ambitious prey was the jackrabbit.

Yet the lowly coyote, the mangy joke animal of Mark Twain and other pioneer humorists, has survived and multiplied. He has the true instinct of a racketeer, and he is the only American predator that has prospered and extended its range since the coming of the white man. A hundred years ago he was found only west of the Mississippi, where he shared the prairie and desert with the great light-gray buffalo wolf, and lived mostly on the smallest of creatures with an occasional bit of carrion. Now the wolf is almost extinct, the mountain lions are going, and not a single grizzly bear remains over wide areas. On the other hand, the coyote has crossed the Mississippi and invaded the East. He is found from Mexico to the edge of the Arctic Circle and from sea-level desert to timberline. In many places he scorns his erstwhile diet of rodents and grasshoppers and feasts like an epicure on deer, antelope and turkey.

Every now and then I read that the coyote is being persecuted and may become extinct. Such stuff is nonsense. Thus far in the war between man and this little fellow, the tide has mostly gone against the human beings. Coyotes raid the melon patches of the farmer, kill the lambs of the sheepmen, destroy the game of the sportsmen, dodge the bullets of the riflemen, and spurn the lures of the trapper. In this never-ending battle there are casualties, of course, but there are in any war. While coyotes are being killed off in one section, they are increasing in another; and as far as I can tell there are as many or more of them as there ever were out here in my native Arizona.

Don Coyote's most faithful defenders are the "balance-of-nature" boys, who say these jolly little animals go about like Pollyannas eating destructive rodents and killing the aged and diseased members of the game herds. They declare they never do any harm. Such nonsense is sickening. True, in many sections the coyote is an asset. In a strictly desert country where there is little big game, the animals serve to keep the rodents in control and thereby probably pay for the quail they destroy.

In the forested areas, however, it is a different matter. In such areas there is little natural coyote food. Prairie dogs and packrats are seldom found there, rabbits are scarce and squirrels far too agile. Once in the woods, the coyote must either turn game-killer or starve.

Oldtimers tell me that fifty years ago very few coyotes were found on the big-game ranges. Now it is another case of man's destroying the balance of nature. Coyotes followed flocks of sheep into the higher elevations and stayed to prey on mule and whitetail deer, on turkeys, and on the young of elk and antelope. Ten deer are killed by coyotes for every one killed by man, and if left unchecked coyotes will exterminate wild turkeys. In our national forests the coyote is a villain with not a single redeeming feature. If he were exterminated over the entire timbered area of the Southwest I for one would not shed a single tear. But the coyote is too smart to be exterminated anywhere. All we can do is to trap him and shoot him and thereby keep his numbers down and save the game.

Many writers have described the coyote as a mean and mangy-looking creature always on the verge of starvation. On the contrary, the coyote is usually sleek and fat, and in the higher elevations where winters are long and cold his thick glossy coat is a thing of beauty. If a thin coyote is taken it means either that he is a very old animal or that there is nothing left to eat in the country. If there is something edible, he will find it. Snow may be deep, turkeys and deer may be so weak they can hardly run, but the coyote is always in the pink of condition.

A coyote is almost as omnivorous as a raccoon. His first preference is good fat game, but if he can't get that he will eat rodents, lizards, birds' eggs, fruit and melons, juniper and manzanita berries —even carrion. It has been proved time and time again that on a range covered with dead cattle and well stocked with prairie dogs and rabbits he will kill game in preference.

Many subspecies of coyotes range through the Southwest, and there is considerable variation in the same species. I have seen coyotes almost as dark as timber wolves and I have seen them almost white. I have also seen three coyotes in widely separated areas—one in the Kaibab, one in the pine woods near Flagstaff, Arizona, and one near Phoenix—that were almost as red as red foxes. Unfortunately I was unable to kill any of the three. As a general rule, though, the desert animals are smaller and lighter than those which live in the mountains.

I have never weighed a coyote, so what information I have as to their size is necessarily second-hand. I have been told that a few mountain coyotes may weigh as much as forty-five pounds, though the ones I have killed appeared to me to go not much over thirty. With the hide off, the carcass of even the largest coyote is surprisingly small—often appearing not much bigger than that of one of the large Western jackrabbits.

But what the coyote lacks in size he makes up in intelligence and teamwork. Alone he cannot hope to kill a big mule deer, but in a pack he hunts the larger game animals skillfully and ruthlessly. I remember seeing one such hunt. A couple of years ago I went out into the woods on snowshoes with a rifle. The winter had been long and severe, and even in the cedars, where the deer were wintering, the snow was two feet deep—and crusted. I had not gone far before I saw what was left of a doe that had been killed by coyotes. Sign of the wolves was abundant. Coming toward me I heard the crash of brush and saw a big buck with a magnificent set of antlers running through the snow. At each bound he sank through the crust. As he came closer I could tell he was about done. His legs were badly cut from the crust and he was staggering with fatigue. I stepped behind a tree and waited for a few seconds before the coyotes came into view, running swiftly and uttering little yelps of excitement. Then I cut loose. My first shot went just under the leader, which jumped into the air about three feet and streaked over the crust in full retreat. My second shot broke his back and my third killed one of his mates. I only wish I could have got the others in the pack. The only other opportunity I had was at one sneaking through low thick cedars. I missed. The buck ran up a little ridge and stopped not more than a hundred yards from where I stood. He was thin and gaunt from a hard winter and much running by coyotes. I only hope he got through until the thaw.

One spring in the Kaibab I saw a sight that brought tears to my eyes. A couple of coyotes had hunted out a hidden fawn and killed it just before its last panic-stricken bleat summoned its mother. And there she was—a picture of blind infuriated mother-love—trying to keep the coyotes from feasting on the body of her babe. (I saw no sign of a second fawn. Mule deer always have twins, so the coyotes had probably got that one, too.) The coyotes were obviously enjoying their game. The doe would drive the coyotes away from the body of the fawn, striking out viciously with her front feet. Then, while one engaged her attention, the other would sneak up behind her and nip her legs, seemingly with no intention of hamstringing her. As she turned to defend herself the first would start to devour the fawn. After I watched for a moment I rushed out shouting and waving my hat. Both coyotes and the doe fled, but the doe did not go far and returned soon to her dead fawn. I left her alone with her grief.

Coyotes readily adapt themselves to every kind of country, from open plains to the thick spruce and aspen forests high in the mountains. When food is plentiful they are almost entirely nocturnal in habits, and one is seldom seen except at dawn and dusk when they are foraging. During the day they prefer to lie down for a nap in a patch of brush or weeds or among the rocks of some hillside. Occasionally, even in midday, a hunter will kick one out of its bed and get a shot or two. They are among the noisiest of animals and they can be heard almost any night. Just at dusk they often give a short yipping bark that echoes and re-echoes through the canyons so that a half-dozen coyotes will sound like a hundred to the uninitiated. Like dogs and wolves they seem to be excited by a full moon. Then their cry is a *yip-yi-yao-o-o* that falls off almost to a moan toward the end. But when serious business is on hand they are seldom noisy. They run game silently except for little half-suppressed yelps of excitement.

Villain though he is, the coyote is an excellent spouse and parent. Perhaps that is one of the reasons his tribe increases and prospers. Pairs seem to mate for life, and the male helps the female care for the young, bringing quail, prairie dogs and rabbits to the den.

As a homesite coyotes usually select some natural cave or crevice in rough country. However, they sometimes enlarge the retreat of some burrowing animal or dig their own den. The young are born in March or in April. The litters run from four to eight in size. By midsummer the half-grown animals leave their dens, and by the following fall they are almost as large as they ever get and are successful and dangerous hunters of everything from grasshoppers to deer. I have heard that the parents train their broods by bringing home game still alive, so the little ones can practice killing for themselves even when they are so small they cannot run game down.

In spite of his reputation as a speedster, the coyote is not a particularly fast animal. His top speed is just about that of a jackrabbit—thirty-five miles an hour. He has an advantage over the big hares, however, in that he is more enduring; and if he really wants a meal of rabbit-meat he can usually get it. But coyotes hate to use brawn when they can substitute brains. They usually hunt rabbits in pairs.

One turns the rabbit, while the other lies in wait. Then they share their feast.

Several times I have had opportunities to check the speed of coyotes against the speedometer of an automobile, and in every case I have found that their top speed is slightly over thirty-five miles an hour. I have even chased down and run over coyotes on smooth open plains.

I remember one three-quarters-grown coyote that surely was the fool of his family. I shall tell an incredible tale. I was driving one night just east of Van Horn in Texas when I saw a coyote by the headlights. I grabbed a rifle I had back of the seat and jumped out to shoot. By that time the coyote was out of the light. Deciding he had given me the slip, I started the car again and drove on. Presently I came across the same coyote running as fast as it could straight up the road. I followed, keeping the animal in the glare of the head-lights. For more than a mile the speedometer stayed on thirty-five. Then the coyote began to slow down, from thirty-five to twenty, then to fifteen. Finally it stopped in the middle of the road, completely exhausted. I got out and killed it. That is my story and I'll stick to it.

Because it is almost entirely nocturnal, the coyote is only casually a sporting proposition for the rifleman. I have shot perhaps fifty in my time, and nearly all of them came by pure chance. A couple of times when hunting jackrabbits I have surprised coyotes doing the same thing, and have shot them. I have also had a few shots when I was out after deer and turkey. Most of the animals that have fallen to my rifle I encountered while driving over lonely desert and mountain roads in the early morning and late afternoon. The best sport

I have ever had was in the Navajo country of northern Arizona, where there is little cover and a coyote can be kept in sight for miles. A friend of mine and I spent every Sunday there for several months hunting coyotes. We killed many—some, O miracle of miracles!— at nearly 400 yards. I was using a .270 then, and he a .30–'06. We were both better-than-average shots, yet I imagine every coyote we killed cost us ten dollars in cartridges, gasoline and repairs to the car.

Hunting coyotes with greyhounds is more certain but just as exciting and even more expensive. No coyote has a chance against a pack of wolfhounds. The dogs can run circles around Don Coyote and whip him in a fair fight. Riding some fast sure-footed Western cowhorse behind a pack of fleet rangy "wolfers," going hell-bent over rough country to see the last thrilling finish, is something that has always appealed to me as being about ten times as much fun as a foxhunt, red coats, thoroughbred horses and all! However, a pack of greyhounds is an expensive thing to keep up. I have ambitions along that line, but not the money.

Like all intelligent animals, coyotes are filled with a vast curiosity about the world and its ways. Once when picnicking with my wife and little boy I returned from a walk to find a coyote observing them carefully from behind a bush. He had no designs on them, of course. To him they were simply curious creatures and he was trying to find out their habits. Often this curiosity gets them into difficulties. My wife's first coyote was an inquisitive fellow we met as we drove along a desert road. He trotted along beside our slow-moving car looking us over. He was paying most of his attention to me and my wife was able to shoot him with a .22. He was an old male that had lost one foot in a trap and had at one time been peppered with bird shot. Surely he knew something of man, but he wanted to know more.

Coyotes are highly migratory and for that reason I have always been somewhat skeptical of the numerous subspecies the biologists assign to the race. A coyote nourished on plentiful venison will naturally be a larger animal than one who makes a precarious living hunting packrats, cottontails and jumping mice. One that lives in cold timbered country will naturally grow a longer and thicker coat than a desert dweller.

If food is plentiful, coyotes are on hand. Where a game range becomes pretty well shot out by hunters and hunted hard by lions and coyotes, the little animals desert it. On the other hand, when in time game becomes plentiful, the coyotes return. The migration of the sheep herds from the deserts into the mountains is accompanied by a constant escort of coyotes who prey on stragglers and make quick effective raids into the flocks in spite of everything the herders and the dogs can do. I have no doubt that coyotes follow an easy food supply two or three hundred miles. When the deer in the Kaibab became plentiful they moved into that beautiful forest from all over northern Arizona and Utah. With so much moving about, it seems that local subspecies would not form easily.

The coyote is a picturesque fellow, no doubt of that. The sight of his slinking form and his bushy dragging tail slipping into some desert draw does lend mystery and enchantment to the country. Seeing him is a pleasant experience for the tourist and amateur naturalist.

But on the other hand the coyote is a real and ever-present problem to the sportsman. Admire him for his brains and his ability to adapt himself to changed conditions if you will, the fact remains that he and man are natural enemies. Both are predatory animals and their interests everywhere conflict. If we want enough deer and turkeys to make hunting productive instead of being merely an excuse for an armed walk, then coyotes must be thinned. If we want the antelope to come back in such numbers that they can once more be real game animals over the Southwest instead of rare and picturesque additions to the scenery, again Don Coyote must be shot, trapped and hunted. I for one am heartily tired of protecting antelope only to furnish coyote meat. I am weary of game preserves that become happy hunting grounds for the coyotes.

CHAPTER XIX

RETROSPECT AND SURVEY

SO I bring to a close the portion of the book about the game birds and animals themselves. In it I have tried to include those things about them which the sportsman-naturalist wants to know. I have tried to make it realistic. I hope I have not sounded cold-blooded, for I am not. Sportsmen are romantics, and I am no exception.

It is even yet a common notion throughout America that the days of large and even small game are numbered, that the time must eventually come when even the whitetail deer must join the heath hen, the great auk, the Merriam elk and the passenger pigeon. Men who should know better wail almost monthly in the pages of the general magazines about the passing of wildlife. For the most part the non-sportsman lends a sympathetic if half-hearted ear to these prophets of doom, shakes his head sadly, and then forgets all about it.

But these gloomy fellows do not realize that with few exceptions the game animals of America are on the increase, and that in many places they are probably more numerous than they were under wilderness conditions. What of the Pennsylvania and Michigan whitetail herds? What of the mule deer in the Kaibab and in certain localities in New Mexico? What of the tremendous numbers of deer both in Texas and California, and of the reports which show increase in the national forests almost annually? All these point the way to the future.

All that is needed by the game of the Southwest, and by the game of the United States as a whole, is a little realistic understanding—not maudlin sentimentality, but understanding. Game, after all, is a crop. Like domestic animals, game needs food, cover, and protection from its natural enemies. When it has those things it will increase astonishingly. We can have all the deer we really want, all the elk, all the antelope, all the bighorns, all the bear. Further, we can have them without much trouble. When, under good conditions at almost no expense, a herd of 100 antelope increases to 5,000 in a decade, I don't think we need to worry about the antelope becoming extinct. When 40 elk become 4,000 in a little over twenty years as they did on Arizona's Mogollon Rim, it seems to me that our mourning has been premature.

But we cannot pass laws to protect game and then sit back satisfied, our duty done. An unenforced law has yet to save a species. Legislators passed laws "protecting" the passenger pigeon and the buffalo, but they have made no attempt to enforce them. The same holds true with the bighorn sheep of the Southwest. The laws protecting them have only served to make every sheep range a preserve for the prospector, the Indian and the meat-hunter. Even yet, however, the sheep of the deserts can be saved, and there are encouraging signs that they will be saved.

And those who save the game will be in the future as in the past the intelligent, unsentimental, well-informed sportsmen of America, the men who can see that game is primarily a crop, romantic and interesting though it may be. It is a crop to be harvested by shotgun and rifle instead of scythe and mowing machine. Exactly the same principles apply to game management as apply to cattle raising, with the exception that game is usually hardier and easier to raise under natural conditions.

The rancher who would get the legislature to pass a law protecting his herd and then go off and leave it, expecting it to have increased and multiplied when he came back, would be considered insane. So would the man who tried to keep a thousand cattle in an area that showed it could support but two hundred. So would the rancher who, though he had but one hundred cattle and wanted more, would refuse to kill off his barren cows and his aged impotent bulls. Yet in our fumbling efforts at political game management we have done all these things. I am convinced that in Arizona foolish laws and hidebound sentimentalists have killed more game in the last twenty years than all the sportsmen combined. But we are learning, and I face the future with optimism, certain that for the most part the game of the Southwest has gone through its dark days and is on the increase. The Southwest was once one of the great game sections of the continent. It is good game country now and it is getting better.

CHAPTER XIX

RETROSPECT AND SURVEY

Part II, An Update (1977)

I N the original edition of *Game in the Desert*, Chapter XIX (this one) was full of sweetness and light. It seems to me now to be full of stilted writing and trite and windy observation. I have come a long way since 1938. I am, I believe, a good deal more skillful as a writer and I have a more skeptical intelligence. Much of my early stuff, including some of this book, brings me down with chills and fever when I read it over. When I wrote it, I was still learning my craft. My style and (alas!) many of my ideas were derivative. I think individual style for the expository writer consists of writing as much like the way he talks as possible. I have learned to try to write simply and honestly and to keep my ideas uncluttered and my sentence structure simple.

Reading the chapter called "Retrospect and Survey" over has made me take down my sign as a prophet. When I wrote the individual chapters, mostly as articles for *Field & Stream*, the Southwest was thinly populated. Hunting pressure was light. The first fumbling steps in research in game management were being made. The attitude of the hunters in the Southwest had shifted. During the early part of the century they were meat hunters and game hogs. Along in the 1920's they began organizing in an attempt to preserve the game, to administer wise game laws. Once it was accepted practice for one man—if he had the opportunity—to kill deer for four or five companions. Many boasted of having done so. By 1930 this practice was frowned upon. As the result of better law enforcement and possibly better range practice game, particularly deer, began to increase.

Back forty years ago most of us were optimistic. We had seen game come back from scarcity to relative plenty. Many of us had learned that it was possible for game to be too plentiful for its own good. We had seen the Rocky Mountain mule deer in the Kaibab forest north of the Grand Canyon increase to an estimated 100,000, eat their range up and starve by the thousands. We saw the same thing happen on a smaller scale in an antelope herd near Flagstaff. Most of us were still anti-mountain lion. We looked upon the big cats as competitors for *our* deer and not as fine trophies and great sporting animals. We thought that every deer that mountain lions took meant one less buck for Joe Doak, license-buying sportsman. This notion of game management ruled in the Kaibab (or the Grand Canyon National Game Preserve) as, I believe, was its official title. The famous Jack Butler had a fine pack of hounds and hunted lions there. He was so successful that there were not enough of these natural predators to keep deer in check and they just about ate up their environment.

Game in the Desert appeared in 1939, at a time when World War II was waiting in the wings. None of us in the Southwest foresaw that tremendous convulsion. None of us realized the profound effect it would have on the world and on our Southwest.

The war was the beginning of the end of the Southwest I had grown up in. Training camps for tanks and infantry were set up. All of the West was spotted with airfields where bomber and fighter pilots trained. Young men were jerked out of their niches in Eastern cities and set down in the West at Uncle Sam's expense. Many decided to return after the war.

I began to realize early in the war years that the Southwest I had grown up in was finished. By 1945 I knew it. By that time I had worked myself into a full-time position as shooting editor on *Outdoor Life*. I resigned from the faculty of the University of Arizona at the end of the Spring term. When the war became officially over, I was in White-horse, Y.T., getting ready for my first hunt for white sheep. In 1948 I moved my family to Lewiston, Idaho and bought a house overlooking the Snake River. That has been my headquarters ever since.

In 1939 Phoenix had about 50,000 people, Tucson perhaps 35,000. Today the population of metropolitan Phoenix is well over a million and that of Tucson is around 500,000. When I was teaching at the University of Arizona the enrollment was around 3,000. Today, I understand it is over 30,000.

A good friend of mine, a physician who practiced both in Tucson and in Beverly Hills, retired some years ago to a lovely spot near a little Mormon village where he had built a modest summer home. He had chosen the area because, when he bought his little piece of land, he was close to good trout fishing plus elk, mule deer, and wild turkey hunting. Today the whole area swarms with service stations, ham-burger joints, bars, motels, golf courses, and restaurants. If my friend wants to hunt elk or turkey, he must go through a drawing. Now he must even draw for a deer license. In my day of few people, plenty of wide-open country, and plenty of game, that was inconceivable.

In my youth in the Southwest there was no such thing as land posted against hunting. Most cattle ran on land owned by the state of Arizona or by the Federal government. The unreserved land (the Pub-lic Domain) was not fenced. Cattlemen rounded up once a year, sorted out their herds, quarreled (and sometimes shot each other) over grass and water. Hunters were not only welcome to hunt but, if the ranchers saw them, they were usually invited to the midday meal. If I shot a deer in a tough spot, I would go to a ranch and borrow a horse to pack it out. No one ever thought of asking permission to hunt anywhere, on cattle range or on farm land. I never saw a "Posted" sign in Arizona until I returned to Arizona in 1931.

When I was putting *Game in the Desert* together, the population of Arizona was, I believe, something over 100,000. Today it is over 2,000,000. People have moved to Arizona for the wide-open spaces, for the freer life, for pure air and they have worked hard at destroying what they came west to find.

But I must quit shedding tears for the good old days. If this book has any value, it is because it is to some extent a record of the unspoiled Southwest by a young, enthusiastic, but unsophisticated man who loved it.

CHAPTER XX

THE SOUTHWESTERN BATTERY

SPORTING calendars, the horse-operas that come from the Hollywood mill, and magazine illustrations for Western stories almost invariably show the Southwestern armed with a light, short carbine, usually a .30–30 Winchester. Many think the .30–30 the one and only rifle used in the West. It is the most widely distributed, and it is almost universally employed for casual ranch and saddle use. There is at least one .30–30 in almost every ranch house, and down in Sonora the *ranchero* who possesses a *"treinta-treita"* considers himself armed like a king. I have no quarrel with the old reliable "thurty-thuty," as some gun editors call it. It has its advantages. It is cheap, it will stand constant neglect, and ammunition of that caliber may be purchased at any crossroads store. Even in Mexico, where ammunition is scarce and expensive, a peon with a few cartridges can usually be located, and storekeepers, even in remote hamlets, can often dig up a box if you have plenty of pesos to exchange for them.

To give the .30–30 its due, it is a far better cartridge than that ranch favorite of the nineties, the .40–40, and its 170-grain bullet properly placed will kill anything from a big buck mule deer on down. Now, however, the old Model '94 carbines are carried mostly by cowboys, who are only casually hunters, and by those who take a week off every couple of years for a deer hunt and who don't know much difference between rifles or care greatly either. The more serious sportsmen have abandoned them because they have very serious faults, as compared to more modern rifles—high trajectories, poor killing-power except at relatively short range and with very well placed shots, and mediocre accuracy.

More .30–30 cartridges are still sold throughout the Southwest than those in any other caliber, but that is because of the enormous number of ancient '94 carbines still in use. The .30–'06 is the nearest competitor, with the .30–40 Krag coming next. As far as new rifles go, far more are sold in .30–'06 than in any other caliber. The popularity of the .30–40 is explained by the great number of converted army Krags which were procured cheaply from the government, and also by the fact that it is a good cartridge.

Yet the crack big-game hunters of the Southwest have in recent years gone more and more into high velocity, flat trajectory, and great accuracy in their rifles, as these are the qualities in a rifle and cartridge which the Southwestern hunter needs. Shots are mostly long. Often they can be fairly deliberate. The hunter in the thick Eastern woods nearly always kills his whitetail buck at less than 100 yards. Out West, the average shot is around 200 yards, and if you can connect at 300 or even 400, you'll get plenty of opportunities. In the thickly wooded East, the typical shot at deer is a quick snap at a vanishing flag, often at under 50 yards; but in the West most game is hunted in relatively open country, often broken by hills and deep canyons. No two styles of rifle-shooting could be more different than those practiced in the two sections. In the East, speed of fire is all-important and accuracy and flat trajectory are secondary. In the West, accuracy and flat trajectory come first, and speed of fire is a secondary consideration. In the brush and timber, nearly all shots must necessarily be taken offhand; but in mountains or canyons, the

en a good friend of mine.
addicted to the .30–30.
he was still too stubborn
m he was swearing by a
he perfect rifle. But now
ighted .270 Winchester,
or coyotes. His evolution
esterners who take big-

g-game hunters demand
h velocity so that their
nized and they will not
game. They want high
a relatively long, sharp-
hat velocity and which
here the game is. They
velocity but which are
ortion to expand reliably
ccuracy, all the accuracy
ullet acts when it lands
accurate to get there. A
minimum for the West-

e the best cartridges for
West? I'll list them in
hester, the .30–'06, the
the .250–300 and the
ous special hand-loaded

ng himself.
essive shots
f game, but
e consistent
il are more
o-yard shot
quence, the
West needs
ge from the
ests.
ers choose?
outhwestern
m thirty to
n big-game
tween them
every vari-
e older ones
wder pump-
the calibers
two in .300
and one in
-actions and
lever-action
to that type
'06's are old
operated, of
to knock the

The oldest hunter of the ten has long be
When I first knew him, years ago, he was
Then he bought himself a .300 Savage, as
to use a bolt-action. The next time I saw h
7 mm. Mauser and claimed he had found t
he does almost all his hunting with a 'scope-
and he is thinking of buying a .220 Swift fe
has been the same as that of most Southw
game hunting seriously.

What qualities, then, do these expert bi
in the cartridges they use? They want hig
mistakes in estimating range will be mini
have to allow so much for lead on running
velocity, too, for shocking power. They wan
pointed "spitzer" bullet which will keep
will deliver that shock 'way out yonder w
want bullets which will not only retain
lightly enough constructed in the forward p
at long range. And beyond that they want a
that can be had. No matter how well the l
on game at 350 to 400 yards, it has to be
velocity of 2,700 feet per second is about the
ern rifle; 3,000 and more is better.

What, then, has experience proved to l
the medium-sized, lightly built game of th
the order of their excellence: the .270 Win
7 mm., the .257 Roberts, the .300 Savage
.30–40 Krag. In addition, there are nume

cartridges which are excellent except that ammunition is hard to obtain. Among them, the .276 and .280 Dubliel should be ideal. The .256 Newton is good, but no factory rifle is made for it, and as a consequence the cartridge is becoming obsolete. I have heard many excellent reports on the .220 Swift, but most hunters remain skeptical of its tiny bullet. The .300 Magnum may come into popularity as a long-range hunting rifle, but just now the fact that the ammunition is not so generally stocked as that of the other calibers, together with the hearty recoil, has dissuaded a good many Westerners.

I have owned and used every one of the calibers I have listed in the preferred class except the .300 Savage, with which I have seen considerable game killed. Of all of them the .270 Winchester is easily the best. With the 130-grain Winchester load, it is the most accurate and deadly rifle I have ever turned on game. That Winchester bullet expands most reliably. It has a sectional density almost equal to the 180-grain .30-caliber bullet and a beautifully shaped spitzer point. As a consequence, it shoots flat and sustains well its high muzzle-velocity of 3,160 feet per second. I have killed mule deer, whitetails and antelope with the .270, one of the deer being, I believe, the first to fall to the cartridge in the entire Southwest. I haven't tried out the new .270 Winchester loads with the 100-grain bullets which travel at 3,520 feet per second—a speed which almost puts the .270 into the .220 Swift class—but I see no reason why they shouldn't prove first-rate on lighter game such as small whitetails, Columbian blacktails and antelope. However, I'd hate to bang into the rear end of a bighorn ram or a big buck mule deer with one, as I'd be afraid of too much expansion and not enough penetration.

With the 150-grain bullets at 3,000 feet per second, the old reliable .30–'06 is second only to the .270 on Western game, and no man who chooses a rifle in that caliber is making a mistake. I have owned four rifles in .30–'06, and the one I have now has accounted for seven mule deer, twenty-two whitetails, five antelope, two big-horns and four javelinas, in my hands and in the hands of friends. Only two animals hit have got away. But after experimenting with other bullets in previous rifles I have stuck to the 150-grain loads at 3,000 feet. Use the 180-grain loads if you must, but by all means avoid the slower 190-, 200- and 220-grain bullets for anything except brush-country use. The .30–'06 will serve for everything from woodchucks to elk, but it must be used with suitable bullets.

For several reasons the 7 mm. Mauser is a favorite among the do-or-die head-hunters of the Southwest. In the first place, with the 139-grain bullet at about 2,800 feet per second in a 24-inch barrel, it is a most excellent cartridge. In the second place, it lacks the recoil of the .270 and the .30–'06 and does the work almost as well. In addition, there is an interesting historical reason for the popularity of the 7 mm. It is the Mexican army cartridge, and hundreds of 7 mm. rifles were left in the hands of Southwesterners by fugitive Mexican soldiers who fled across the border during the various revolutions. Sportsmen tried them out, liked them, and the popularity of the caliber has increased ever since the high-speed 139-grain loads came out. Some authorities have declared the 7 mm. relatively inaccurate with the 139-grain bullets. I must disagree, as my own fine 'scope-sighted Mauser is as accurate as any Springfield I have ever owned, and in addition it is a very pleasant rifle to shoot. Of the various high-speed loads, I like the Western best, as the bullet is better shaped to sustain velocity and it expands more reliably in game. For the woman, for the small man—for anyone sensitive to recoil yet wanting a relatively powerful rifle with a good choice of bullet weights—the 7 mm. is a fine choice.

These three cartridges—the .270, the .30–'06, and the 7 mm.—are the leaders. The .257 Roberts is also good, but it could stand a bit more bullet weight and its bullets also need sharper points to sustain velocity. Of the three bullets made for the caliber in 87-, 100- and 117-grain weight, the 100-grain seems to be the best for animals of the deer class. They travel at around 3,000 feet per second, and rifles in that caliber have very light recoil.

The .300 Savage is a good cartridge, no doubt of it, and for the man who loves the lever-action it is practically the only choice for Western hunting, as the fairly sharp 150-grain bullet sustains its velocity better than its only rival, the .348 Winchester of the same weight. The .30–'06 in the Model '95 Winchester lever-action is now no longer made. The .30–40 in the Krag or in the Model '95 has killed thousands of heads of Western game, but it is a bit shy on velocity to be among the leaders. The little .250–3,000 has many devotees among real hunters, but though it has the speed, it in turn lacks bullet weight, and is somewhat less effective than the .257. Up to around 225 yards it will kill very dead, but beyond that it has often failed.

The .300 Magnum, now that a rifle to shoot it is made commercially in this country, should be a most excellent Southwestern rifle. However, the Winchester Model 70 in that caliber is made only with the 26-inch barrel, and as the .300 kicks like a mule and bellows like a bull, cutting that 26-inch barrel off much is not to be advised. The .300 is really a sort of a super .30–'06, and it ought to extend the range of that cartridge by a full 100 yards. *But*—and this is something to consider—very few sportsmen can use the full range and accuracy of the .30–'06. If a man can't, it is futile for him to go to the .300.

The .35 Whelen is an excellent choice for the man who wants but one rifle for all Western game from antelope to elk and grizzlies. With the 275-grain bullet, it is almost equal to the .375 Magnum for really big game. With the 250-grain .35 Newton bullet at 2,750 it has the ballistics of the 180-grain .30–'06 with far more power, and can be used on anything on the continent. One of the most spectacularly deadly loads for medium game I have ever seen in my life is the 250-grain Winchester soft-point as loaded into the .35 Whelen case at 2,750 feet per second. The 220-grain Western Tool and Copper Co. bullet can be boosted to above 2,800 in the .35 Whelen. That is a load of high velocity, flat trajectory and terrific power, about as good a heavy long-range load as I know of. I own a .35 Whelen with a fairly heavy 24-inch barrel. It is astonishingly accurate with anything I put in it. Furthermore, it will throw bullets of the three weights almost into the same hole at 100 yards. Perhaps I sound enthusiastic about the .35 Whelen. I am. It is a bit severe for most Southwestern shooting, but for the man who wants to own but one rifle for everything I cannot think of a better.

The ideal mountain and open-country rifle to be used on light and medium game is as specialized as the cartridges it is built to fire, but before I describe it, let's consider what the foreign mountaineers use. The chamois hunters of the Alps seem to prefer light, very short Mannlichers in calibers like the .256. On the other hand, the English who seek the wild sheep of the Indian frontier choose long-barreled rifles in heavier calibers. Both are right. The alpine chamois hunter carries his own weapon and hunts an animal about the size of a domestic goat. The Anglo-Indian, on the other hand, has a gun-bearer to do the carrying for him, and so the weight of his weapon makes but little difference.

What the American mountaineer needs is a compromise. If he had a caddy to carry his rifle, the weight and the length of barrel would make but little difference. Since he hasn't, he ought to choose a rifle which weighs between 7½ and 8 pounds and which has a barrel between 22 and 24 inches in length. Barrels shorter than 22 inches in the .270 and the .30–'06 lead to loud report and unpleasant muzzle-blast. Longer barrels simply get in the way. But remember —every inch you cut off the barrel reduces the velocity about 25 feet per second.

Yet short barrels are handier in very rough country, no doubt of that! When you're high in the crags for sheep, for example, you'll often find it necessary to strap your rifle to your back so both hands will be free to aid you in climbing. When you do, you'll curse every inch of superfluous barrel length, as the barrel catching on a rock you haven't seen may unbalance you and threaten to send you tumbling a couple of hundred feet down a cliff. The chamois hunters of the Alps don't carry short barrels without reason. Then, too, any man who does much hunting in the West will spend considerable time on a horse with his rifle in a scabbard, and he'll find that the shorter weapons are handier, easier to put in and take out, less liable to catch on brush. So never have a rifle with a barrel longer than 24 inches; a length of 22 is handy but a bit noisier in the heavier calibers; with a rifle in .250–3,000, .257 or even 7 mm. you may well cut the barrel down to 20 or 21 inches, but at the loss of about 100 feet per second in velocity.

If you can afford it, a telescope sight is ideal for mountain hunting, as no other sight shows up the game so clearly or enables the hunter to take full advantage of the flat trajectory and wonderful accuracy of the modern high-intensity cartridges we have been discussing. For hunting on horseback and for everything except the very roughest country, the 'scope should be mounted right down on the receiver, but little higher than iron sights, and left on all the time. If you are extra cautious and fear some possible injury to the 'scope, you can carry the slide of the receiver sight under the trap of the buttplate in case you meet with an accident. However, I think it is better simply to forget iron sights in most cases. Keep a spare rifle in camp, if you want to, but don't switch from iron to glass and back again.

Any man who hunts much on horseback has to make up his mind if he is really going to use his 'scope or simply carry it around. If he is, he must leave that 'scope on his rifle when it is in the scabbard. If he tries to carry the 'scope in a case at his belt and then attach it when he jumps game, he isn't going to use it much. If you don't believe me, try putting on your 'scope sometime while a big buck races up the side of a canyon 250 yards away. Get a good 'scope mounted low in strong mounts, *and then leave it on the rifle*. I'll admit that your horse may fall down sometime, but that happens rarely, and when you strike country where an accident might occur, get off, take your rifle out of the scabbard, and lead your horse.

The low Neidner mounts and any of the small German 'scopes are good for the Western horseback hunter. Perhaps the Redfield and Stith mounts, which are of the bridge type, are even better, as they lend the 'scope more support against strains. Mounts with big windage knobs ought to be avoided, as they are apt to turn when the rifle is being put in the scabbard and taken out. For my own horse-back hunting, I use a Noske 'scope on Noske mounts. I've ridden over some tough country in Arizona and Sonora with it and have never had trouble with its coming out of adjustment.

Carrying a 'scope-sighted rifle successfully on a horse calls for a special scabbard. Get one made to fit your rifle with the 'scope attached. Have it tight enough to support it, yet loose enough so that it will never bind coming in or going out. Have it big enough to come up well over the comb and protect both 'scope and action from rain and snow. Then carry the rifle top side up, with the butt to the rear at an angle of about 45 degrees. When you have the scabbard made, a couple of dollars extra invested in a piece to slip over the butt will convert it into a carrying case as well.

No mountain rifle should be without a light gun sling of the Whelen type for both shooting and carrying. With such a sling, a man can carry a relatively heavy rifle all day and not mind it. He can strap his rifle to his back to leave both hands free. By using the so-called "hasty sling adjustment" he can hold more steadily for that long shot across the canyon.

The rifle I have described will do excellently for 90 per cent of all Western hunting. For antelope, a man might well use higher powered 'scopes and heavier barrels, perhaps, and for the occasional brush hunting which is apt to be encountered anywhere, he might well carry a box of heavier round-nosed bullets, such as the 220-grain soft-point in the .30–'06 and the 175-grain for the 7 mm.

But what of the other 10 per cent of mountain hunting—going after bighorn sheep and the deer that are sometimes found in very rough country? For one thing, the sheep hunter must use his rifle a great deal as an alpenstock as he climbs. He cannot avoid bumping it against rocks, and as he may slip at any time, he may have to drop it to save himself. As a consequence, it has always seemed to me that carrying a rifle with the 'scope attached into sheep country is a far riskier business than carrying one in a saddle scabbard. For this reason, it seems wise to equip the sheep rifle with a receiver sight and a 'scope on mounts that clear it. Then the hunter can use his iron sights on the occasional short shots that present themselves even in sheep hunting and put the 'scope on for the long ones. Another reason why the 'scope should be left off the rifle in very rough country is that the 'scope comes at the point of balance, where the hand naturally grasps the rifle to carry it. When a man needs both hands free to keep from falling a few hundred feet and often has to carry his weapon across his back with the sling over his chest, the 'scope had better remain in a case at the belt.

Several times I have taken some very nice tumbles while sheep hunting—tumbles which would possibly have meant the ruin of an expensive glass sight if it had been left on the rifle. But since it hadn't, the only damage was a few dents in the stock and some scratches on the blueing. I remember seeing a friend of mine skating a couple of hundred feet down a rock slide with his rifle in the air in an effort to protect the 'scope. He did protect it, but at the cost of the seat of his trousers and many bruises.

When a man who hunts the mountains and plains has selected his rifle and cartridge, he should take pains to target his weapon most carefully. Without exception, he should sight it in for the longest possible range. If he picks the .270, for example, he can sight it in to strike the point of aim at 250 yards. In that case the bullet will go but 2½ inches high at 140 yards and 4 inches low at 300. At a range of 400 yards, the bullet will strike within the vital chest cavity if aim is taken on the backbone of the animal. The .270 might well be sighted in even for 300 yards, as in that case the bullet will strike only about 5 inches high midway. The .30–'06 and the 7 mm. should be sighted in for from 200 to 225 yards, as they don't quite have the range of the .270.

Anyone who hunts the plains and mountains of the West, will find the conditions he faces very different from those of the heavily wooded East, and he'll also find that he can do much better if he has the proper cartridge, the proper rifle and the proper sights. So if you get a rifle for Western hunting, don't put it away. Shoot it occasionally throughout the year, and when that big buck or big ram jumps up across the canyon, you'll find that if you can do your part, your rifle will do the rest.

Selecting a suitable rifle for Southwestern hunting may well prove difficult for the Easterner, but the shotgun is more or less a matter of choice. I'll not go into the respective merits of 12- and 20-gauge weapons here, as that constitutes an ancient argument. I use a light 20 for most of my shooting, largely because I am used to one. For the hunter of desert quail the shotgun should be light— light enough so that it may be carried many miles with as little fatigue as possible, light enough so that it will come up to cover an unexpected flush of which you have no dog to warn you. This same light gun, be it a 12, a 16 or a 20, also serves excellently for decoy shooting on ducks or for water-hole shooting on doves or whitewings. However, when it comes to flight shooting, where shots of fifty yards must be taken, the 20 is better left behind. The medicine then is a full-choked 12. I own one, and I am convinced that it will reach out a full 10 yards farther than my favorite 20.

If I were making a Southwestern hunting trip, then, I'd bring along a fairly light, bolt-action rifle with a good telescope sight in some such caliber as .30–'06, .270 or 7 mm., a light shotgun, and either a .22 pistol for rabbits (if you can use it) or a light .22 rifle. As I write this, I have just read that one of the big arms companies is shortly to put on the market a weapon which can be either a single-shot .30–30 rifle or a 20-gauge shotgun with the interchange of barrels. Such a gun would be a happy combination for a Mexican or Southwestern trip—a spare rifle and a light shotgun for camp meat —all at small cost.

CHAPTER XX

THE SOUTHWESTERN BATTERY

Part II, An Update (1977)

The first article I ever sold to an outdoor magazine (as a matter of fact, it was the first article I ever wrote) was called "Rifles and Cartridges for Southwestern Game". It appeared in *Sports Afield*. That piece came out a long time ago, but my opinions today have not changed much in spite of the fact that in the intervening years I have accumulated vastly more hunting experience not only in North America but on other continents. The reason my opinions have changed little is that the game animals are still the same and are hunted under much the same conditions. In reality changes in rifles and cartridges are minor. A cartridge that was a good one forty years ago is still suitable today.

But there *have* been changes. In 1938 probably more .30/30 rifles were carried afield than rifles of any other caliber. Today over most of the West the .30/30 has slipped in both rifle and cartridge sales. Probably the .30/06, which was popular in the 1930's, is even more popular today. I would guess that more .30/06 rifles are taken out each fall than anything else. In 1938 the .270 was just beginning to show up in fair numbers among Southwestern hunters. Today it is one of the most widely used cartridges. I may have had something to do with the popularity of the cartridge because I used it widely on a variety of animals from javelinas and coyotes to moose and grizzly bears and wrote about my experiences in the pages of *Outdoor Life* with considerable enthusiasm.

When asked what the most popular cartridges were among Arizona hunters, a gun writer who had moved to Arizona about the time I fled to Idaho answered that the two most used were the .30/30 because it could be had in the shape of a light, flat carbine ideal for saddle use and the .270 because there had formerly lived in the state a blow-hard and phony who had led his fellow Arizonians down the primrose path by his praise of a completely inadequate cartridge. This man said the .270 was a "fair" cartridge for whitetail deer, goats, and sheep, but that it was entirely inadequate for mule deer, black bear, and elk. I thought this passing strange, since a Rocky Mountain white goat bears the reputation of being a pretty tough animal and since the average big northern ram is generally heavier than the run-of-the-mill mule deer. I wrote this man and asked him just where he had done his sheep and goat hunting. He told me that he had shot dozens of each species in Saskatchewan and Manitoba. This struck me as being odd indeed because neither province has wild sheep or goats.

In the middle 1930's the .300 Savage cartridge in the Model 99 Savage was exceedingly popular. It is much less so today, as its place in the Model 99 line has been taken by the .308 Winchester. The .308 is, I understand, widely used not only in bolt actions, but in such rifles as the Browning lever action and the Remington Model 742 automatic and Model 760 pump. Newcomers that have won their place in the Southwest are the .243 Winchester and the 6 mm. Remington, both of which I consider entirely adequate for deer, sheep, black bear, and antelope. The use of the two 6 mms. is prohibited on elk. Nuttier gun nuts among Southeastern hunters are going more and more to the 7 mm. Remington Magnum, a fine cartridge but one which is a bit formidable for Southwestern use.

In the 1930's telescope sights in the game fields were a rarity. Today most big game rifles are equipped with them. Since most Southwestern game is shot at fairly long range, I think a 4-x is about right. For Arizona whitetail or antelope, a 6-x scope would be very useful. The variable power scopes are very popular but such scopes are heavier, more complicated, and at any one power not quite the equal of the fixed power scope. My pick would be a bolt-action rifle to weigh no more than eight pounds with scope and sling, with a 22-inch barrel and 4-x scope with crosswire reticule. For all around use in the Southwest the .270 is hard to beat!

CHAPTER XXI

HINTS ON CAMPING AND TRAVEL

SOME of those who have read this book may feel the urge to hunt in the Southwest, to try their skill on its birds and big game. Accordingly this chapter will make some suggestions as to how to go about it. If one happens to be a wealthy man who can engage guides and outfitters and leave the details to them, his problem is simple. On the other hand, the man who wants to hunt in the Southwest may be a person of moderate means, with more time than money. In that case he must choose his own country, select his own equipment.

State game departments are eager for the extra revenue from out-of-state licenses; and they are always very helpful, and glad to give advice as to localities and to recommend local ranchers who are willing to earn a few extra dollars by acting as guides. Letters to the supervisors of the various national forests can bring much usable but relatively general information. Once in the Southwest, the visitor will find that the local sportsmen are for the most part a hospitable race. Nearly all of them have the notion that there is game enough for everyone, and the most casual acquaintance will direct you to good local hunting country. Hunting, too, is almost entirely on national forest land and on the public domain.

Here are a few general hints. If you want mule deer alone, the Kaibab Forest in northern Arizona is by far the best bet. The deer there are plentiful and have the best heads in the section. For a combination of mule deer and turkey, the mountainous area of Arizona from Williams east to the New Mexico border is good. So are the mountains of central and northern New Mexico. In the chapter on elk, I have very definitely located the herds of those animals. Bears and lions are dog-and-horse propositions and a guide is always necessary. A letter to either the state game departments or the forest offices will bring good accurate information about ranchers with dogs.

Quail and doves are found all over the lower elevations of both Arizona and New Mexico, and a winter visitor who likes to shoot birds can find good hunting close to the larger cities such as Albuquerque, El Paso, Phoenix and Tucson. In addition, although the deer and bird seasons no longer overlap, the man who spends the fall in Phoenix can shoot desert mule deer, and if he stays in Tucson he can find the interesting little Arizona whitetails. If he doesn't care to camp out, he can drive out, hunt, and return that same evening to a luxurious hotel.

Hunting in Mexico is far more complicated. The government of Mexico is a federal bureaucracy with many different departments and many regulations. Crossing the border legally requires a sheaf of papers an inch thick which it usually takes two days to collect. Coming out is almost as complicated. Further, the regulations change so fast that they are usually out-dated by the time they find publication in the United States. I won't waste time here telling prospective Mexican hunters how to go in. I make several trips into Sonora annually and every time I run into different regulations and strange and wonderful interpretations of old ones.

However, I'll give a few directions as to the game country. Whitetail deer are found literally all over Mexico, often surprisingly close to large towns, from the highest peaks of the Sierra

Madres to the lowest, hottest coastal deserts. Lions are found wherever there are deer, and they are usually more plentiful than they are in the United States, because few Mexicans own good hounds and they are seldom hunted. Tigres are wide rangers and may occasionally turn up anywhere, but the man who has his heart set on one has to go about 200 miles south of the border. The country along the Rio Yaqui at the foot of the Sierras is good. It also contains lions, ocelots, worlds of whitetail deer, doves, whitewings and masked bob-white quail, with some Mearn's and Benson quail at higher elevations.

Mule deer are found in the lower elevations in all the border states—Sonora, Chihuahua and Coahuila, but the country along the Sonora coast produces the best heads. At the present time, bighorn sheep and antelope can be taken only on special permits. There are antelope in scattered bunches all along the border, but the sheep are found only in western Sonora, as the Mexican bighorn (*Ovis mexicanus*) has become extinct in the foothills of the Sierras and exists only in New Mexico. Sonora sheep and antelope are found roughly in the same area—a strip of country bounded by the American border to the north, Hermosillo to the south, the Gulf of California to the west, and the railroads to the east. This whole section is a fine mixed-game country away from the larger towns, with the exception that quail are surprisingly scarce because of the great numbers of smaller predators. In one day I have several times seen mule and whitetail deer, sheep, javelinas and antelope out of one camp and within a few miles.

The hunter who goes to Mexico always needs a guide and outfitter of some sort unless he speaks Spanish and knows the country himself. However, a good many of the guides are pretty shady individuals, and the man planning a Mexican trip should always demand references from sportsmen and from banks. Mexico is a great hunting country. Its only disadvantages are the complicated regulations and the fact that nearly all Mexicans think Americans rich and crazy.

CLOTHES AND EQUIPMENT

Even in the high mountains of the Southwest, the hunting seasons come before winter weather really sets in, and as a consequence the hunter does not need to be dressed like an arctic explorer. Nights, even at the beginning of the seasons, are nippy and go below freezing, but days are warm and pleasant.

Here is how I ordinarily dress for deer and turkey hunting on foot at altitudes of around 7,000 feet: light underwear, khaki cotton trousers, wool socks, Munson army-last shoes, light slip-over sweater, wool shirt. If I go out on horseback I usually add a leather windbreaker. Later in the season, when the days and nights are colder, I put on long, light wool underwear. That is as much as I ever wear, and I have hunted in zero weather in that outfit. More clothes, I find, simply make the hunter awkward and keep him no warmer. I usually wear a hat of the ten-gallon cowboy variety. It keeps the sun out of my eyes and the snow and rain from going down my neck. It also shields my face and eyes from branches when I'm out on a horse.

The same outfit that I wear for deer and turkey hunting early in the season does well for quail hunting later. On exceptionally warm days I sometimes change from a wool shirt to a cotton one, and on very chilly ones—and there are chilly days even in the desert —I again put on the long underwear.

The man who hunts extensively in the Southwest needs a variety of footgear to match his terrain. In the pine country, I like the Munson army shoe with corrugated composition soles that will not slip on pine needles. Short hobnails also serve the purpose, though they are noisy on rocks. For the flat desert I know of nothing better than a plain shoe with a light leather sole. However, the man who is not used to dodging cactus when hunting quail, had better wear some boot like the Goeke. The ability to watch subconsciously for cholla and other sharp-thorned cactus is acquired from long and painful experience. Nearly all Southwesterners have it, but sportsmen from the East get it only by coming often to grief, so boots are a good idea. The same sort of boot is also handy for horseback hunting. Most natives wear leather chaps, but they are exceedingly clumsy, heavy and noisy for the occasional forays on foot which even the horseback hunter must make. For the man who hunts sheep there is but one type of suitable footwear—a heavy basketball shoe worn with thick wool socks and a heavy leather innersole. With such shoes, one can climb over the desert mountains as sure-footedly as the sheep themselves. With anything else, one is noisy and insecure. I made my first Mexican sheep-hunt wearing the hobnails recommended for Canadian sheep-hunting, and found them noisy and, compared to basketball shoes, slippery. These same shoes, by the way, are satisfactory for still-hunting the big desert mule deer which are often found adjacent to sheep mountains.

For a hunting knife the sportsman should choose a good substantial pocket knife, and he should never be without it. With it he can field-dress his game, bore holes in leather, and remove cholla balls from his anatomy. The absurd toad-stabbers advertised as "hunting knives" look ferocious and delight the heart of the theatrical novice who invades the woods in red cap, heavy mackinaw, high laced boots, riding pants, hunting knife and revolver. But such hunting knives are easily lost; they can do nothing in the field that a pocket knife won't do and nothing in camp that cannot be accomplished with a cheap butcher knife. Furthermore they might easily injure a hunter who happened to fall down on one.

Binoculars are something which are often very handy for the Southwestern big-game hunter, even though he already has a telescope sight on his rifle. Good glasses are often almost worth their weight in gold; poor ones are useless. Anyone planning to acquire a pair should get nothing but the standard makes—Zeiss, Hensoldt, or Bauch & Lomb. There are good French glasses, but mostly they are to be avoided. Many sportsmen recommend the little Mirakel Daylux, which can be carried in the shirt pocket. But for my part, I think the Southwestern hunter should own a good full-sized glass like the new Bauch & Lomb 8 x 30 or 7 x 35, or a good German glass of the same general type. If he is on horseback he can carry his binoculars in saddlebags, and if he hunts sheep or antelope he can let the guide take care of them. A glass which is not A-1 in field, in magnification and in resolving power is simply no good, no matter how portable it is. When a man hunts on foot and alone, he can depend on his rifle 'scope.

In the chapter on the Southwestern battery, I have described the proper sort of saddle scabbard. Every man planning to hunt in the Southwest should have one made. Another gadget of value is a leather cartridge-box to be worn on the belt. Have it made so that a full box of big-game cartridges may be slipped in after the top or outside portion is removed. Such a box is very satisfactory for carrying cartridges. A cartridge belt may make a hunter look rough and tough and Western, but the cartridges carried in one are easily lost and easily damaged. Further, the belt is heavy and clumsy, and in the way. Carrying cartridges loose in the pocket is unsatisfactory. So is the habit of putting a carton in the rear pocket. Such a box can be used for a variety of cartridges as a rule—7 mm., 8 mm., .270, .35 Whelen, .256 Newton—anything based on the .30–'06 case.

A good pair of saddlebags tends to make the life of the Southwestern hunter easier and more pleasant. Mine lace on behind the cantle of the saddle. I had them made in Mexico for ten pesos, and in them I can keep lunch, extra cartridges, a tape measure, camera, filter, film, and so on.

CAMERAS

I am tempted here to say something about cameras—a subject on which I am surely no authority. However, I have long since learned that the only camera worth much to the hunter is the one he can take with him wherever he goes, on foot or on a horse. Big cameras have to be left in camp.

For the man who does his own developing and enlarging, a miniature is the answer. One of my friends, an ardent sportsman, uses a Leica, and with it he has produced some of the finest game and hunting-scene photographs I have ever run across. I have a Contax and a little Welti, both taking 35 mm. motion picture film, of course. With either of them I can shoot three dozen pictures without having to stop every few minutes to change rolls, as one has to do with larger cameras—something which is surely an advantage in the field. The fast lenses, the long rolls, the ease of carrying—all make the miniature a good instrument for the sportsman. However, anyone who hunts on foot and plans to carry a miniature should have a little leather belt case made for it, as the ever-ready cases, no matter how convenient for ordinary use, are an abomination when you are climbing about in the cliffs or even sneaking through the timber. The self-timer on the Contax puts it ahead of the Leica as a sportsman's camera in my estimation, as with it the sportsman can take his picture as he gloats over that big ram or lordly buck he has just shot.

However, the man who has neither the time nor the inclination to do his own photographic work should stay away from the miniature, as few photo-finishers can be depended on to process miniature film with the necessary care. So if the sportsman plans to have the corner drugstore do his work, he should go to a larger film area. The Super Iknota B made by Zeiss is a first-class camera in every way, and its $2\frac{1}{4}$ x $2\frac{1}{4}$ negative area makes it less tricky to handle. One of the most satisfactory field cameras I have ever owned is an Eastman 620 with an f: 4.5 lens and a Compur shutter with a self-timer. It is fairly small, fairly light, and with it I have got many pictures I would have missed with a larger and heavier instrument. It could use more lens speed, however, and one of the many German cameras with 3.5 lens would be even better. The reflex and ground-glass focusing cameras like the National Graflex and the Rolleiflex are out because of their relative bulkiness. They are excellent for camp and for use when photography is the only objective, but for knocking around in the hills when you are already burdened by a rifle with 'scope, a rucksack and a pair of binoculars, they are cumbersome.

I have mentioned heretofore the time I went up into sheep country without the bulky camera I had taken on the trip and got above a feeding bighorn ewe. How I wished then I had a more portable camera! The chance has never come again.

Another little lesson I have learned is to take two cameras on important trips. Once a shutter failed me and I didn't get a single picture. Another time I got the lens of my camera dusty and all my pictures were practically beyond redemption. Of the sixty I took, only three or four were fit for magazine reproduction. One of them, by the way, was an excellent picture of a couple of mule deer fawns. By the greatest of care, enlargements good enough for reproduction can be made from it. Since then I never go on an important trip without a camera in reserve, and curiously enough, I have never had a shutter fail me. You know how it is—carry an umbrella and it never rains!

BEDDING AND TENTS

Once, when I was young and very foolish, I was hard bitten by the he-man complex, and as a consequence I felt that the lighter I traveled the more masculine I was. Without exception my adolescent deer-hunts left me weary and exhausted, as my friends and I tried to get by with a couple of blankets apiece. We were very hearty fellows, we thought, when as a matter of fact we were simply silly youngsters. We would hit for the mountains with two blankets apiece, salt, flour and bacon. We took no cooking utensils but a skillet and a coffeepot. We froze, starved, grew weary, ill and constipated. We were poor hunters simply because we were tired.

I am convinced now that every sportsman should be as comfortable as possible. Take an air mattress, an eiderdown robe if you can afford one, good light blankets if you cannot. Get yourself a good sleeping bag with a sort of pillow you are used to. Don't be ashamed to use a cot if you like it. Remember, too, that pajamas are a sign of good common sense, not of femininity. No man can sleep well in the damp underwear in which he has hunted all day long.

Comfort is a relative thing. A Mexican *vaquero* can make a night of it in his clothes on a saddle blanket beside a fire. He can walk in worn-out flimsy shoes without socks all day long. He seems content with his beans, meat and tortillas. Seeing this, Americans are often consumed with envy at his seeming hardiness. Yet that proves nothing. At home, in his mud and ocatilla *jacal*, he also sleeps on the ground with a couple of blankets. Furthermore, he is usually a broken-down old man by middle age.

My advice to any wilderness hunter is to be as comfortable as possible—not to try to disrupt habits of a lifetime for two weeks or two months just because it may seem romantically hardy. Sleep in pajamas in a comfortable bed on a comfortable pillow. If you habitually eat at noon take a lunch along when you go out. Take care of your feet and give yourself an occasional sponge-bath. If you sleep well and eat good food, you'll really enjoy your trip and you'll come back fresh and rejuvenated. Take a tent along. You won't ordinarily need one in the Southwest, but when you do you'll be miserable without one.

On the other hand, the occasion may arise when you may have to back-pack into country, eat little and travel light. But when you do, you have to take it as a necessity and make the best of it. I have often done it, but I have done it under no illusions that a bed of pine boughs before a fire was as satisfactory as an air mattress and a couple of blankets. It isn't.

After all, hunting is simply a game. Observing birds and animals and shooting at them serves to let us escape from complex reality to the illusion of simplicity. And when we're doing it we ought to have the grand fun which we count on when we plan those trips.

A SELECTED BIBLIOGRAPHY ON THE GAME BIRDS AND ANIMALS OF THE SOUTHWEST

BAILEY, FLORENCE. Birds of New Mexico. Santa Fe, Department of Fish and Game, 1915. A good general book, with chapters on the various Southwestern quail.

BAILEY, VERNON. Mammals of New Mexico. *North American Fauna*, No. 53. Washington, United States Department of Agriculture, Bureau of Biological Survey, 1931. Best available material on the extinct Merriam elk, good chapters on the other game and predatory animals.

DIXON, JOSEPH S. A study of the life history and food habits of mule deer in California. Sacramento, California State Game Department, 1934. An exhaustive study of California mule deer. Much of it may be applied to the Rocky Mountain mule deer of other sections.

GORSUCH, DAVID. Life study of the Gambel's quail in Arizona. Tucson, University of Arizona, 1934. The first really good and thorough study of the Gambel's quail.

HORNADAY, WILLIAM T. Campfires on desert and lava. New York, 1909. An account of a sheep hunt in the Pinacate Mountains, Sonora, back in the days when the Pinacates were virgin desert sheep country. Brief discussions of Sonora whitetail and antelope are included. Some of the geography is wrong, but the book is interesting and for the most part accurate.

KEITH, ELMER. Big game rifles and cartridges. Onslow County, N. C., Small-Arms Technical Publishing Co., 1936. A good discussion of American big-game cartridges, 'scopes, and rifles, by a man who goes in for power and who knows whereof he speaks.

MEARNS, E. A. Mammals of the Mexican boundary. Washington, U. S. National Museum (Bulletin No. 56), 1907. The real source book about Southwestern game.

NELSON, E. W. Status of the pronghorned antelope, 1922–24. Washington, U. S. Department of Agriculture (Bulletin No. 1346), 1925. A survey of the pronghorn when the herds were just about at their lowest ebb.

NICHOL, ANDREW A. Large game mammals. In: University of Arizona. *Arizona and its heritage.* Tucson, 1936. A brief and good account of the distribution of deer, antelope and sheep in Arizona.

Large predator mammals. *Ibid.*

SETON, ERNEST THOMPSON. Lives of the game animals. New York, Doubleday, Doran, 1926. 4 vols. A set every amateur naturalist should own. Contains good general discussions of all the large game species, but is written more from the viewpoint of the Northwest.

VAN DYKE, THEODORE S. The still-hunter. New York, Macmillan, 1932. First published in 1882, this is still the classic book on still-hunting of deer and antelope. The chapters on rifles are, of course, badly out of date, but the deer is still the same kind of a creature he was more than fifty years ago.

WHELEN, TOWNSEND. Wilderness hunting and wildcraft. Onslow County, N. C., Small-Arms Technical Publishing Co., 1927. Brief life studies of North American big game, with special attention to hunting. The information is mostly about the game of the Northwest and Canada. The chapters on rifles, photography, tents and equipment are excellent.

In addition, many magazine articles and hunting stories have been published about the game birds and animals of the Southwest. Many of them are true and good, some are indifferent, and others downright bad. I could compile an extensive bibliography of them if I were a diligent fellow, but it would be of little use, as complete files of outdoor magazines are seldom kept.